Lead Petty Officer Marcus Luttrell joined the U.S. Navy in March 1999 and became a combat-trained SEAL in January 2002. After serving in Baghdad, he was deployed to Afghanistan in the spring of 2005. He was awarded the Navy Cross for combat heroism in 2006 by President George W. Bush.

Patrick Robinson is known for his bestselling U.S. Navy-based novels, and the autobiography of Admiral Sir Sandy Woodward, *One Hundred* Days, which he cowrote, was an international bestseller. He lives in England and spends his summers on Cape Cod, Massachusetts, where he and Luttrell wrote *Lone Survivor*.

LONE SURVIVOR

The Eyewitness Account of Operation Redwing and the Lost Heroes of SEAL Team 10

MARCUS LUTTRELL

with PATRICK ROBINSON

sphere

SPHERE

First published in the United States of America in 2007
by Little, Brown and Company
First published in Great Britain in 2008 by Sphere
Reprinted 2008 (twice)

A CIP catalogue record for this book
is available from the British Library.

ISBN 978-0-7515-4098-7

Map by George W. Ward

Typeset in Caslon by M Rules
Printed and bound in Great Britain by Clays Ltd, St Ives plc

Papers used by Sphere are natural, renewable and recyclable
products made from wood grown in sustainable forests and certified
in accordance with the rules of the Forest Stewardship Council.

Mixed Sources
Product group from well-managed
forests and other controlled sources
www.fsc.org Cert no. SGS-COC-004081
© 1996 Forest Stewardship Council

Sphere
An imprint of
Little, Brown Book Group
100 Victoria Embankment
London EC4Y 0DY

An Hachette Livre UK Company
www.hachettelivre.co.uk

www.littlebrown.co.uk

This book is dedicated to the memory of
Murph, Axe, and Danny Boy, Kristensen, Shane,
James, Senior, Jeff, Jacques, Taylor, and Mac.
These were the eleven men of Alfa and Echo Platoons
who fought and died in the mountains of Afghanistan
trying to save my life, and with whom I was honored
to serve my country. There is no waking hour when
I do not remember them all with the deepest
affection and the most profound,
heartbreaking sadness.

Contents

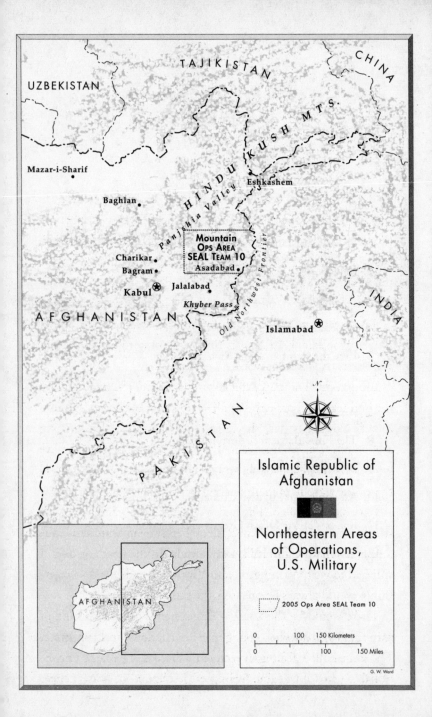

UZBEKISTAN

TAJIKISTAN

CHINA

Mazar-i-Sharif

HINDU KUSH MTS.

Eshkashem

Baghlan

Panjshia Valley

Mountain Ops Area SEAL Team 10

Charikar

Asadabad

Bagram

Jalalabad

Old Northwest Frontier

Kabul

Khyber Pass

AFGHANISTAN

Islamabad

INDIA

PAKISTAN

N

Islamic Republic of Afghanistan

Northeastern Areas of Operations, U.S. Military

2005 Ops Area SEAL Team 10

0   100   150 Kilometers
0   100   150 Miles

AFGHANISTAN

G. W. Ward

Prologue

Would this ever become easier? House to house, freeway to freeway, state to state? Not so far. And here I was again, behind the wheel of a hired SUV, driving along another Main Street, past the shops and the gas station, this time in a windswept little town on Long Island, New York, South Shore, down by the long Atlantic beaches. Winter was coming. The skies were platinum. The whitecaps rolled in beneath dark, lowering clouds. So utterly appropriate, because this time was going to be worse than the others. A whole lot worse.

I found my landmark, the local post office, pulled in behind the building, and parked. We all stepped out of the vehicle, into a chill November day, the remains of the fall leaves swirling around our feet. No one wanted to lead the way, none of the five guys who accompanied me, and for a few moments we just stood there, like a group of mailmen on their break.

I knew where to go. The house was just a few yards down the street. And in a sense, I'd been there before—in Southern California, northern California, and Nevada. In the next few days, I still had to visit Washington and Virginia Beach. And so many things would always be precisely the same.

There would be the familiar devastated sadness, the kind of pain that wells up when young men are cut down in their prime. The same hollow feeling in each of the homes. The same uncontrollable tears. The same feeling of desolation, of brave people trying to be brave, lives which had uniformly been shot to pieces. Inconsolable. Sorrowful.

As before, I was the bearer of the terrible news, as if no one knew the truth until I arrived, so many weeks and months after so many funerals. And for me, this small gathering in Patchogue, Long Island, was going to be the worst.

I tried to get a hold of myself. But again in my mind I heard that terrible, terrible scream, the same one that awakens me, bullying its way into my solitary dreams, night after night, the confirmation of guilt. The endless guilt of the survivor.

"Help me, Marcus! Please help me!"

It was a desperate appeal in the mountains of a foreign land. It was a scream cried out in the echoing high canyons of one of the loneliest places on earth. It was the nearly unrecognizable cry of a mortally wounded creature. And it was a plea I could not answer. I can't forget it. Because it was made by one of the finest people I ever met, a man who happened to be my best friend.

All the visits had been bad. Dan's sister and wife, propping each other up; Eric's father, an admiral, alone with his grief; James's fiancée and father; Axe's wife and family friends; Shane's shattered mother in Las Vegas. They were all terrible. But this one would be worse.

I finally led the way through the blowing leaves, out into the cold, strange street, and along to the little house with its tiny garden, the grass uncut these days. But the lights of an illuminated American flag were still right there in the front window. They were the lights of a patriot, and they still shone defiantly, just as if he were still here. Mikey would have liked that.

We all stopped for a few moments, and then we climbed the little flight of steps and knocked on the door. She was pretty, the lady who answered the door, long dark hair, her eyes already brimming with tears. His mother.

She knew I had been the last person to see him alive. And she stared up at me with a look of such profound sadness it damn near broke me in half and said, quietly, "Thank you for coming."

I somehow replied, "It's because of your son that I am standing here."

As we all walked inside, I looked straight at the hall table and on it was a large framed photograph of a man looking straight at me, half grinning. There was Mikey, all over again, and I could hear his mom saying, "He didn't suffer, did he? Please tell me he didn't suffer."

I had to wipe the sleeve of my jacket across my eyes before I answered that. But I did answer. "No, Maureen. He didn't. He died instantly."

I had told her what she'd asked me to tell her. That kind of tactical response was turning out to be essential equipment for the lone survivor.

I tried to tell her of her son's unbending courage, his will, his iron control. And as I'd come to expect, she seemed as if she had not yet accepted anything. Not until I related it. I was the essential bearer of the final bad news.

In the course of the next hour we tried to talk like adults. But it was too difficult. There was so much that could have been said, and so much that would never be said. And no amount of backup from my three buddies, plus the New York City fireman and policeman who accompanied us, made much difference.

But this was a journey I had to complete. I had promised myself I would do it, no matter what it took, because I knew what it would mean to each and every one of them. The sharing of personal anguish with someone who was there. House to house, grief to grief.

I considered it my sworn duty. But that did not make it any easier. Maureen hugged us all as we left. I nodded formally to the photograph of my best friend, and we walked down that sad little path to the street.

Tonight it would be just as bad, because we were going to see Heather, Mikey's fiancée, in her downtown New York City apartment. It wasn't fair. They would have been married by now. And the day after this, I had to go to Arlington National Cemetery to visit the graves of two more absent friends.

By any standards it was an expensive, long, and melancholy journey across the United States of America, paid for by the organization for which I work. Like me, like all of us, they understand. And as with many big corporations which have a dedicated workforce, you can tell a lot about them by their corporate philosophy, their written constitution, if you like.

It's the piece of writing which defines their employees and their standards. I have for several years tried to base my life on the opening paragraph:

"In times of uncertainty there is a special breed of warrior ready to answer our Nation's call; a common man with uncommon desire to succeed. Forged by adversity, he stands alongside America's finest special operations forces to serve his country and the American people, and to protect their way of life. I am that man."

My name is Marcus. Marcus Luttrell. I'm a United States Navy SEAL, Team Leader, SDV Team 1, Alfa Platoon. Like every other SEAL, I'm trained in weapons, demolition, and unarmed combat. I'm a sniper, and I'm the platoon medic. But most of all, I'm an American. And when the bell sounds, I will come out fighting for my country and for my teammates. If necessary, to the death.

And that's not just because the SEALs trained me to do so; it's because I'm willing to do so. I'm a patriot, and I fight with the Lone Star of Texas on my right arm and another Texas flag over my heart. For me, defeat is unthinkable.

Mikey died in the summer of 2005, fighting shoulder to shoulder with me in the high country of northeast Afghanistan. He was the best officer I ever knew, an iron-souled warrior of colossal, almost unbelievable courage in the face of the enemy.

Two who *would* believe it were my other buddies who also fought and died up there. That's Danny and Axe: two American heroes, two towering figures in a fighting force where valor is a common virtue. Their lives stand as a testimony to the central paragraph of the philosophy of the U.S. Navy SEALs:

"I will never quit. I persevere and thrive on adversity. My Nation expects me to be physically harder and mentally stronger than my enemies. If knocked down, I will get back up, every time. I will draw on every remaining ounce of strength to protect my teammates and to accomplish our mission. I am never out of the fight."

As I mentioned, my name is Marcus. And I'm writing this book because of my three buddies Mikey, Danny, and Axe. If I don't write it, no one will ever understand the indomitable courage under fire of those three Americans. And that would be the biggest tragedy of all.

1

To Afghanistan...
in a Flying Warehouse

This was payback time for the World Trade Center. We were coming after the guys who did it. If not the actual guys, then their blood brothers, the lunatics who still wished us dead and might try it again.

Good-byes tend to be curt among Navy SEALS. A quick back-slap, a friendly bear hug, no one uttering what we're all thinking: *Here we go again, guys, going to war, to another trouble spot, another half-assed enemy willing to try their luck against us...they must be out of their minds.*

It's a SEAL thing, our unspoken invincibility, the silent code of the elite warriors of the U.S. Armed Forces. Big, fast, highly trained guys, armed to the teeth, expert in unarmed combat, so stealthy no one ever hears us coming. SEALs are masters of strategy, professional marksmen with rifles, artists with machine guns, and, if necessary, pretty handy with knives. In general terms, we believe there are very few of the world's problems we could not solve with high explosive or a well-aimed bullet.

We operate on sea, air, and land. That's where we got our name. U.S. Navy SEALs, underwater, on the water, or out of the water. Man, we can do it all. And where we were going, it was likely to be strictly out of the water. Way out of the water. Ten thousand feet up some treeless moonscape of a mountain range in one of the loneliest and sometimes most lawless places in the world. Afghanistan.

"'Bye, Marcus." "Good luck, Mikey." "Take it easy, Matt." "See you later, guys." I remember it like it was yesterday, someone pulling open the door to our barracks room, the light spilling out into the warm, dark night of Bahrain, this strange desert kingdom, which is joined to Saudi Arabia by the two-mile-long King Fahd Causeway.

The six of us, dressed in our light combat gear—flat desert khakis with Oakley assault boots—stepped outside into a light, warm breeze. It was March 2005, not yet hotter than hell, like it is in summer. But still unusually warm for a group of Americans in springtime, even for a Texan like me. Bahrain stands on the 26° north line of latitude. That's more than four hundred miles to the south of Baghdad, and that's hot.

Our particular unit was situated on the south side of the capital city of Manama, way up in the northeast corner of the island. This meant we had to be transported right through the middle of town to the U.S. air base on Muharraq Island for all flights to and from Bahrain. We didn't mind this, but we didn't love it either.

That little journey, maybe five miles, took us through a city that felt much as we did. The locals didn't love us either. There was a kind of sullen look to them, as if they were sick to death of having the American military around them. In fact, there were districts in Manama known as black flag areas, where tradesmen, shopkeepers, and private citizens hung black flags outside their properties to signify *Americans are not welcome.*

I guess it wasn't quite as vicious as *Juden Verboten* was in Hitler's Germany. But there are undercurrents of hatred all over the Arab world, and we knew there were many sympathizers with the Muslim extremist fanatics of the Taliban and al Qaeda. The black flags worked. We stayed well clear of those places.

Nonetheless we had to drive through the city in an unprotected vehicle over another causeway, the Sheik Hamad, named for the emir. They're big on causeways, and I guess they will build more, since there are thirty-two other much smaller islands forming the low-lying Bahrainian archipelago, right off the Saudi western shore, in the Gulf of Iran.

Anyway, we drove on through Manama out to Muharraq, where the U.S. air base lies to the south of the main Bahrain International Airport. Awaiting us was the huge C-130 Hercules, a giant turbo-prop freighter. It's one of the noisiest aircraft in the stratosphere, a big, echoing, steel cave specifically designed to carry heavy-duty freight—not sensitive, delicate, poetic conversationalists such as ourselves.

We loaded and stowed our essential equipment: heavy weaps (machine guns), M4 rifles, SIG-Sauer 9mm pistols, pigstickers (combat knives), ammunition belts, grenades, medical and communication gear. A couple of the guys slung up hammocks made of thick netting. The rest of us settled back into seats that were also made of netting. Business class this wasn't. But frogs don't travel light, and they don't expect comfort. That's frogmen, by the way, which we all were.

Stuck here in this flying warehouse, this utterly primitive form of passenger transportation, there was a certain amount of cheerful griping and moaning. But if the six of us were inserted into some hellhole of a battleground, soaking wet, freezing cold, wounded, trapped, outnumbered, fighting for our lives, you would not hear one solitary word of complaint. That's the way of our brotherhood. It's a strictly American brotherhood, mostly forged in blood. Hard-won, unbreakable. Built on a shared patriotism, shared courage, and shared trust in one another. There is no fighting force in the world quite like us.

The flight crew checked we were all strapped in, and then those thunderous Boeing engines roared. Jesus, the noise was unbelievable. I might just as well have been sitting in the gearbox. The whole aircraft shook and rumbled as we charged down the runway, taking off to the southwest, directly into the desert wind which gusted out of the mainland Arabian peninsula. There were no other passengers on board, just the flight crew and, in the rear, us, headed out to do God's work on behalf of the U.S. government and our commander in chief, President George W. Bush. In a sense, we were all alone. As usual.

We banked out over the Gulf of Bahrain and made a long, left-hand swing onto our easterly course. It would have been a whole hell of a lot quicker to head directly northeast across the gulf. But that would have taken us over the dubious southern uplands of the Islamic Republic of Iran, and we do not do that.

Instead we stayed south, flying high over the friendly coastal deserts of the United Arab Emirates, north of the burning sands of the Rub al Khali, the Empty Quarter. Astern of us lay the fevered cauldrons of loathing in Iraq and nearby Kuwait, places where I had previously served. Below us were the more friendly, enlightened desert kingdoms of the world's coming natural-gas capital, Qatar; the oil-sodden emirate of Abu Dhabi; the gleaming modern high-rises of Dubai; and then, farther east, the craggy coastline of Oman.

None of us were especially sad to leave Bahrain, which was the first place in the Middle East where oil was discovered. It had its history, and we often had fun in the local markets bargaining with local merchants for everything. But we never felt at home there, and somehow as we climbed into the dark skies, we felt we were leaving behind all that was god-awful in the northern reaches of the gulf and embarking on a brand-new mission, one that we understood.

In Baghdad we were up against an enemy we often could not see and were obliged to get out there and find. And when we found him, we scarcely knew who he was—al Qaeda or Taliban, Shiite or Sunni, Iraqi or foreign, a freedom fighter for Saddam or an insurgent fighting for some kind of a different god from our own, a god who somehow sanctioned murder of innocent civilians, a god who'd effectively booted the Ten Commandments over the touchline and out of play.

They were ever present, ever dangerous, giving us a clear pattern of total confusion, if you know what I mean. Somehow, shifting positions in the big Hercules freighter, we were leaving behind a place which was systematically tearing itself apart and heading for a place full of wild mountain men who were hellbent on tearing us apart.

Afghanistan. This was very different. Those mountains up in the northeast, the western end of the mighty range of the Hindu Kush, were the very same mountains where the Taliban had sheltered the lunatics of al Qaeda, shielded the crazed followers of Osama bin Laden while they plotted the attacks on the World Trade Center in New York on 9/11.

This was where bin Laden's fighters found a home training base. Let's face it, *al Qaeda* means "the base," and in return for the Saudi fanatic bin Laden's money, the Taliban made it all possible. Right now these very same guys, the remnants of the Taliban and the last few tribal warriors of al Qaeda, were preparing to start over, trying to fight their way through the mountain passes, intent on setting up new training camps and military headquarters and, eventually, their own government in place of the democratically elected one.

They may not have been the precise same guys who planned 9/11. But they were most certainly their descendants, their heirs, their followers. They were part of the same crowd who knocked down the North and South towers in the Big Apple on the infamous Tuesday morning in 2001. And our coming task was to stop them, right there in those mountains, by whatever means necessary.

Thus far, those mountain men had been kicking some serious ass in their skirmishes with our military. Which was more or less why the brass had sent for us. When things get very rough, they usually send for us. That's why the navy spends years training SEAL teams in Coronado, California, and Virginia Beach. Especially for times like these, when Uncle Sam's velvet glove makes way for the iron fist of SPECWARCOM (that's Special Forces Command).

And that was why all of us were here. Our mission may have been strategic, it may have been secret. However, one point was crystalline clear, at least to the six SEALs in that rumbling Hercules high above the Arabian desert. This was payback time for the World Trade Center. We were coming after the guys who did it. If not the actual guys, then their blood brothers, the lunatics who still wished us dead and might try it again. Same thing, right?

We knew what we were coming for. And we knew where we were going: right up there to the high peaks of the Hindu Kush, those same mountains where bin Laden might still be and where his new bands of disciples were still hiding. Somewhere.

The pure clarity of purpose was inspirational to us. Gone were the treacherous, dusty backstreets of Baghdad, where even children of three and four were taught to hate us. Dead ahead, in Afghanistan, awaited an ancient battleground where we could match our enemy, strength for strength, stealth for stealth, steel for steel.

This might be, perhaps, a little daunting for regular soldiers. But not for SEALs. And I can state with absolute certainty that all six of us were excited by the prospect, looking forward to doing our job out there in the open, confident of our ultimate success, sure of our training, experience, and judgment. You see, we're invincible. That's what they taught us. That's what we believe.

It's written right there in black and white in the official philosophy of the U.S. Navy SEAL, the last two paragraphs of which read:

We train for war and fight to win. I stand ready to bring the full spectrum of combat power to bear in order to achieve my mission and the goals established by my country. The execution of my duties will be swift and violent when required, yet guided by the very principles I serve to defend.

Brave men have fought and died building the proud tradition and feared reputation that I am bound to uphold. In the worst of conditions, the legacy of my teammates steadies my resolve and silently guides my every deed. I will not fail.

Each one of us had grown a beard in order to look more like Afghan fighters. It was important for us to appear nonmilitary, to not stand out in a crowd. Despite this, I can guarantee you that if three SEALs were put into a crowded airport, I would spot them all, just by their bearing, their confidence, their obvious discipline, the way they walk. I'm not saying anyone else could recognize them. But I most certainly could.

The guys who traveled from Bahrain with me were remarkably diverse, even by SEAL standards. There was SGT2 Matthew Gene Axelson, not yet thirty, a petty officer from California, married to Cindy, devoted to her and to his parents, Cordell and Donna, and to his brother, Jeff.

I always called him Axe, and I knew him well. My twin brother, Morgan, was his best friend. He'd been to our home in Texas, and he and I had been together for a long time in SEAL Delivery Vehicle Team 1, Alfa Platoon. He and Morgan were swim buddies together in SEAL training, went through Sniper School together.

Axe was a quiet man, six foot four, with piercing blue eyes and curly hair. He was smart and the best Trivial Pursuit player I ever saw. I loved talking to him because of how much he knew. He would come out with answers that would have defied the learning of a Harvard professor. Places, countries, their populations, principal industries.

In the teams, he was always professional. I never once saw him upset, and he always knew precisely what he was doing. He was just one of those guys. What was difficult and confusing for others was usually a piece of cake for him. In combat he was a supreme athlete, swift, violent, brutal if necessary. His family never knew that side of him. They saw only the calm, cheerful navy man who could undoubtedly have been a professional golfer, a guy who loved a laugh and a cold beer.

You could hardly meet a better person. He was an incredible man.

Then there was my best friend, Lieutenant Michael Patrick Murphy, also not yet thirty, an honors graduate from Penn State, a hockey player, accepted by several law schools before he turned the rudder hard over and changed course for the United States Navy. Mikey was an inveterate reader. His favorite book was Steven Pressfield's *Gates of Fire,* the story of the immortal stand of the Spartans at Thermopylae.

He was vastly experienced in the Middle East, having served in Jordan, Qatar, and Djibouti on the Horn of Africa. We started our careers as SEALs at the same time, and we were probably flung together by a shared devotion to the smart-ass remark. Also, neither of us could sleep if we were under the slightest pressure. Our insomnia was shared like our humor. We used to hang out together half the night, and I can truthfully say no one ever made me laugh like that.

I was always razzing him about being dirty. We'd sometimes go out on patrol every day for weeks, and there seems to be no time to shower and no point in showering when you're likely to be up to your armpits in swamp water a few hours later. Here's a typical exchange between us, petty officer team leader to commissioned SEAL officer:

"Mikey, you smell like shit, for Christ's sake. Why the hell don't you take a shower?"

"Right away, Marcus. Remind me to do that tomorrow, willya?"

"Roger that, *sir!*"

For his nearest and dearest, he used a particularly large gift shop, otherwise known as the U.S. highway system. I remember him giving his very beautiful girlfriend Heather a gift-wrapped traffic cone for her birthday. For Christmas, he gave her one of those flashing red lights which fit on top of those cones at night. Gift-wrapped, of course. He once gave me a stop sign for my birthday.

And you should have seen his traveling bag. It was enormous, a big, cavernous hockey duffel bag, the kind carried by his favorite team, the New York Rangers. The single heaviest piece of luggage in the entire navy. But it didn't sport the Rangers logo. On its top were two simple words: *Piss off.*

There was no situation for which he could not summon a really smart-ass remark. Mikey was once involved in a terrible and almost fatal accident, and one of the guys asked him to explain what happened.

"C'mon," said the New York lieutenant, as if it were a subject of which he was profoundly weary. "You're always bringing up that old shit. Fuggeddaboutit."

The actual accident had happened just two days earlier.

He was also the finest officer I ever met, a natural leader, a really terrific SEAL who never, ever bossed anyone around. It was always *Please*. Always *Would you mind?* Never *Do that, do this*. And he simply would not tolerate any other high-ranking officer, commissioned or noncommissioned, reaming out one of his guys.

He insisted the buck stopped with him. He always took the hit himself. If a reprimand was due, he accepted the blame. But don't even try to go around him and bawl out one of his guys, because he could be a formidable adversary when riled. And that riled him.

He was excellent underwater, and a powerful swimmer. Trouble was, he was a bit slow, and that was truly his only flaw. One time, he and I were on a two-mile training swim, and when I finally hit the beach I couldn't find him. Finally I saw him splashing through the water about four hundred yards offshore. *Christ, he's in trouble*—that was my first thought.

So I charged back into the freezing sea and set out to rescue him. I'm not a real fast runner, but I'm quick through the water, and I reached him with no trouble. I should have known better.

"Get away from me, Marcus!" he yelled. "I'm a race car in the red, highest revs on the TAC. Don't mess with me, Marcus, not now. You're dealing with a race car here."

Only Mike Murphy. If I told that story to any SEAL in our platoon, withheld the name, and then asked who said it, everyone would guess Mikey.

Sitting opposite me in the Hercules was Senior Chief Daniel Richard Healy, another awesome Navy SEAL, six foot three, thirty-seven, married to Norminda, father of seven children. He was born in New Hampshire and joined the navy in 1990, advancing to serve in the SEAL teams and learning near-fluent Russian.

Danny and I served in the same team, SDV Team 1, for three years. He was a little older than most of us and referred to us as his kids—as if he didn't have enough. And he loved us all with equal passion, both big families, his wife and children, sisters, brothers, and parents, and the even bigger one hitherto based on the island of Bahrain. Dan was worse than Mikey in his defense of his SEALs. No one ever dared yell at any of us while he was around.

He guarded his flock assiduously, researched every mission with complete thoroughness, gathered the intel, checked the maps, charts, photographs, all reconnaissance. Also, he paid attention to the upcoming missions and made sure his kids were always in the front line. That's the place we were trained for, the place we liked to go.

In many ways Dan was tough on everyone. There were times when he and I did not see eye to eye. He was unfailingly certain that his way was the best way, mostly the only way. But his heart was in the right place at all times. Dan Healy was one hell of a Navy SEAL, a role model for everything a senior chief should be, an iron man who became a strategist and who knew his job from A to Z. I talked face to face with big Dan almost every day of my life.

Somewhere up above us, swinging in his hammock, headset on, listening to rock-and-roll music, was Petty Officer Second Class Shane Patton, twenty-two-year-old surfer and skateboarder originally from Las Vegas, Nevada. My protégé. As the primary communications operator, I had Shane as my number two. Like a much younger Mike Murphy, he too was a virtuoso at the smart-ass remark and, as you would expect, an outstanding frogman.

It was hard for me to identify with Shane because he was so different. I once walked into the comms center, and he was trying to order a leopard-skin coat on the Internet.

"What the hell do you want that for?" I asked.

"It's just so cool, man," he replied, terminating further discussion.

A big, robust guy with blond hair and a relatively insolent grin, Shane was supersmart. I never had to tell him anything. He knew what to do at all times. At first, this slightly irritated me; you know, telling a much junior guy what you want done, and it turns out he's already done it. Every time. Took me a while to get used to the fact I had an assistant who was damn near as sharp as Matt Axelson. And that's as sharp as it gets.

Shane, like a lot of those beach gods, was hugely laid back. His buddies would probably call it supercool or some such word.

But in a comms operator, that quality is damn near priceless. If there's a firefight going on, and Shane's back at HQ manning the radio, you're listening to one ultracalm, very measured SEAL communicator. Sorry, I meant *dude*. That was an all-purpose word for Shane. Even I was a dude, according to him. Even the president of the United States was a dude, according to him. Actually he accorded President Bush the highest accolade, the gold-plated Congressional Medal of Honor awarded by the surf gods: *He's a real dude, man, a real dude.*

He was the son of a Navy SEAL, and his quiet, rarely uttered ambition was to be just like his dad, James J. Patton. He wanted to be a member of the navy jump team, as his father had once been. He completed basic airborne training at Fort Benning, Georgia, before he passed his SEAL qualification exams and accepted orders to SDV Team 1, Alfa Platoon. Five months later he joined us on the flight to Afghanistan.

Everything Shane did, all through his short life, was outstanding. In high school he was the star pitcher and the best outfielder. He could play the guitar really well, ran a band called True Story, the quality of which remains a bit of a mystery. He was a super photographer and a skilled mechanic and engineer; he'd single-handedly restored and customized two old Volkswagen Bugs. He had acquired another one that he told me would become "the ultimate customized Bug, dude. That's what I'm all about."

Shane was as good on a computer as anyone at the base. He spent hours on it, some website called MySpace, always keeping in touch with his friends: *Hey, dude, howya been?*

The sixth member of our group was James Suh, a twenty-eight-year-old native of Chicago who was raised in south Florida. James had been with SDV Team 1 for three years before we left for Afghanistan, and during that time he became one of the best-liked guys on the base. He had only one sibling, an older sister, but he had about three hundred cousins, every one of whom he was sworn to protect.

James, like his close buddy Shane, was another inordinately tough SEAL, a petty officer second class. Like Shane, he'd gone through basic airborne training at Fort Benning and gone forward to join Alfa Platoon.

His early ambition had been to become a veterinarian, a dog specialist. But James was born to be a SEAL and was passionately proud of his membership in one of the most elite combat outfits in the world and in his ability to defy the limits of physical and mental endurance.

Like Shane, he was a star high school athlete, outstanding on both the swim and tennis teams. Academically, he was constantly in the gifted and advanced classes. In our platoon, James was right up there with Axe and Shane as a SEAL of high intelligence and supreme reliability under fire. I never met one person with a bad word to say about him.

It took us almost three hours to reach the Gulf of Oman. We'd cut south of the Strait of Hormuz, staying well away from the superhighway of world oil and gas tankers moving to and from the massive loading docks of the Gulf of Iran. The Iranian navy does its exercises down there, operating out of their main base at Bandar Abbas and also farther down the coast, at their increasingly active submarine base.

Not that we imagined some trigger-happy Iranian missile director might take a pop at us with some fast heat-seeking weapon.

But caution was usually advisable around there, despite the fact we had a very tough man in the White House who'd made clear his policy of harsh retaliation at the merest suggestion of an attack on U.S. air traffic, civilian or military.

You had to serve out here in the Middle East to understand fully the feeling of danger, even threat, that was never far away, even in countries generally regarded as friendly to America. Like Bahrain.

The rugged part of the Omani coast I mentioned earlier is around the point of land at Ras Musandam, with its deep fjords. This most northerly rocky shelf which juts out into the Gulf of Hormuz is the closest foreign point to the Iranian base at Bandar Abbas. The stretch of coastline running south from that point is much flatter, sloping down from the ancient Al Hajar Mountains. We began our long ocean crossing somewhere down there, north of Muscat, close to the Tropic of Cancer.

And as we crossed that coastline heading out toward the open ocean, it really was good-bye, from me at least, to the Arabian Peninsula and the seething Islamic states at the north end of the gulf, Kuwait, Iraq, Syria, and Iran, that had dominated my life and thoughts for the past couple of years. Especially Iraq.

I had first arrived there to join Team 5 back on April 14, 2003, coming into the U.S. air base fifteen minutes out of Baghdad with twelve other SEALs from Kuwait in an aircraft just like this C-130. It was one week after the U.S. forces launched their opening bombardment against the city, trying to nail Saddam before the war really started. The Brits had just taken Basra.

On the same day I arrived, U.S. Marines took Tikrit, Saddam's hometown, and a few hours later the Pentagon announced that major combat had concluded. None of which had the slightest bearing on our mission, which was to help root out and if necessary destroy what little opposition was left and then help with the search for weapons of mass destruction.

I had been in Baghdad just one day when President Bush declared Saddam Hussein and his Ba'ath Party had fallen, and my colleagues swiftly captured, that same day, Abu Abbas, leader of the Palestinian Liberation Front, which attacked the Italian cruise ship *Achille Lauro* in the Mediterranean in 1985.

Forty-eight hours later, on April 17, U.S. forces captured Saddam's half brother, the infamous Barzan Ibrahim al-Tikriti. That was the kind of stuff I was instantly involved in. I was one of 146,000 American and coalition troops in there, under the command of General Tommy Franks. It was my first experience of close-quarter combat. It was the place where I learned the finer points of my trade.

It was also the first inkling we had of the rise from the ashes of Osama bin Laden's followers. Sure, we knew they were still around, still trying to regroup after the United States had just about flattened them in Afghanistan. But it was not long before we began to hear of an outfit called al Qaeda in Iraq, a malicious terrorist group trying to cause mayhem at every conceivable opportunity, led by the deranged Jordanian killer Abu Musab al-Zarqawi (now deceased).

Our missions in the city were sometimes interrupted by intense searches for whatever or whoever happened to be missing. On my first day, four of us went out to some huge Iraqi lake area looking for a missing F-18 Super Hornet fighter bomber and its U.S. pilot. You probably remember the incident. I'll never forget it. We came in low over the lake in our MH-47 Chinook helicopter and suddenly we spotted the tail of an aircraft jutting out of the water. Right after that, we found the body of the pilot washed up on the shore.

I remember feeling very sad, and it would not be for the last time. I'd been in the country for less than twenty-four hours. Attached to Team 5, we were known as straphangers, extra muscle drafted in for particularly dangerous situations. Our primary mission was special surveillance and reconnaissance, photographing hot spots and danger areas using unbelievable photographic lenses.

We carried out everything under the cover of darkness, waiting patiently for many hours, watching our backs, keeping our eyes on the target, firing computerized pictures back to base from virtually inside the jaws of the enemy.

We worked usually in a very small unit of four SEALs. Out on our own. This kind of close-quarter recon is the most dangerous job of all. It's lonely and often dull, and fraught with peril should we be discovered. Sometimes, with a particularly valuable terrorist leader, we might go in and get him, trying to yank him out of there alive. Brutal, no mercy. Generally speaking, the Navy SEALs train the best recon units in the world.

It always makes me laugh when I read about "the proud freedom fighters in Iraq." They're not proud. They'd sell their own mothers for fifty bucks. We'd go into some house, grab the guy we believed was the ringleader, and march him outside into the street. First thing he'd say was "Hey, hey, not me. You want those guys in that house down the street." Or "You give me dollars, I tell you what you want to know."

They would, and did. And what they told us was very often extremely valuable. Most of those big military coups, like the elimination of Saddam's sons and the capture of Saddam himself, were the result of military intel. Somebody, someone from their own side, shopped them, as they had shopped hundreds of others. Anything for a buck, right? Pride? Those guys couldn't even spell it.

And that grade of intelligence is often hard-won. We'd go in fast, driving into the most dangerous districts in the city, screaming through the streets in Humvees, or even fast-roping in from helicopters if necessary. We'd advance, city block by city block, moving carefully through the dark, ready for someone to open fire on us from a window, a building, somewhere on the opposite side of the street, even a tower. It happened all the time. Sometimes we returned fire, always to much more deadly effect than our enemy could manage.

And when we reached our objective, we'd either go in with sledgehammers and a hooley—that's a kind of a crowbar that will rip a door right off its hinges—or we'd wrap the demo around the lock and blast that sucker straight in. We always made certain the blast was aimed inward, just in case someone was waiting behind the door with an AK-47. It's hard to survive when a door comes straight at you at one hundred miles an hour from point-blank range.

Occasionally, if we had an element of doubt about the strength of the opposition behind that door, we would throw in a few flash-crashes, which do not explode and knock down walls or anything but do unleash a series of very loud, almost deafening bangs accompanied by searing white flashes. Very disorienting for our enemy.

Right then our lead man would head the charge inside the building, which was always a shock for the residents. Even if we had not used the flash-crashes, they'd wake up real quick to face a group of big masked men, their machine guns leveled, shouting, daring anyone to make a move. Although these city houses were mostly two-story, Iraqis tend to sleep downstairs, all of them crowded together in the living room.

There might be someone upstairs trying to fire down on us, which could be a massive pain in the ass. We usually solved that with a well-aimed hand grenade. That may sound callous, but your teammates are absolutely relying on the colleague with the grenade, because the guy upstairs might also have one, and that danger must be taken out. For your teammates. In the SEALs, it's *always* your teammates. No exceptions.

However, in the room downstairs, where the Iraqis were by now in surrender mode, we'd look for the ringleader, the guy who knew where the explosives were stored, the guy who had access to the bomb-making kit or the weapons that would be aimed straight at American soldiers. He was usually not that difficult to find. We'd get some light in there and march him directly to the window so the guys outside with the intel could compare his face with photographs.

Often the photographs had been taken by the team I worked in, and identification was swift. And while this process happened, the SEAL team secured the property, which means, broadly, making darned sure the Iraqis under this sudden house arrest had no access to any form of weaponry whatsoever.

Right then what the SEALs call A-guys usually showed up, very professional, very steely, steadfast in their requirements and the necessary outcome of the interrogation. They cared, above all, about the quality of the informant's information, the priceless data which might save dozens of American lives. Outside we usually had three or four SEALs patrolling wide, to keep the inevitable gathering crowd at bay. When this was under control, with the A-guidance, we would question the ringleader, demanding he inform us where his terrorist cell was operating.

Sometimes we would get an address. Sometimes names of other ringleaders. Other times a man might inform us about arms dumps, but this usually required money. If the guy we'd arrested was especially stubborn, we'd cuff him and send him back to base for a more professional interrogation.

But usually he came up with something. That's the way we gathered the intelligence we needed in order to locate and take out those who would still fight for Saddam Hussein, even if his government had fallen, even if his troops had surrendered and the country was temporarily under American and British control. These were dangerous days at the conclusion of the formal conflict.

Fired on from the rooftops, watching for car bombs, we learned to fight like terrorists, night after night, moving like wild animals through the streets and villages. There is no other way to beat a terrorist. You must fight like him, or he will surely kill you. That's why we went in so hard, taking houses and buildings by storm, blowing the doors in, charging forward, operating strictly by the SEAL teams' tried-and-trusted methods, ingrained in us by years of training.

Because in the end, your enemy must ultimately fear you, understand your supremacy. That's what we were taught, out there in the absolute front line of U.S. military might. And that's probably why we never lost one Navy SEAL in all my long months in Iraq. Because we played it by the book. No mistakes.

At least nothing major. Although I admit in my first week in Iraq we were subject to ... well ... a minor lapse in judgment after we found an Iraqi insurgent ammunition dump during a patrol along a river as sporadic shots were fired at us from the other side. There are those military officers who might have considered merely capturing the dump and confiscating the explosive.

SEALs react somewhat differently and generally look for a faster solution. It's not quite, *Hey, hey, hey... this lot's gotta go.* But that will do for broad guidelines. We planted our own explosives in the building and then deferred to our EOD guy (explosive ordnance disposal). He positioned us a ways back, but a couple of us did wonder if it was quite far enough.

"No problem. Stay right where you are." He was confident.

Well, that pile of bombs, grenades, and other explosives went up like a nuclear bomb. At first there was just dust and small bits of concrete flying around. But the blasts grew bigger and the lumps of concrete from the building started to rain down on us.

Guys were diving everywhere, into trucks, under trucks, anywhere to get out of the way. One of our guys jumped into the Tigris! We could hear these rocks and lumps of hard mud walls raining down on us, hitting the trucks. It was amazing no one was killed or hurt out there.

Eventually it all went quiet, and I crawled out, unscathed. The EOD maestro was standing right next to me. "Beautiful," I said. "That went really well, didn't it?" I wished Mike Murphy had been there. He'd have come up with something better.

We worked for almost three months with SEAL Team 5 out in the Baghdad suburbs. That was really where we were blooded for battle, combing those urban streets, flushing out insurgents wherever they hid. We needed all our skill, moving up to the corner blocks, opening fire out there in the night as we rounded these strange, dark, foreign street junctions.

The trouble was, the places often looked normal. But up close you realized there were holes straight through the buildings. Some of them just had their front façade, the entire rear area having been blown out by U.S. bombs as the troops fought to run down the murderous Saddam Hussein.

Thus we often found ourselves in what looked like respectable streets but which were in fact piles of rubble, perfect hiding places for insurgents or even Sunni Muslim terrorists still fighting for their erstwhile leader.

On one such night I was almost killed. I had moved out onto the sidewalk, my rifle raised, as I fired to provide cover for my teammates. I remember it vividly. I was standing astride a bomb, directly over it, and I never even saw it.

One of the guys yelled, *"Marcus! Move it!"* and he came straight toward me, hit me with the full force of his body, and the pair of us rolled into the middle of the street. He was first up, literally dragging me away. Moments later, our EOD guys blew it up. Thankfully we were both now out of range, since it was only a small improvised explosive made in someone's kitchen. Nevertheless, it would have killed me, or at the very least inflicted serious damage on my wedding tackle.

It was just another example of how amazingly sharp you need to be in order to wear the SEAL Trident. Over and over during training, we were told never to be complacent, reminded constantly of the sheer cunning and unpredictability of our terrorist enemy, of the necessity for total vigilance at all times, of the endless need to watch out for our teammates. Every night before our mission, one of the senior petty officers would say, "C'mon now, guys. Get your game faces on. This is for real. Stay on your toes. Concentrate. That way you'll live."

I learned a lot about myself out there with Team 5, moving through the dark, zigzagging across the ground, never doing anything the same way twice. That's what the army does, everything the same way. We operate differently, because we are a much smaller force. Even with a major city operation we never travel in groups of more than twenty, and the recon units consist of only four men.

It all causes your senses to go up tenfold, as you move quietly, stealthily through the shadows, using the dead space, the areas into which your enemy cannot see. Someone described us as the shadow warriors. He was right. That's what we are. And we always have a very clear objective, usually just one guy, one person who is responsible for making the problem: the terrorist leader or strategist.

And there's a whole code of conduct to remember when you finally catch up with him. First of all, make him drop his gun and get his ass on the ground. He'll usually do that without much protest. Should he decide against this, we help him get on the ground, quickly. But we never, never, turn around, even for a split second. We never give these guys one inch of latitude. Because he'll pick that rifle up and shoot you at point-blank range, straight in the back. He might even cut your throat if he had a chance. No one can hate quite like a terrorist. Until you've encountered one of these guys, you don't understand the meaning of the word *hate*.

We found half-trained terrorists all over the world, mostly unfit to handle a lethal weapon of any kind, especially those Russian-made Kalashnikovs they use. First of all, the damn thing is inaccurate, and in the hands of an hysteric, which most of them are, the guns spray bullets all over the place. When these guys go after an American, they usually fire blindly around a corner, aiming at nothing in particular, and end up killing three passing Iraqi civilians. Only by pure chance do they hit the American soldier they wanted.

On May 1, 2003, President Bush announced the military phase of the war was over. Four days later it was revealed Saddam and his son had heisted $1 billion in cash from the Central Bank. Around that time, with the search for weapons of mass destruction still under way, we were detailed to the gigantic Lake Buhayrat ath Tharthar, where supposedly a large cache had been hidden by Saddam.

This was a major stretch of water, nearly fifty miles long and in some places thirty miles wide, set on a flat, verdant plain between the Euphrates and the Tigris, south of Tikrit. There's a huge dam at one end, and we were stationed just to the south at a place named Hit. Seemed fitting. So we jocked up and combed the deep, clear waters of that lake for about a week, every inch of it. We were operating out of Zodiacs and found nothing except for a bicycle tire and an old ladder.

As the weeks went by the weather grew hotter, sometimes hitting 115°F. We kept going, working away through the nights. There were times when it all seemed to grow calmer, and then on July 4, a taped voice, which al-Jazeera television said was Saddam, urged everyone to join the resistance and fight the U.S. occupation to the death.

We thought that was kind of stupid, because we weren't trying to occupy anything. We were just trying to stop these crazy pricks from blowing up and wiping out the civilian population of the country we had just liberated from one of the biggest bastards in history.

Didn't much matter what we thought. The very next day a serious bomb went off at a graduation ceremony for the new Iraqi police class, trained by the United States. Seven new cops were killed and seventy more were wounded. God alone understood those to whom that made sense.

We continued our operations, looking for the key insurgents, forcing or bribing the information out of them. But it already seemed their recruiting numbers were limitless. No matter how many we ran to ground, there were always more. It was around this time we first heard of the rise of this sinister group who called themselves al Qaeda in Iraq. It was an undisguised terrorist operation, dedicated to mayhem and murder, especially of us.

However, the whole movement received a severe blow to its morale on July 22, when Saddam's sons, Uday and Qusay, who were at least as evil as their dad, were finally nailed at a house in Mosul. I'm not allowed to speak of this highly classified operation, save to mention the pair of them were killed when U.S. Special Forces flattened the entire building. Their deaths were entirely due to the fact that a couple of their devoted, loyal comrades, full of pride in their fight for freedom, betrayed them. For money. Just as they would later betray Abu Musab al-Zarqawi.

Despite all our efforts, the suicide bombers just continued, young Iraqis convinced by the teachings of the extremist ayatollahs that the murder of their perceived enemies would open the gateway to paradise for them—that the three trumpets would sound and they would cross the bridge into the arms of Allah and everlasting happiness.

So they just went right back at it. A bomb killed a U.S. soldier on August 26, which meant there had now been more U.S. lives lost since the conflict ended than during the battle. On August 29, a massive car bomb exploded outside a Shiite mosque in Najaf and killed eighty people, including the revered and greatly loved Shiite leader Ayatollah Mohammad Baqir al-Hakin.

In our opinion, this was rapidly getting out of hand. It seemed no matter what we did, no matter how many of these nuts we rounded up, how much explosive, bombs, or weapons we located, there was always more. And always more young men quite happy to take that shortcut to the trumpets, get right over that bridge and plug into some quality happiness.

By now, late August, the question of the missing WMDs was growing more urgent. Hans Blix, the United Nations' chief weapons inspector, had retired from public life, and the U.S. Armed Forces were now keeping a careful watch. In our view, the question of whether Saddam Hussein had biological and chemical weapons was answered. Of course he did. He used them in Halabja, right?

I guess by now the issue in the minds of the American public was, Did he have a nuclear weapon, an atom bomb? But, of course, that is not the most significant question. The one that counts is, Did he have a nuclear program?

Because that would mean he was trying to produce weapons-grade uranium-235. You get that from using a centrifuge to spin uranium-238, thus driving the heavy neutrons outward, like water off the lettuce in a salad spinner. It's a hell of a process and takes up to seven years, at which time, if you've had a trouble-free run, you cut off the outside edges of the uranium and there you have a large hunk of heavy-molecule uranium-235. Cut that in half and then slam the two pieces together by high explosive in a confined steel space, like a rocket or a bomb, and right there it's Hiroshima all over again.

And that's the issue: Was Saddam spinning for uranium-235, and if so, where did he get the uranium in the first place? And where was he conducting his program? Remember, there is no other reason on this earth to want uranium-235 except to make an atom bomb.

We knew the American intelligence agencies believed he had such a program, that somewhere in this vast country — it's bigger than Germany, nearly as big as Texas—there were centrifuges trying to manufacture the world's most dangerous substance.

That was all the information we had. But we knew what to look for, and we would most certainly have recognized it if we had found it. Did Saddam actually own the completed article, a finely tuned atomic bomb or missile? Probably not. No one ever thought he did. But as former defense secretary Donald Rumsfeld once remarked, "What do you want to do? Leave him there till he does?"

You may remember the CIA believed they had uncovered critical evidence from the satellite pictures of those enormous government trucks rolling along Iraq's highways: four of them, usually in convoy, and all big enough to house two centrifuges. The accepted opinion was that Saddam had a mobile spinning program which could not easily be found, and in fact could be either lost and buried in the desert or alternatively driven across the border into Syria or even Jordan.

Well, we found those trucks, hidden in the desert, parked together. But the inside of each one had been roughly gutted. There was nothing left. We saw the trucks, and in my opinion someone had removed whatever they had contained, and in a very great hurry.

I also saw the al Qaeda training camp north of Baghdad. That had been abandoned, but it was stark evidence of the strong links between the Iraqi dictator and Osama bin Laden's would-be warriors. Traces of the camp's military purpose were all around. Some of the guys who had been in Afghanistan said it was just about a direct replica of the camp the United States destroyed after 9/11.

There were many times when we really were chasing shadows out there in that burning hot, sandy wilderness. Especially in our coastal searches. Out there, often in uncharted desert waste-land near the water, we'd see rocket launchers in the distance and drive right onto them, only to find they were just decoys, huge fake missile containers pointing at the sky, made out of scrap metal and old iron bars.

After a two-day drive over rough country in unbelievable heat, that counted as a very grave inconvenience. If our team had ultimately found Saddam in his hidey-hole, we'd probably have shot him dead for a lot of reasons but especially on the strength of those wasted desert runs. (Just joking.)

I'll say one thing. That Iraqi president was one wily devil, ducking and diving between his thirteen palaces, evading cap-ture, making tape recordings, urging the dregs of his armed forces to keep killing us, encouraging the insurgents to continue the war against the great Satan (that's us).

It was tough out there. But in many ways I'm grateful for the experience. I learned precisely how seditious and cunning an enemy could be. I learned never to underestimate him. And I learned to stay right on top of my game all of the time in order to deal with it. No complacency.

Looking back, during our long journey in the C-130 to Af-ghanistan, I was more acutely aware of a growing problem which faces U.S. forces on active duty in theaters of war all over the world. For me, it began in Iraq, the first murmurings from the liberal part of the U.S.A. that we were somehow in the wrong, brutal killers, bullying other countries; that we who put our lives on the line for our nation at the behest of our government should somehow be charged with murder for shooting our enemy.

It's been an insidious progression, the criticisms of the U.S. Armed Forces from politicians and from the liberal media, which knows nothing of combat, nothing of our training, and nothing of the mortal dangers we face out there on the front line. Each of the six of us in that aircraft en route to Afghanistan had constantly in the back of our minds the ever-intrusive rules of engagement.

These are drawn up for us to follow by some politician sitting in some distant committee room in Washington, D.C. And that's a very long way from the battlefield, where a sniper's bullet can blast your head, where the slightest mistake can cost your life, where you need to kill your enemy before he kills you.

And those ROE are very specific: we may not open fire until we are fired upon or have positively identified our enemy and have proof of his intentions. Now, that's all very gallant. But how about a group of U.S. soldiers who have been on patrol for several days; have been fired upon; have dodged rocket-propelled grenades and homemade bombs; have sustained casualties; and who are very nearly exhausted and maybe slightly scared?

How about when a bunch of guys wearing colored towels around their heads and brandishing AK-47s come charging over the horizon straight toward you? Do you wait for them to start killing your team, or do you mow the bastards down before they get a chance to do so?

That situation might look simple in Washington, where the human rights of terrorists are often given high priority. And I am certain liberal politicians would defend their position to the death. Because everyone knows liberals have never been wrong about anything. You can ask them. Anytime.

However, from the standpoint of the U.S. combat soldier, Ranger, SEAL, Green Beret, or whatever, those ROE represent a very serious conundrum. We understand we must obey them because they happen to come under the laws of the country we are sworn to serve. But they represent a danger to us; they undermine our confidence on the battlefield in the fight against world terror. Worse yet, they make us concerned, disheartened, and sometimes hesitant.

I can say from firsthand experience that those rules of engagement cost the lives of three of the finest U.S. Navy SEALs who have ever served. I'm not saying that, given the serious situation, those elite American warriors might not have died a little later, but they would not have died right then, and in my view would almost certainly have been alive today.

I am hopeful that one day soon, the U.S. government will learn that we can be trusted. We know about bad guys, what they do, and, often, who they are. The politicians have chosen to send us into battle, and that's our trade. We do what's necessary. And in my view, once those politicians have elected to send us out to do what 99.9 percent of the country would be terrified to undertake, they should get the hell out of the way and stay there.

This entire business of modern war crimes, as identified by the liberal wings of politics and the media, began in Iraq and has been running downhill ever since. Everyone's got to have his little hands in it, blathering on about the public's right to know.

Well, in the view of most Navy SEALs, the public does not have that right to know, not if it means placing our lives in unnecessary peril because someone in Washington is driving himself mad worrying about the human rights of some cold-hearted terrorist fanatic who would kill us as soon as look at us, as well as any other American at whom he could point that wonky old AK of his.

If the public insists it has the right to know, which I very much doubt, perhaps the people should go and face for themselves armed terrorists hell-bent on killing every single American they can.

I promise you, every insurgent, freedom fighter, and stray gunman in Iraq who we arrested knew the ropes, knew that the way out was to announce he had been tortured by the Americans, ill treated, or prevented from reading the Koran or eating his breakfast or watching the television. They all knew al-Jazeera, the Arab broadcasters, would pick it up, and it would be relayed to the U.S.A., where the liberal media would joyfully accuse all of us of being murderers or barbarians or something. Those terrorist organizations laugh at the U.S. media, and they know exactly how to use the system against us.

I realize I am not being specific, and I have no intention of being so. But these broad brushstrokes are designed to show that the rules of engagement are a clear and present danger, frightening young soldiers, who have been placed in harm's way by their government, into believing they may be charged with murder if they defend themselves too vigorously.

I am not a political person, and as a Navy SEAL I am sworn to defend my country and carry out the wishes of my commander in chief, the president of the United States, whoever he may be, Republican or Democrat. I am a patriot; I fight for the U.S.A. and for my home state of Texas. I simply do not want to see some of the best young men in the country hesitating to join the elite branches of the U.S. Armed Services because they're afraid they might be accused of war crimes by their own side, just for attacking the enemy.

And I know one thing for certain. If I ever rounded a mountainside in Afghanistan and came face to face with Osama bin Laden, the man who masterminded the vicious, unprovoked attack on my country, killing 2,752 innocent American civilians in New York on 9/11, I'd shoot him dead, in cold blood.

At which point, urged on by an outraged American media, the military would probably incarcerate me *under* the jail, never mind *in* it. And then I'd be charged with murder.

Tell you what. I'd still shoot the sonofabitch.

2

Baby Seals...
and Big Ole Gators

**I wrestled with one once and was pretty glad when that
sucker decided he'd had enough and took off for calmer
waters. But to this day my brother loves to wrestle alligators, just for fun.**

We flew on, high over the southern reaches of the Gulf of
Oman. We headed east-northeast for four hundred miles, forty-
five thousand feet above the Arabian Sea. We crossed the sixty-
first line of longitude in the small hours of the morning. That
put us due south of the Iranian border seaport of Gavater, where
the Pakistan frontier runs down to the ocean.

Chief Healy snored quietly. Axe did a *New York Times* crossword. And the miracle was that Shane's headset didn't explode,
as loud as his rock-and-roll music was playing.

"Do you really need to play that shit at that volume, kiddo?"

"It's cool, man...dude, chill."

"Jesus Christ."

The C-130 roared on, heading slightly more northerly now,
up toward the coast of Baluchistan, which stretches 470 miles
along the northern shoreline of the Arabian Sea and commands,

strategically, the inward and outward oil lanes to the Persian Gulf. Despite a lot of very angry tribal chiefs, Baluchistan is part of Pakistan and has been since the partition with India in 1947. But that doesn't make the chiefs any happier with the arrangement.

And it's probably worth remembering that no nation, not the Turks, the Tatars, the Persians, the Arabs, the Hindus, or the Brits has ever completely conquered Baluchistan. Those tribesmen even held off Genghis Khan, and his guys were the Navy SEALs of the thirteenth century.

They never tell us, or anyone else, the precise route of U.S. Special Forces into any country. But there's a big American base in the Baluchistan coastal town of Pasni. I guess we made our landfall somewhere along there, long before first light, and then flew on over four mountain ranges for 250 miles up to another U.S. military base near the city of Dalbandin.

We never stopped, but Dalbandin lies only fifty miles south of the Afghan border, and the airspace is safe around there. At least, it's as safe as anything can be in this strange, wild country, which is kind of jammed into a triangle among Iran, Pakistan, and Afghanistan.

Baluchistan, its endless mountains a safe haven for so many fleeing al Qaeda recruits and exiled Taliban fighters, currently provides shelter for up to six thousand of these potential terrorists. And even though Chief Healy, me, and the guys were nine miles above this vast, underpopulated, and secretive land, it still gave me the creeps, and I was pleased when the aircrew finally told us we were in Afghanistan airspace, running north for another four hundred miles, up toward Kabul.

I fell asleep somewhere over the Regestan Desert, east of one of Afghanistan's greatest waterways, the 750-mile-long

Helmand River, which flows and irrigates most of the southern farmlands.

I cannot remember my dreams, but I expect they were of home. They usually are when I'm serving overseas. Home for us is a small ranch out in the piney woods of East Texas, near Sam Houston National Forest. We live down a long, red dirt road in a lonely part of the country, close by another two or three ranches, one of which, our adjoining neighbor, is about four thousand times bigger than ours and sometimes makes us seem a whole lot bigger than we are. I have a similar effect on my identical twin brother, Morgan.

He's about seven minutes older than I am, and around the same size (six feet five inches, 230 pounds). Somehow I've always been regarded as the baby of the family. You wouldn't believe seven minutes could do that to a guy, would you? Well, it did, and Morgan is unflagging in his status as senior man.

He's a Navy SEAL as well, a little behind me in rank, because I joined first. But he still assumes a loose command whenever we're together. And that's pretty often, since we share a house in Coronado, California, hard by the SEAL teams.

Anyway, there's two or three houses on our Texas property, the main one being a single-story stone ranch surrounded by a large country garden, which contains one little plantation for corn and another couple for vegetables. All around us, just about as far as you can see in any direction, there's pasture, studded with huge oak trees and grazing animals. It's a peaceful place for a God-fearing family.

Right from kids, Morgan and I were brought up to believe in the Lord. We weren't compelled to go to church or anything, and to this day the family are not churchgoers. In fact, I'm the only one who does go to church on a somewhat regular basis. On

Sunday mornings when I'm home, I drive over to the Catholic church, where people know me. I was not baptized a Catholic, but it suits me, its beliefs and doctrines sit easily with me. Since I was young, I have always been able to recite the Twenty-third Psalm and several others from beginning to end.

Also, I thought the late Pope John Paul was the holiest man in the world, an uncompromising Vicar of Christ, a man whose guidelines were unshakable. Tough old guy, John Paul. A lot too tough for the Russians. I've always thought if he hadn't been a vicar, he'd have made a good Navy SEAL.

Down home, in our quiet backwoods area, it looks like an untroubled life. There are a few minor irritants, most of those being snakes. However, Dad taught us how to deal with them long ago, especially the coral snakes and those copperhead vipers. There's also rattlesnakes, eastern diamondbacks, and king snakes, which eat the others. In the local lake you can find the occasional water moccasin, and he is one mean little sonofabitch. He'll chase you, and while I don't much like 'em, I'm not scared of them. Morgan goes after them as a sport, likes to hustle 'em up, keep 'em alert.

A mile or so up the road from us, there's a mighty herd of Texas longhorns. Beyond the house there's a half dozen paddocks for my mom's horses, some of them belonging to her, others boarders from other people.

People send horses to her for her near-mystical power to bring sick or weak animals back to full fighting form. No one knows how she does it. She's plainly a horse whisperer. But she has some special ways of feeding them, including, for a certain type of ailing racehorse, some kind of a seaweed concoction she swears to God can turn a cow pony into Secretariat. Sorry, Mom. Didn't mean that. Just joking.

Seriously, Holly Luttrell is a brilliant horsewoman. And she does turn horses that seem very poorly into gleaming, healthy runners again. I guess that's why those horses keep on coming. She can only cope with about ten at a time, and she's out there in the barn at five every morning looking after them. If you take the time, you can see the effect she has on them, the very obvious results of her very obvious skills.

My mom's a seventh-generation Texan, although she did once immigrate to New York City. Around here, that's like moving to Shanghai, but Mom has always been a rather glamorous blonde and she wanted to make a career as an air stewardess. Didn't last long, though. She was back in the big country of East Texas real quick, raising horses. Like all of us, she feels Texas is a part of her spirit. It's in mine, in Dad's, and it sure as hell is the very essence of Morgan.

None of us would live anywhere else. We're right at home down here, with people we have known and trusted for many years. There's no one like Texans for a spirit of expansiveness, optimism, friendship, and decency. I realize that might not be acceptable to everyone, but that's how it seems to us. We're out of place anywhere else. It's no good pretending otherwise.

That might mean we just get real homesick quicker than other people. But I will come back to live here when I'm finished in the military. And I intend, sometime, to die here. Hardly a day goes by, wherever I am in the world, when I don't think of our little ranch and my huge circle of family and friends, of having a beer on the front porch and telling tall stories full of facts, some of 'em true, all of 'em funny.

So while I'm on the subject I'll explain how a farm boy from the backwoods of East Texas came to be made a petty officer first class and a team leader in the U.S. Navy SEALs.

The short explanation is probably talent, but I don't have any more of that than the next guy. In fact, my natural-born assets are very average. I'm pretty big, which was an accident of birth. I'm pretty strong, because a lot of other people took a lot of trouble training me, and I'm unbelievably determined, because when you're as naturally ungifted as I am, you have to keep driving forward, right?

I'll outwork anyone. I'll just go on and on until the dust clears. Then I'm usually the only one left standing. As an athlete, I'm not very fast, but I'm kind of sharp. I know where to be, I'm good at anticipating things, and I guess that's why I was a halfway decent sportsman.

Give me a golf ball and I can hit that sucker a country mile. That's because golf is a game that requires practice, practice, and more practice. That's my brand of doggedness. I can do that. I play to a reasonable handicap, although I wasn't born a Ben Hogan or anything. But Ben came from Texas like me. We were born about ninety-four miles apart, and in my country that's the equivalent of a sand wedge. Ben, of course, was known to practice more than any other golfer who had ever lived. Must be something in the water.

I was born in Houston but raised up near the Oklahoma border. My parents, David and Holly Luttrell, owned a fair-sized horse farm, about 1,200 acres at one time. We had 125 head up there, mostly Thoroughbreds and quarter horses. My mom ran the breeding programs, and Dad took charge of the racing and sales operation.

Morgan and I were brought up with horses, feeding, watering, cleaning out the barns, riding. Most every weekend we'd go in the horse van to the races. We were just kids at the time, and both our parents were excellent riders, especially Mom. That's how we learned. We worked the ranch, mended fences, swinging sledgehammers when we were about nine years old. We loaded the bales into the loft, worked like adults from a young age. Dad insisted on that. And for a lot of years, the operation did very well.

At the time, Texas itself was in a boom-time hog heaven. Out in West Texas, where the oil drillers and everyone surrounding them were becoming multimillionaires, the price of oil went up 800 percent between 1973 and 1981. I was born in 1975, before that wave even started to crest, and I have to say the Luttrell family was riding high.

It was nothing for my dad to breed a good-looking horse from a $5,000 stallion and sell the yearling for $40,000. He did it all the time. And my mom was a pure genius at improving a horse, buying it cheap and devoting months of tender loving care and brilliant feeding to produce a young runner worth eight times what she paid.

And breeding horses was precisely the right line to be in. Horses were right up there with Rolex watches, Rolls-Royces, Learjets, Gulfstream 1s, palaces rather than regular houses, and boats, damn great boats. Office space was at a premium all over the state, and massive new high-rise blocks were under construction. Retail spending was at an all-time high. *Racehorses, beautiful. Give me six. Six fast ones, Mr. Luttrell. That way I'll win some races.*

That oil money just washed right off, and people were making fortunes in anything that smacked of luxury, anything to feed the egos of the oil guys, who were spending and borrowing money at a rate never seen before or since.

It wasn't anything for banks to make loans of more than $100 million to oil explorers and producers. At one time there were

4,500 oil rigs running in the U.S.A., most of them in Texas. Credit? That was easy. Banks would lend you a million bucks without batting an eye.

Listen, I was only a kid at the time, but my family and I lived through the trauma to come, and, boy, I've done some serious reading about it since. And in a way, I'm glad I lived through it, because it taught me to be careful, to earn my money and invest it, get it somewhere secure.

And it taught me to think very carefully about the element of luck, when it's running, and how to keep your life under control. I have long since worked out that when the crash came in Texas, its effects were magnified a thousandfold, because the guys in the oil industry sincerely believed money had nothing to do with luck. They thought their prosperity came from their own sheer brilliance.

No one gave much consideration to the world oil market being controlled in the Middle East by Muslims. Everything that happened had its roots in Arabia, assisted by President Carter's energy policy and the fact that when I was five years old the price per barrel of crude was $40.

The crash, when it came, was caused by the oil embargo and the Iranian revolution, when the ayatollah took over from the shah. The key to it was geopolitical. And Texas could only stand and watch helplessly as the oil glut manifested itself and the price per barrel began to slide downward to an ultimate low of around $9.

That was in 1986, when I was not quite ten. In the meantime, the giant First National Bank of Midland, Texas, collapsed, judged insolvent by government financial inspectors. That was one huge bank to go belly-up, and the ripple effect was statewide. An era of reckless spending and investing was over. Guys building palaces were forced to sell at a loss. You couldn't give away a luxury boat, and Rolls-Royce dealers darned near went out of business.

Along with the commercial giants felled by the oil crash went the horse farm of David and Holly Luttrell. Hard-running colts and mares, which Dad had valued at $35,000 to $40,000, were suddenly worth $5,000, less than they cost to raise. My family lost everything, including our house.

But my dad's a resilient man, tough and determined. And he fought back, with a smaller ranch and the tried-and-trusted techniques of horse raising he and Mom had always practiced. But it all went wrong again. The family wound up living with my grandfather, Morgan sleeping on the floor.

My dad, who had always kept one foot in the petrochemical business ever since he came back from Vietnam, went back to work, and in a very short time he was on his feet, with a couple of huge deals. We moved out of Grandfather's place into a grand four-story house, and the good times seemed to be back.

Then some giant deal went south and we somehow lost it all again, moved back out to a kind of rural skid row. You see, my dad, though born over the border in Oklahoma, is a Texan in his soul. He was as brave as a lion when he was a navy gunner in Vietnam. And in Texas, real men don't sit on their money. They get back out there, take risks, and when they hit it big, they just want to hit it bigger. My dad's a real man.

You could tell a lot about him just by the names he gave the ranches, big or small—Lone Star Farms, North Fork Ranch, Shootin' Star. Like he always said, "I'd rather shoot for a star and hit a stump than shoot for a stump and miss."

I cannot describe how poor we were during the time Morgan and I were trying to get through college. I had four jobs to pay tuition and board and make my truck payment. I was the lifeguard in the college pool and I worked with Morgan on construction, landscaping, cutting grass, and yard work. In the evening I was a bouncer in a rough local bar full of redneck cowboys. And I was still starving, trying to feed myself on about twenty dollars a week.

One time, I guess we were around twenty-one, Morgan snapped his leg playing baseball, sliding into second. When they got him to the hospital Morgan just told them we didn't have any money. Eventually the surgeon agreed to operate and set the leg on some kind of long-term credit. But the anaesthetist would not administer anything to Morgan without payment.

No one's tougher than my brother. And he eventually said, "Fine. I don't need anaesthetic. Set the leg without it. I can take the pain." The surgeon was aghast and told Morgan he could not possibly have such an operation without anaesthesia. But Morgan stuck to his guns. "Doc, I don't have any money. Fix my leg and I'll handle the pain."

No one was crazy about that, especially the surgeon. But then Jason Miller, a college buddy of Morgan's, turned up, saw that he was in absolute agony, and gave him every last dollar of his savings to pay the anaesthetist. At which point they put Morgan back together.

But I'm getting ahead of myself. When we were young, working the horses, my dad was very, very tough on us. He considered that good grades were everything, bad ones were simply unacceptable. I once got a C in conduct, and he beat me with a saddle girth. I know he was doing it for our own good, trying to instill discipline in his sons, which would serve them well in later life.

But he ruled our lives with an iron fist. He would tell us: "One day I'm not gonna be here. Then it's gonna be you two, by yourselves, and I want you to understand how rough and unfair this world is. I want you both prepared for whatever the hell might come your way."

He tolerated nothing. Disobedience was out of the question. Rudeness was damn near a hanging offense. There was no leeway. He insisted on politeness and hard work. And he didn't let up even when we were all broke. Dad was the son of an Arkansas woodsman, another amazingly tough character, and he brought that stand-on-your-own-feet ruggedness into our lives at the earliest opportunity.

We were always out in the woods, in rough country in the East Texas pines, the red oaks, and the sweet gum trees. Dad taught us to shoot straight at the age of seven, bought us a .22 rifle, a Nylon 66. We could hit a moving Miller High Life beer can from 150 yards. Now that's redneck stuff, right? Redneck kids in redneck country, learning life's skills.

He taught us how to survive out there. What you could eat and what you couldn't. He showed us how to build a shelter, taught us how to fish. He even taught us how to rope and kill a wild boar: drop a couple of long loops around his neck and pull, then hope to hell he doesn't charge straight at you! I still know how to butcher and roast one.

At home, on any of the ranches, Dad showed us how to plant and grow corn and potatoes, vegetables and carrots. A lot of times when we were really poor we just about lived on that. Looking back, it was important training for a couple of farm boys.

But perhaps most important of all, he taught us to swim. Dad himself was an all-American swimmer and this really mattered to him. He was superb in the water and he made me that good. In almost everything, Morgan is naturally better than I am. He's very gifted as a runner, a fighter, a marksman, a navigator on land or water. He always sails through his exams, whereas I have to slog it out, studying, practicing, trying to be first man in and last man out. Morgan does not have to strive.

He was honor man after his SEAL BUD/S (Basic Underwater Demolition/Seals) class, voted for by his peers. I knew he would be before he even started. There's only one discipline at which he can't beat me. I'm faster in the water, and I have the edge underwater. He knows it, though he might not admit it.

There was a huge lake near where we lived, and that's where Dad trained us. All through the long Texas summers we were out there, swimming, racing, diving, practicing. We were just like fish, the way Dad wanted it.

He spent months teaching us to dive, deep, first on our own, then with our scuba gear on. We were good, and people would pay us to try and retrieve keys and valuables thrown into deep water. Of course, Dad considered this might be too easy, and he stipulated we only got paid if we found the correct object.

During this time we had the occasional brush with passing alligators, but one of my great Texas friends, Tray Baker, showed us how to deal with them. I wrestled with one once and was pretty glad when that sucker decided he'd had enough and took off for calmer waters. But to this day my brother loves to wrestle alligators, just for fun. He is, of course, crazy. But we sometimes take an old flat-bottomed boat fishing in the lake, and one of those big ole gators will come sliding up alongside the boat.

Morgan makes a quick assessment—*Nostrils about eight or nine inches from his eyes, so he's eight or nine feet long.* Morgan executes a ramrod-straight low-angled dive right on top of the gator, clamping its jaws shut with his fists, then he twists it and turns it, gets on its back, all the while holding those huge jaws tight shut and laughing at the panic-stricken beast of the deep.

After a few minutes they both get fed up with it, and Morgan lets it go. I always think this is the most dangerous part. But I never saw a gator who felt like having another go at Morgan. They always just turn around and swim away from the area. He only misjudged it once, and his hand bears a line of alligator-teeth scars.

You know, I think Dad always wanted us to be Navy SEALs. He was forever telling us about those elite warriors, the stuff they did and what they stood for. In his opinion they were all that is best in the American male—courage, patriotism, strength, determination, refusal to accept defeat, brains, expertise in all that they did. All through our young lives he told us about those guys. And over the years, it sunk in, I suppose. Morgan and I both made it.

I was about twelve when I realized beyond doubt that I was going to become a Navy SEAL. And I knew a lot more about it than most kids of my age. I understood the brutality of the training, the level of fitness required, and the need for super skills in the water. I thought I would be able to handle that. Dad had told us of the importance of marksmanship, and I knew I could do that.

SEALs need to be at home in rough country, able to survive, live in the jungle if necessary. We were already good at that. By the age of twelve, Morgan and I were like a couple of wild animals, at home in the great outdoors, at home with a fishing pole and gun, easily able to live off the land.

But deep down I knew there was something more required to make it into the world's top combat teams. And that was a level of fitness and strength that could only be attained by those who actively sought it. Nothing just happens. You always have to strive.

In our part of East Texas, there are a lot of past and present special forces guys, quiet, understated iron men, most of them unsung heroes except among their families. But they don't serve in the U.S. Armed Forces for personal recognition or glory.

They do it because deep in their granite souls they feel a slight shiver when they see Old Glory fluttering above them on the parade square. The hairs on the backs of their necks stand up when these men hear the national anthem of the United States. When the president walks out to the strains of a U.S. military band's "Hail to the Chief," there's a moment of solemnity for each and every one of them — for our president, our country, and what our country has meant to the world and the many people who never had a chance without America.

These men of the special forces have had other options in their lives, other paths, easier paths they could have taken. But they took the hardest path, that narrow causeway that is not for the sunshine patriot. They took the one for the supreme patriot, the one that may require them to lay down their lives for the United States of America. The one that is suitable only for those who want to serve their country so bad, nothing else matters.

That's probably not fashionable in our celebrity-obsessed modern world. But special forces guys don't give a damn about that either. I guess you have to know them to understand them. And even then it's not easy, because most of them are shy, rather than taciturn, and getting any of them to say anything self-congratulatory is close to impossible. They are of course aware of a higher calling, because they are sworn to defend this country and to fight its battles. And when the drum sounds, they're going to come out fighting.

And when it does sound, the hearts of a thousand loved ones miss a beat, and the guys know this as well as anyone. But for them, duty and commitment are stronger than anyone's aching heart. And those highly trained warriors automatically pick up their rifles and ammunition and go forward to obey the wishes of their commander in chief.

General Douglas MacArthur once warned the cadets of West Point that if they should become the first to allow the Long Gray Line to fail, "a million ghosts in olive drab, brown khaki, in blue and gray, would rise from their white crosses thundering those magic words, *Duty, Honor, and Country*." No need for ghosts in the U.S. Navy SEALs. Those words are engraved upon our hearts.

And many such men way down there in East Texas were willing to give up their time for absolutely no reward to show kids what it takes to become a SEAL, a Ranger, or a Green Beret. The one we all knew about was a former Green Beret sergeant who lived close by. His name was Billy Shelton, and if he ever sees this, he'll probably die of embarrassment, seeing his name in print on the subject of valor.

Billy had a glittering army career in combat with the Green Berets in Vietnam and, later, serving on a government SWAT team. He was one of the toughest men I ever met, and one afternoon just before my fifteenth birthday, I plucked up my courage and went to his house to ask if he could train me to become a Navy SEAL. He was eating his lunch at the time, came to the door still chewing. He was a bull of a man, rippling muscles, fair skin, not carrying one ounce of fat. To my eyes he looked like he could have choke slammed a rhino.

I made my hesitant request. And he just looked me up and down and said, "Right here. Four, tomorrow afternoon." Then he shut the door in my face. I was a bit young at the time, but the phrase I was groping for was *No bullshit, right?*

Now, everyone in the area knew that Billy trained kids for the special forces. And when he had a group of us running down the street, cars driving by would blow their horns and cheer us on.

He always ignored that, and he showed us no mercy. Our program included running with heavy concrete blocks on our shoulders. When Billy thought we were strong enough, we stepped up the pace, running with rubber tires, which felt like they'd just come off the space shuttle or at least that big ole tractor out back.

Billy did not hold an exercise class; he operated a full pre-SEAL training program for teenagers. Over the years he had us in the gym pumping iron, hauling the torture machine, the ergometer, pounding the roads, driving our bodies, sweating and straining.

Morgan and I were terrified of him. I used to have nightmares when we were due to report to him the next morning, because he drove us without mercy, never mind our extreme youth. We were in a class of maybe a dozen guys, all midteens.

"I'm gonna break you down, mentally and physically," he yelled at us. "Break you down, hear me? Then I'm gonna build you right back up, as one fighting unit—so your mind and body are one. Understand me? I'm gonna put you through more pain than you've ever been in."

Right about then, half the class ran for their lives rather than face this bulldog, this ex–Texas Tech tailback who could run like a Mack truck going downhill. He had the support of a local high school, which allowed him to use their gym free of charge to train future special forces from our part of the world.

"I'm not your friend," he'd shout. "Not right here in this gym. I'm here to get you right—fit, trained, and ready for the SEALs, or the Berets, or the Rangers. I'm not getting one dime from anyone to do this. And that's why you're gonna do it right, just so you don't waste my time.

"Because if any one of you fails to make the grade in the special forces, it will not be because you were too weak. Because that would mean I'd failed, and I'm gonna make sure that cannot happen, because right here, failure's not an option. I'm gonna get you right. All of you. Understand?"

He'd take us on twelve-mile runs, hauling the concrete blocks till we nearly collapsed. Guys would have blood on the backs of their heads from the chafing. And he never took his eyes off us, never tolerated idleness or lack of concentration. He just made us grind it out, taking it to the limit. Every time.

That's what built my strength, gave me my basis. That's how I learned the fitness creed of the SEALs. Billy was extremely proud of that; proud to pass on his knowledge.

And he asked only for undying devotion to the cause, the discipline of a samurai warrior, and lungs like a pair of bagpipes. He was absolutely relentless, and he really loved Morgan and me, two of only six survivors in the class.

Once, when I came back from a tour of duty in Iraq, I went to see him after a couple of weeks' easy living and Mom's cooking, and he threw me out of the gym!

"You're a goddamned fat, pitiful excuse for a SEAL, and I can't stand to look at you!" he yelled. "Get out of my sight!" Holy shit! I was out of there, ran down the stairs, and didn't dare go back until I'd dropped eight pounds. No one around here argues with Billy Shelton.

The other skill I needed was still to come. No Navy SEAL can operate without a high level of expertise in unarmed combat. Billy told me I'd need to take martial-arts classes as soon as possible. And so I found a teacher to work with. All through my grade school and college career, I studied and learned that strange, rather mystical Asian skill. I worked at it for many years instead of becoming involved in other sports. And I attained all of my goals.

Morgan says the real truth is I don't know my own strength and should be avoided at all times.

By any standards, I had a head start in becoming a Navy SEAL. I was made aware of the task at a young age, and I had two strong engines driving me forward: my dad and Billy Shelton. Everything I learned beyond the schoolroom, down from my early years, seems to have directed me to Coronado. At least, looking back now it seems that way.

Everyone understands why there's a huge rate of dropouts among applicants for the SEALs. And when I think of what I went through in the years before I got there, I can't even imagine what it must be like for guys who try out with no prior training. Morgan and I were groomed to be SEALs, but it was never easy. The work is brutally hard, the fitness regimes are as harsh and uncompromising as any program in the free world. The examinations are searching and difficult. Nothing but the highest possible standard is acceptable in the SEAL teams.

And perhaps above all, your character is under a microscope at all times; instructors, teachers, senior chiefs, and officers are always watching for the character flaw, the weakness which may one day lead to the compromise of your teammates. We can't stand that. We can stand damn near anything, except that.

When someone tells you he is in the SEAL teams, it means he has passed every test, been accepted by some of the hardest taskmasters in the military. And a short nod of respect is in order, because it's harder to become a Navy SEAL than it is to get into Harvard Law School. Different, but harder.

When someone tells you he's in a SEAL team, you know you are in the presence of a very special cat. Myself, I was just born lucky, somehow fluked my way in with a work ethic bequeathed to me by my dad. The rest of those guys are the gods of the U.S. Armed Forces. And in faraway foreign fields, they serve their nation as required, on demand, and mostly without any recognition whatsoever.

They would have it no other way, because they understand no other way. Accolades just wash off them, they shy away from the spotlight, but in the end they have one precious reward—when their days of combat are over, they know precisely who they are and what they stand for. That's rare. And no one can buy it.

Back in the C-130, crossing into the southern wastes of the Regestan Desert, the gods of the U.S. Armed Forces with whom I traveled were asleep, except for the beach god Shane, who was still rockin'.

Somewhere out in the darkness, to our starboard side, was the Pakistani city of Quetta, which used to be quite important when the Brits ran the place. They had a big army staff college down there, and for three years in the mid-1930s, Field Marshal Viscount Montgomery, later the victor of the Battle of Alamein, taught there. Which proves, I suppose, that I'm as much addicted to military trivia as I am to the smart-ass remark.

However, we stayed on the left-hand, Afghanistan side of the border, I think, and continued on above the high western slopes of the great range of the Hindu Kush mountains. The most southerly peak, the one nearest the desert, is 11,000 feet high. After that it gets pretty steep, and it was to those mountains we were headed.

Way below us was the important city of Kandahar, which a few weeks later, on June 1, 2005, was the scene of one of the most terrible Taliban attacks of the year. One of their suicide bombers killed twenty people in Kandahar's principal mosque. In that central-city disaster, they killed the security chief of Kabul, who was attending the funeral of an anti-Taliban cleric who had been killed three days earlier by a couple of guys on a motorbike.

I think that Chief Healy and myself, in particular, were well aware of the dangers in this strife-torn country. And we realized the importance of our coming missions, to halt the ever-burgeoning influx of Taliban recruits streaming in over the high peaks of the Hindu Kush and to capture their leaders for interrogation.

The seven-hour journey from Bahrain seemed endless, and we were still an hour or more south of Kabul, crawling north high above the treacherous border that leads directly to the old Khyber Pass and then to the colossal peaks and canyons of the northern Hindu Kush. After that, the mountains swerve into Tajikstan and China, later becoming the western end of the Himalayas.

I was reading my guidebook, processing and digesting facts like an Agatha Christie detective. Chaman, Zhob, key entry points for the Taliban and for bin Laden's al Qaeda as they fled the American bombs and ground troops. These tribesmen drove their way over sixteen-thousand-foot mountains, seeking help from the disgruntled Baluchistan chiefs, who were now bored sideways by Pakistan and Afghanistan, Great Britain, Iran, the U.S.A., Russia, and anyone else who tried to tell them what to do.

Our area of operations would be well north of there, and I spent the final hours of the journey trying to glean some data.

But it was hard to come by. Trouble is, there's not much happening in those mountains, not many small towns and very few villages. Funny, really. Not much was happening, and yet, in another way, every damn thing in the world was happening: plots, plans, villainy, terrorism, countless schemes to attack the West, especially the United States.

There were cells of Taliban warriors just waiting for their chance to strike against the government. There were bands of al Qaeda swarming around a leader hardly anyone had seen for several years. The Taliban wanted power in Afghanistan again; bin Laden's mob wanted death and destruction of U.S. citizens, uniformed or not. One way or another, they were all a goddamned nightmare, and one that was growing progressively worse. Which was why they sent for us.

In the weeks before our arrival, there had been widespread incidents of violence, confirming everyone's dread that the generally hated Taliban was once more on the rise and a serious threat to the new government of Afghanistan. Even with the support of thirty thousand U.S. and NATO troops, President Hamid Karzai struggled to control the country anywhere outside of Kabul.

A few weeks earlier, in February, the Taliban flatly announced they were increasing their attacks on the government as soon as the weather improved. And from then on they launched a series of drive-by shootings and bombings, usually directed at local officials and pro-government clergy. In the south and over to the east, they started ambushing American soldiers.

It's a strange word, *Taliban*. Everyone's heard it, like *insurgent, Sunni, ayatollah,* or *Taiwan*. But what does Taliban really stand for? I've suffered with them, what you might describe as close encounters of the most god-awful type. And I've done a lot of reading. The facts fit the reality. Those guys are evil, murderous religious fanatics, each one of them with an AK-47 and a blood-lust. You can trust me on that one.

The Taliban have been in prominence since 1994. Their original leader was a village clergyman named Mullah Mohammad Omar, a tough guy who lost his right eye fighting the occupying forces of the Soviet Union in the 1980s. By the mid-'90s, the Taliban's prime targets in Afghanistan—before I showed up—were the feuding warlords who (a) formed the mujahideen and (b) threw the Soviets out of the country.

The Taliban made two major promises which they would carry out once in power: to restore peace and security, and to enforce sharia, or Islamic law. Afghans, weary of the mujahideens' excesses and infighting, welcomed the Taliban, which enjoyed much early success, stamping out corruption, curbing lawlessness, and making the roads safe for commerce to flourish. This applied to all areas that came under their control.

They began their operation in the southwestern city of Kandahar and moved quickly into other parts of the country. They captured the province of Herat, which borders Iran, in September 1995. And one year later, their armies took the Afghan capital of Kabul, overthrowing the regime of President Burhanuddin Rabbani and his defense minister, Ahmed Shah Massoud. By 1998, they were in control of almost 90 percent of the country.

Once in power, however, the Taliban showed their true colors. They set up one of the most authoritarian administrations on earth, one that tolerated no opposition to their hard-line policies. Ancient Islamic punishments, like public executions for convicted murderers and amputations at the wrist for those charged with theft, were immediately introduced. I cannot even think about the penalty a rapist or an adulterer might anticipate.

Television, music, sports, and cinema were banned, judged

by the Taliban leaders to be frivolities. Girls age ten and above were forbidden to go to school; working women were ordered to stay at home. Men were required to grow beards, women had to wear the burka. These religious policies earned universal notoriety as the Taliban strived to restore the Middle Ages in a nation longing to join the twenty-first century. Their policies concerning human rights were outrageous and brought them into direct conflict with the international community.

But there was another issue, which would bring about their destruction. And that was their role in playing host to Osama bin Laden and his al Qaeda movement. In August 1998 Islamic fanatics bombed the U.S. embassies in Kenya and Tanzania, killing more than 225 people. Washington immediately presented the Taliban leaders with a difficult choice—either expel bin Laden, who was held responsible for the bombings by the U.S. government, or face the consequences.

The Taliban flatly refused to hand over their Saudi-born guest, who was providing them with heavy funding. President Bill Clinton ordered a missile attack on the main bin Laden training camp in southern Afghanistan, which failed to kill its leader. Then in 1999 the United States persuaded the U.N. Security Council to impose sanctions on Taliban-ruled Afghanistan. Two years later, even harsher sanctions were put in place in another attempt to force the Taliban to hand over bin Laden.

Nothing worked. Not sanctions nor the denial of Afghanistan's U.N. seat. The Taliban were still in power, and they were still hiding Osama bin Laden, but their isolation, political and diplomatic, was becoming total.

But the Taliban would not budge. They took their isolation as a badge of honor and decided to go whole hog with an even more fundamentalist regime. The poor Afghan people realized too late what they had done: handed over the entire country to a group of bearded lunatics who were trying to inflict upon them nothing but stark human misery and who controlled every move they made under their brutal, repressive, draconian rule. The Taliban were so busy trying to enslave the citizens, they forgot about the necessity for food, and there was mass starvation. One million Afghans fled the country as refugees.

All of this was understood by the West. Almost. But it took horrific shock, delivered in March 2001, to cause genuine international outrage. That was when the Taliban blasted sky-high the two monumental sixth-century statues of the Bamiyan Buddhas, one of them 180 feet high, the other 120 feet, carved out of a mountain in central Afghanistan, 143 miles northwest of Kabul. This was tantamount to blowing up the Pyramids of Giza.

The statues were hewn directly from sandstone cliffs right in Bamiyan, which is situated on the ancient Silk Road, the caravan route which linked the markets of China and central Asia with those of Europe, the Middle East, and south Asia. It was also one of the revered Buddhist religious sites, dating back to the second century and once home to hundreds of monks and many monasteries. The two statues were the largest standing Buddha carvings on earth.

And their summary destruction by the Taliban rulers of Afghanistan caused museum directors and curators all over the world to have about four hemorrhages apiece. The Taliban effectively told the whole lot of them to shove it. Whose statues were they, anyway? Besides, they were planning to destroy all the statues in Afghanistan, on the grounds they were un-Islamic.

The Bamiyan Buddhas were destroyed in accordance with sharia law. Only Allah the Almighty deserves to be worshipped, not anyone or anything else. Wraps that up then, right? Praise Allah and pass the high explosive.

The blasting of the Buddhas firmed up world opinion that something had to be done about Afghanistan's rulers. But it took another explosion to provoke savage action against them. That took place on September 11, the same year, and was the beginning of the end for the Taliban and bin Laden's al Qaeda.

Before the dust had settled on lower Manhattan, the United States demanded the Taliban hand over bin Laden for masterminding the attack on U.S. soil. Again the Taliban refused, perhaps not realizing that the new(ish) U.S. president, George W. Bush, was a very different character from Bill Clinton.

Less than one month later, on October 7, the Americans, leading a small coalition force, unleashed an onslaught against Afghanistan that shook that area of the world to its foundations. U.S. military intelligence located all of the al Qaeda camps in the mountains of the northeast part of the country, and the military let fly with one of the biggest aerial bombardments in modern warfare.

It began with fifty cruise missiles launched from U.S. warships and Royal Navy submarines. At the same time, long after dark in Afghanistan, twenty-five carrier-based aircraft and fifteen land-based bombers took off and destroyed Taliban air defenses, communications infrastructure, and the airports at Kabul, Jalalabad, Kandahar, and Herat. The U.S. bombs blasted the big radar installations and obliterated the control tower in Kandahar. This was the city where Mullah Omar lived, and a navy bomber managed to drop one dead in the middle of his backyard. That one-eyed ole bastard escaped, though.

The Taliban, its military headquarters now on fire, did own a somewhat insignificant air-strike capacity, just a few aircraft and helicopters, and the U.S. Air Force wiped that right out with smart bombs as a matter of routine.

Navy bombers taking off from the carriers targeted the Taliban's other military hardware, heavy vehicles, tanks, and fuel dumps. Land-based B-1, B-2, and B-52 bombers were also in the air, the B-52s dropping dozens of five-hundred-pound gravity bombs on al Qaeda terrorist training camps in eastern Afghanistan, way up in the border mountains where we would soon be visiting.

One of the prime U.S. objectives was the small inventory of surface-to-air missiles and shoulder-fired antiaircraft missiles, stolen from either the Russians or the old mujahideen. These were hard to locate, and various caches were removed by the tribesmen and hidden in the mountains. Hidden, sadly, for use another day.

One hour after that nighttime bombardment began, the Northern Alliance opened fire with a battery of rockets from an air base twenty-five miles north of Kabul. They aimed them straight at Taliban forces in the city. There were five thunderous explosions and all electric power was knocked out throughout the capital.

But the United States never took its eye off the ball. The true objective was the total destruction of al Qaeda and the leader who had engineered the infamous attack on the Twin Towers—"the Pearl Harbor of the twenty-first century," as the president described it. And that meant a massive strike on the sinister network of caves and underground tunnels up in the mountains, where bin Laden made his headquarters.

The cruise missiles had softened up the area, but that was only the start. The real heavyweight punch from the world's only superpower would come in the form of a gigantic bomb—the

BLU-82B/C-130, known as Commando Vault in Vietnam and now nicknamed Daisy Cutter. This is a high-altitude, fifteen-thousand-pound conventional bomb that needs to be delivered from the huge MC-130 aircraft because it is far too heavy for the bomb racks on any other attack aircraft.

This thing is awesome. It was originally designed to create instant clearings for helicopter landings in the jungle. Its purpose in Afghanistan was as an antipersonnel weapon up in those caves. Its lethal radius is colossal, probably nine hundred feet. Its flash and sound is obvious from literally miles away. The BLU-82B is the largest conventional bomb ever built and, of course, leaves no nuclear fallout. (For the record, the Hiroshima atom bomb was a thousand times more powerful.)

On the upside, the Daisy Cutter is extremely reliable, no problems with wind speed or thermal gradient. Its conventional explosive technique incorporates both agent and oxidizer. It is not fuel-air explosive, like the old FAE systems used for much, much smaller bombs. It's nearly twelve feet long and more than four feet wide.

The BLU-82B depends on precise positioning of the delivery aircraft, coordinates gotten from fixed ground radar or onboard navigation equipment. The aircraft must be perfectly positioned prior to final countdown and release. The navigator needs to make dead-accurate ballistic and wind computations.

The massive blast effect of the bomb means it cannot be released below an altitude of 6,000 feet. Its warhead, containing 12,600 pounds of low-cost GSX slurry (ammonium nitrate, aluminum powder, and polystyrene), is detonated by a 38-inch fuse extender a few feet above ground level, so it won't dig a crater. The entire blast blows outward, producing overpressure of 1,000 pounds per square inch. Hence the nickname Daisy Cutter.

The United States has never specified how many of these things were dropped on the Tora Bora area of the White Mountains, where the al Qaeda camps were located. But there were at least four, maybe seven. The first one, according to a public announcement by the Pentagon, was dropped after a reported sighting of bin Laden. We can only imagine the crushing effect such a blast would have inside the caves where the al Qaeda high command and senior leadership operated. Wouldn't have been too good even if you were standing in the middle of a field — but a cave! Jesus, that's brutal. That thing wiped out hundreds of the enemy at a time.

The United States really did a number on the Taliban, flattened their stronghold in Kunduz in the north, shelled them out of the Shomali Plains north of Kabul, carpet bombed them anywhere they could be located around the Bagram air base, where, four years later, we were headed in the C-130.

In the fall of 2001, the Taliban and al Qaeda were mostly fleeing the U.S. offensive or surrendering. In the subsequent years, they drifted together on the other side of the Pakistani border, reformed, and began their counteroffensive to retake Afghanistan.

Somehow these hickory-tough tribesmen not only survived the onslaught of American bombing and escaped from the advancing Northern Alliance, but they also evaded one of the biggest manhunts in the history of warfare as an increasingly frustrated United States moved heaven and earth to capture bin Laden, Mullah Omar, and the rest. I guess their propensity to run like hell from strong opposition and their rapid exit into the Pakistani mountains on the other side of the border allowed them to limit their human and material resources.

It also bought them time. And while they undoubtedly lost many of their followers after a front-row view of what the American military could and would do, they also had many months to begin recruiting and training a brand-new generation of supporters. And now they were back as an effective fighting army, launching guerrilla operations against the U.S.-led coalition forces only four years after they'd lost power, been driven into exile, and had nearly been annihilated.

As we prepared for our final approach to the great, sprawling U.S. base at Bagram, the Taliban were once again out there, killing aid workers and kidnapping foreign construction workers. Parts of eastern and southern Afghanistan have been officially designated unsafe due to increasingly daring Taliban attacks. There was evidence they were extending their area of influence, working closely again with bin Laden's al Qaeda, forging new alliances with other rebel groups and anti-government warlords. Same way they'd grabbed power last time, right? Back in 1996.

Only this time they had one principal ambition before seizing power, and that was to destabilize the U.S.-led coalition forces and eventually drive them out of Afghanistan forever.

I ought to mention the Pashtuns, the world's oldest living tribal group; there are about forty-two million of them. Twenty-eight million live in Pakistan, and 12.5 million of them live in Afghanistan; that's 42 percent of the entire population. There are about 88,000 living in Britain and 44,000 in the U.S.A.

In Afghanistan, they live primarily in the mountains of the northeast, and they also have heavily populated areas in the east and south. They are a proud people who adhere to Islam and live by a strict code of honor and culture, observing rules and laws known as *Pashtunwalai,* which has kept them straight for two thousand years.

They are also the quintessential supporters of the Taliban. Their warriors form the backbone of the Taliban forces, and their families grant those forces shelter in high mountain villages, protecting them and providing refuge in places that would appear almost inaccessible to the Western eye. That, by the way, does not include U.S. Navy SEALs, who do have Western eyes but who don't do inaccessible. We can get in anywhere.

It's easy to see why the Pashtuns and the Taliban get along just fine. The Pashtuns were the tribe who refused to buckle under to the army of the Soviet Union. They just kept fighting. In the nineteenth century, they fought the British to the verge of surrender and then drove them back into Pakistan. Three hundred years before that, they wiped out the army of Akbar the Great, the most fearsome of India's Mogul rulers.

Those Pashtuns are proud of their stern military heritage, and it's worth remembering that in all the centuries of bitter, savage warfare in Baluchistan, during which time they were never subdued, half the population was always Pashtun.

The concept of tribal heritage is very rigid. It involves bloodlines, amazing lineages that stretch back through the centuries, generation after generation. You can't join a tribe in the way you can become an American citizen. Tribes don't hand out green cards or passports. You either are, or you aren't.

Language, traditions, customs, and culture play a part, but, I repeat, you can't join the Pashtuns. And that gives them all a steel rod of dignity and self-esteem. Their villages may not be straightforward military strongholds as the Taliban desire, but the Pashtuns are not easily intimidated.

The people are organized strictly by relationships; male relationships, that is. The tribal lineage descends from the father's side, the male ancestors. I understand they don't give a damn for Mom and her ancestors. Inheritances are strictly for the boys, and land rights go directly to sons.

They have a proverb that says a lot: I against my brothers; my brothers and I against my cousins; my brothers, my cousins, and I against the world. That's how they do it. The tight military formation has, again and again, allowed them to knock eight bells out of more sophisticated invaders.

The tribal code, *Pashtunwalai*, has heavy demands: hospitality, generosity, and the duty to avenge even the slightest insult. Life among the Pashtuns is demanding—it depends on the respect of your peers, relatives, and allies. And that can be dangerous. Only the tribe's principles of honor stand in the way of anarchy. A tribesman will fight or even kill in order to avoid dishonor to himself and his family.

And killing throws the whole system into confusion, because death must be avenged; killers and their families are under permanent threat. Which puts a big air brake on violence. According to the learned Charles Lindhorn, a professor of anthropology at Boston University, homicide rates among the Pashtun tribes are way lower than homicide rates in urban areas of the United States. I am grateful to the professor for his teachings on this subject.

The Taliban creed comes right out of the Pashtun handbook: women are the wombs of patrilineage, the fountainheads of tribal honor and continuity. Their security and chaste way of life is the only guarantee of the purity of the lineage. This seclusion of women is known as purdah, and it is designed to keep women concealed, maintaining the household, and it gives them a high sense of honor.

Purdah represents the status of belonging. A woman's husband can go fight the invaders while she controls the household, enjoying the love and respect of her sons, expecting one day to rule as matriarch over her daughters-in-law and their children.

That's the basis of the Taliban view of women. And I guess it works fine up in the Hindu Kush, but it might not go over too well in downtown Houston.

Anyway, there's been a lot of terrible fighting on the Pashtuns' lands, mostly by outsiders. But the ole *Pashtunwalai* has kept them intact. Their tradition of generous hospitality, perhaps their finest virtue, includes the concept of *lokhay warkawal*. It means "giving of a pot." It implies protection for an individual, particularly in a situation where the tribe might be weaker than its enemies. When a tribe accepts *lokhay*, it undertakes to safeguard and protect that individual from an enemy at all costs.

I, perhaps above all other Western visitors, have reason to be eternally grateful for it.

We were on our final approach to the enormous U.S. base at Bagram. Everyone was awake now, seven hours after we left Bahrain. It was daylight, and down below we could see at last the mountains we had heard so much about and among which we would be operational in the coming weeks.

There was still snow on the high peaks, glittering white in the rising sun. And below the snow line, the escarpments looked very steep. We were too high to pick up villages on the middle slopes, but we knew they were there, and that's where we were probably going in the not too distant future.

The huge runway at Bagram runs right down the side of the complex, past hundreds and hundreds of bee huts, lines and lines of them. On the ground we could see parked aircraft and a whole lot of Chinook helicopters. We didn't worry about whom we'd have to share with. SEALs are always billeted together, separate from anyone else, thus avoiding loose talk about highly classified missions. All of our missions are, of course, highly classified, and we do not talk loosely, but other branches of the services are not so stringently trained as we are, and no one takes any chances.

Here we were at last, in the Islamic Republic of Afghanistan, a country the size of Texas, landlocked on all sides, protected by the granite walls of mountains, war torn for years and years and still at it. Just like always, warlords were trying to drive out the usurpers. Us. And we weren't even usurping, just trying to stop another bloody tribal upheaval and another regime change from the elected to the dictators.

Boy. It seemed like a hell of a task. But we were excited. This was what we joined for. In truth, we could hardly wait to get down there and get on with it. And in a sense, it was pretty simple. We somehow had to get out into those infamous mountain passes and put a stop to this clandestine infiltration of faceless tribal warriors making their way across the border, doggedly, silently, prepared to fight at the drop of a turban.

We knew their track record, and we knew they could move around the mountains very quickly. They had dominated those slopes, caves, and hideouts for centuries, turning them into impregnable military strongholds against all comers.

And they had already faced the SEALs in open combat up there, because the SEALs had been first in. They would be prepared, we knew that. But like all SEAL operational teams, we believed we were better than everyone else, so the goddamned Taliban had better watch it.

Danny, Shane, James, Axe, Mikey, and I. We were here on business, trained to the minute, armed to the teeth, all set to drive the armies of the Taliban and al Qaeda right back to where they came from, seize the leaders, and get rid of anyone too dangerous to live. And restore order to the mountains.

I was eight thousand miles from home, but I could e-mail my family and loved ones. I was a bit light on home comforts, but I had in my rucksack a DVD player and a DVD of my favorite movie, *The Count of Monte Cristo*, from the novel by Alexandre Dumas *père*. It's always an inspiration to me, always raises my spirits to watch one brave, innocent man's lonely fight against overpowering forces of evil in an unforgiving world.

That's my kind of stuff. Backs to the wall. Never give in. Courage, risks, daring beyond compare. I never thought my own problems would very shortly mirror, albeit briefly, those of Edmond Dantès and the hopelessness of his years in the grim island fortress of Chateau d'If.

And I never thought those unforgettable words he carved with flintstones, into the granite walls of the cruelest of jails, would also provide me with hope; a forlorn hope, but hope nonetheless. During the peril of my own darkest hours, I thought of those words over and over, more times than I care to admit: *God will give me justice.*

3

A School for Warriors

It was pitch dark, and he was wearing sunglasses, wraparound, shiny black... "Most of you aren't going to
be here in a couple of months," said Instructor Reno...
"If you guys don't start pulling together as a team, none
of you will be here."

The six SEALs from Bahrain landed in Bagram, in northeast
Afghanistan, shortly after first light. I realize I have just spent
two entire chapters essentially pointing out what a momentous event that was, our arrival to work with the elite mountain
troops of the U.S. Army. It has occurred to me that you might
be wondering why we thought we were so goddamned superior
to everyone else, why we felt entitled to our own private brand of
arrogance.

Not wishing to be haunted by anyone's doubts about me and
my teammates, I propose to explain right now, before we get
moving, precisely why we felt this way about the world. It's not
some form of premature triumph, and it would be absurd to call
it mere confidence. That would be like calling the Pacific wet.

It's a higher form of consciousness, and I do not mean that to
be pretentious. It's been said that only the very rich understand
the difference between themselves and the poor, and only the

truly brilliant understand the difference between themselves and the relatively dumb.

Well, only men who have gone through what we went through can understand the difference between us and the rest. In the military, even the rest understand what it takes to scale the heights of combat excellence. And in my case, it started inauspiciously. Way down on the ranch, with Mom in tears, refusing to leave the house to see me go. March 7, 1999. I was twenty-three.

To say that I was not making amazing headway in my hometown would be an understatement. The reputation Morgan and I had was not assisting either of us. There were always guys showing up wondering how tough we really were. I guess my dad considered it a matter of time before one of us was faced with a low-flying pugilist and either hurt someone badly or got badly hurt himself. And so I decided to get out of town and join the U.S. Navy SEALs. Morgan thought it was a great idea, and he introduced me to a recruiting officer in a nearby town, Petty Officer First Class Beau Walsh. He steered me down to the military enlistment processing station in Houston; that's navy recruitment.

Naturally, I told them immediately there was no need for me to attend boot camp. I was already way too advanced for that. Yessir, I'll go straight to Coronado, where the big dogs eat. That's what I'm all about, I'm a half-trained SEAL already.

They sent me directly to boot camp. I signed the papers and prepared to report for duty in a few days. As I left the ranch, it was not a real ceremony of departure, but everyone was there, including Beau Walsh and Billy Shelton. As previously stated, Mom caved in and retreated to the house, unable to witness the departure of her baby. That was me.

My destination was more than a thousand miles to the north, Navy Recruit Training Command (RTC) in Great Lakes, Illinois. And I can truthfully say, it was where I spent the most miserable eight weeks of my entire life. I had never even seen snow, and I arrived in the middle of the worst blizzard that boot camp had seen in eleven years. It was like sending a Zulu to the North Pole.

That wind and snow came howling in across Lake Michigan, blasting its way onto the western shore where we were situated, thirty-five miles north of Chicago. Right on the water. I could not believe the sheer misery of that freezing weather. The camp was a gigantic place, with hundreds of recruits trying to make that miraculous transformation from civilian to U.S. Navy sailor. It was a drastic metamorphosis, both mental and physical, and it would have been difficult enough in fine weather. But in that ice, snow, and wind, Jesus. Words fail me.

I'd never needed winter clothes, and I had none. I remember being extremely pleased when the navy issued everyone the right gear—thick socks, boots, dark blue trousers, shirts, sweaters, and coats. They told us how to fold and store everything, showed us how to make our bunks every morning. Without missing a beat, they put us straight into physical training, running, working out, marching, drilling, and many classes.

I didn't have much trouble, and I excelled in the swimming pool. The requirements were to enter the water feetfirst from a minimum height of five feet, remain afloat for five minutes, and then swim fifty yards using any stroke. I could have done that in my sleep, especially without having to worry about the occasional alligator or water moccasin.

The running would not have been that bad in decent weather, but the campus was absolutely frigid, and the wind off the lake was cutting. A penguin would have had trouble out there. We ran through snow, marched through snow, and made our way to classes through snow.

In that first week, while we were trying to avoid freezing to death, they instilled in us three words which have been with me ever since. *Honor, Courage, Commitment,* the motto of the United States Navy, the core values that immediately became the ideals we all lived by. I can remember to this day an instructor telling us, "What you make of this experience here at Great Lakes is what will make you as a person." He was right. I hope.

In the second week, they put us through the Confidence Course. This is designed to simulate emergency conditions in a U.S. Navy warship. They taught us to be sharp, self-reliant, and, above all, to make key decisions on which our lives and those of our shipmates might depend. That word: *teamwork.* It dominates and infiltrates every single aspect of life in the navy. In boot camp, they don't just tell you, they indoctrinate you. Teamwork. It was the new driving force in all of our lives.

Week three, they put us on board a landbound training ship. Everything was hands-on training. We learned the name of nearly every working part of that ship. They taught us first aid techniques, signaling ship to ship with flags (semaphore). We spent a lot of time in the classroom, where we focused on navy customs and courtesies, the laws of armed conflict, shipboard communication, ship and aircraft identification, and basic seamanship.

All this was interspersed with physical training tests, sit-ups, sit-reaches, and push-ups. I was fine with all of those, but the one-and-a-half-mile run in that weather would have tested the stamina of a polar bear. They told us anyone who failed could come back and take it again. I decided I would rather run barefoot across the Arctic than take it again. Gave it my all. Passed, thank God.

During week four, we got our hands on some weaponry for the first time—the M16 rifle. I was pretty quick with that part of the course, especially on the live-fire range. After that, the navy concentrated on which path through the service everyone wanted to take. That was also easy for me. Navy SEALs. No bullshit, right?

The firefighting and shipboard damage-control course came next. And we all learned how to extinguish fires, escape smoke-filled compartments, open and close watertight doors, operate the oxygen breathing apparatus, and move fire hoses around. The last part was the worst—the Confidence Chamber. You get in there with your class and put on a gas mask. Then someone unleashes a tear-gas tablet, and you have to take off your mask, throw it in a trash can, and recite your full name and Social Security number.

Every single recruit who joins the navy has to endure that exercise. At the end, the instructors make it clear: you have what it takes. There's a place in the navy for you.

The final task is called battle stations. Teams are presented with twelve situations, all of which have been addressed during the previous weeks. This is where they grade the recruits, individually and as teams. When you've completed this, the trainers present you with a U.S. Navy ball cap, and that tells the world you are now a sailor. You have proved you belong, proved you have the right stuff.

The following week, I graduated, in my brand-new dress uniform. I remember passing the mirror and hardly recognizing myself. Standing tall, right there. There's something about graduating from boot camp; I guess it's mostly pride in yourself.

But you also know a lot of people couldn't have done it. Makes you feel pretty good. Especially someone like me, whose major accomplishment thus far had involved hurling some half-drunk cowboy out of an East Texas bar and into the street on his ear.

After I graduated, I flew immediately to San Diego, headed to Coronado Island and the navy amphibious base. I made my way there alone, a couple of weeks early, and spent my time organizing my uniforms, gear, and rooms, and trying to get into some sort of shape.

Most of us had lost a lot of condition at boot camp because the weather was so bad. You couldn't just jog outside and go for a run because of the blizzards and the deep snow. Perhaps you remember that very brave guy who made the journey to the South Pole with the Royal Navy officer, Robert Falcon Scott, in 1912. He believed he was hindering the entire team because of his frostbite. Captain Oates was his name, and he crawled out into a raging blizzard one night with the immortal words, "I am going outside now. I may be gone for some time."

They never found his body, and I have never forgotten reading his words. Guts-ball, right? Well, going outside at Great Lakes would have been a bit like that, and almost as brave. Unlike the gallant captain, we stayed by the heater.

And now we were going for runs along the beach, trying to get in shape for the first week of Indoctrination. That's the two-week course known as Indoc, where the SEALs prepare you for the fabled BUD/S course (Basic Underwater Demolition/SEALs). That one lasts for seven months and is a lot harder than Indoc. But if you can't get through the initial pretraining endurance test, then you ought not to be in Coronado, and they don't want you anyway.

The official navy literature about the reason for Indoc reads:

"To physically, mentally and environmentally prepare qualified SEAL candidates to begin BUD/S training." Generally speaking, the instructors do not turn on the pressure during Indoc. You're only revving up for the upcoming trial by fire.

But they still make it very tough for everyone, officers and enlisted men alike. The SEAL programs make no distinction between commissioned officers coming in from the fleet and the rest of us. We're all in it together, and the first thing they instill in you at Indoc is that you will live and train as a class, as a team. Sorry. Did I say *instill in you?* I meant, *ram home with a jackhammer.* Teamwork. They slam that word at you every other minute. *Teamwork. Teamwork. Teamwork.*

This is also where you first understand the concept of a swim buddy, which in SEAL ethos is an absolutely gigantic deal. You work with your buddy as a team. You never separate, not even to go to the john. In IBS (that stands for "inflatable boat, small") training, if one of you falls over the side into the freezing ocean, the other joins him. Immediately. In the pool, you are never more than an arm's length away. Later on, in the BUD/S course proper, you can be failed out of hand, thrown out, for not staying close enough to your swim buddy.

This all comes back to that ironclad SEAL folklore—we never leave a man behind on the battlefield, dead or alive. No man is ever alone. Whatever the risk to the living, however deadly the opposing fire, SEALs will fight through the jaws of death to recover the remains of a fallen comrade. It's a maxim that has survived since the SEALs were first formed in 1962, and it still applies today.

It's a strange thing really, but it's not designed to help widows and parents of lost men. It's designed for the SEALs who actually do the fighting. There's something about coming home, and we all want to achieve that, preferably alive. But there is a certain private horror about being killed and then left behind in a foreign land, no grave at home, no loved ones to visit your final resting place.

I know that sounds kind of nuts, but nonetheless, it's true. Every one of us treasures that knowledge: No matter what, I will not be left behind, I will be taken home. We are all prepared to give everything. And in the end it does not seem too much to ask in return, since we fight, almost without exception, on the enemy's ground, not our own.

That World War I English poet and serving soldier Rupert Brooke understood the Brits do not traditionally bring home their war dead. And he expressed it right: "If I should die, think only this of me: / That there's some corner of a foreign field / That is forever England." There's not a Navy SEAL anywhere in the world who does not understand those lines and why Brooke wrote them.

It's a sacred promise to us from our high command. That's why it gets drummed into us from the very first day in Coronado—you are not going to be alone. Ever. And you're not going to leave your swim buddy alone.

I suffered a minor setback in the early part of that summer when I was in Class 226. I managed to fall from about fifty feet up a climbing rope and really hurt my thigh. The instructor rushed up to me and demanded, "You want to quit?"

"Negative," I responded.

"Then get right back up there," he said. I climbed again, fell again, but somehow I kept going. The leg hurt like hell, but I kept training for another couple of weeks before the medics diagnosed a cracked femur! I was immediately on crutches but still hobbling along the beach and into the surf with the rest of them. Battle conditions, right?

Eventually, when the leg healed, I was put back and then joined BUD/S Class 228 in December for phase two. We lived in a small barracks right behind the BUD/S grinder. That's the blacktop square where a succession of SEAL instructors have laid waste to thousands of hopes and dreams and driven men to within an inch of their lives.

Those instructors have watched men drop, watched them fail, watched them quit, and watched them quietly, with ice-cold, expressionless faces. That's not heartless; it's because they were only interested in the others, the ones who did not crack or quit. The ones who would rather die than quit. The ones with no quit in them.

It was only the first day of Indoc, and my little room was positioned right next to the showers. *Showers,* by the way, is a word so polite it's damn near a euphemism. They were showers, okay, but not in the accepted, civilized sense. They were a whole lot closer to a goddamn car wash and were known as the decontamination unit. Someone cranked 'em up at around 0400, and the howl of compressed air and freezing cold pressurized water forcing its way through those pipes sounded like someone was trying to strangle a steam engine.

Jesus. First time I heard it, I thought we were under attack.

But I knew the drill: get into my canvas UDT swim trunks and then get under those ice-cold water jets. The shock was unbelievable, and to a man we hated it, and we hated it for as long as we were forced through it. The damn thing was actually designed to power wash our sand-covered gear when we returned from the beach. The shock was reduced somewhat then because everyone had just been in the Pacific Ocean. But right out of bed at four o'clock in the morning! Wow! That was beyond reason, and I can still hear the sound of those screaming, hissing water pipes.

Freezing cold and wet, we reported to the training pool to roll and stow the covers. Then, shortly before 0500, in the pitch dark, we lined up on the grinder and sat in rows, chest to back, very close, to conserve body heat. There were supposed to be 180 of us, but for various reasons there were only 164 of us assigned.

We had a class leader by now, Lieutenant David Ismay, a Naval Academy man and former Rhodes Scholar who'd had two years at sea and was now a qualified surface warfare officer. David was desperate to achieve his lifelong dream of becoming a SEAL. He had to do this right. Officers only got one shot at BUD/S. They were supposed to know better than to waste anyone's time if they weren't up to it.

The man we all awaited was our proctor. That's the instructor assigned to guide us, teach us, torture us, observe us, and get rid of us, if necessary. He was Instructor Reno Alberto, a five-foot-six man-mountain of fitness, discipline, and intelligence. He was a ruthless, cruel, unrelenting taskmaster. And we all grew to love him for two reasons. He was scrupulously fair, and he wanted the best for us. You put out for Instructor Reno, he was just a super guy. You failed to give him your absolute best, he'd have you out of there and back to the fleet before you could say, "Aye, aye, sir."

He arrived at 0500 sharp. And we'd have a ritual which was never broken. This was how it went:

"Feet!" shouted the class leader.

"Feet!" An echoing roar ripped into the still night air as nearly

164 of us responded and jumped to our feet, attempting to move into ranks.

"In-structor Ree-no!" called the class leader.

"Hooyah, Instructor Ree-no!" we bellowed as one voice.

Get used to that: *hooyah*. We don't say yes, or right away, or thanks a lot, or understand and will comply. We say *hooyah*. It's a BUD/S thing, and its origins are lost in antiquity. There's so many explanations, I won't even go there. Just so you know, that's how students respond to an instructor, in greeting or command acceptance. *Hooyah*.

For some reason, Instructor Reno was the only one who was unfailingly addressed by his first name. All the others were Instructor Peterson or Matthews or Henderson. Only Reno Alberto insisted on being called by his first name. I always thought it was good they didn't call him Fred or Spike. Reno sounded good on him.

When he walked onto the grinder that morning, we could tell we were in the presence of a major man. As I mentioned, it was pitch dark and he was wearing sunglasses, wraparound, shiny black. It seemed he never took them off, night or day. Actually, one time I did catch him without them, and as soon as he saw me, he reached into his pocket and immediately put 'em on again.

I think it was because he never wanted us to see the expression in his eyes. Beneath that stern, relentless exterior, he was a superintelligent man—and he could not have failed to be amused at the daily Attila the Hun act he put on for us. But he never wanted us to see the amusement in his eyes, and that was why he never showed them.

On this dark, slightly misty morning he stood with his arms folded and gazed at the training pool. Then he turned back to us and stared hard.

We had no idea what to expect. And Instructor Reno said without expression, "Drop."

"Drop!" we roared back. And we all struggled down to the concrete and assumed a position for push-ups, arms extended, bodies outstretched, rigid.

"Push 'em out," said Reno.

"Push-ups," snapped the class leader.

"Push-ups," we responded.

"Down."

"One."

"Down."

"Two."

We counted out every one of the twenty push-ups in the set then returned to the rest position, arms outstretched. The class leader called out, "In-structor Ree-no."

"Hooyah, Instructor Ree-no," we roared.

He ignored us. Then said quietly, "Push 'em out." As he did twice more, at which point he left us with muscles on fire in the straight-arm, outstretched rest position. He actually left us there for almost five minutes, and everyone's arms were throbbing. Eighty push-ups and now this new kind of agony, which ended only when he said, very slowly, very quietly, "Recover."

We all yelled, *"Feet!"* in response, and somehow we stood up without falling over. Then David Ismay called out the wrong number of men present. Not his fault. Someone had simply vanished. Reno was onto young Dave in a flash. I don't quite remember what he said, but his phrase contained the loud pronunciation of the word *wrong.*

And he ordered Lieutenant Ismay and our leading petty officer student, "Drop, and push 'em out." I remember that first day like it happened this week. We sat and watched Dave complete his push-ups. And when they'd done it, damn near exhausted, they called out, "*Hooyah,* Instructor Reno!"

"Push 'em out," said Reno softly. And, somehow, they set off on twenty more repetitions of this killer discipline. Finally they finished, doubtless wondering, like the rest of us, what the hell they had let themselves in for. But I bet they never called out the wrong number of men present ever again.

I now understand that SEAL ethos—every officer, commissioned or noncommissioned, must know the whereabouts of every single one of his men. No mistakes. At that early stage in our training, our class leader, David Ismay, did not know. Reno, who'd only been with us for about fifteen minutes, did.

Again, he surveyed his kingdom and then spoke flatly. "Most of you aren't going to be here in a couple of months," said Instructor Reno. And, as if blaming each and every one of us individually for the wrong head count, he added, "If you guys don't start pulling together as a team, none of you will be here."

He then told us we were again about to take the basic BUD/S screening test. I graphically recall him reminding us we'd all passed it once in order to make it this far. "If you can't pass it again this morning," he added, "you'll be back in the fleet as soon as we can ship you out."

At this stage, no one was feeling . . . well . . . wanted. In fact, we were beginning to feel abandoned in this world-renowned military coliseum—a coliseum where someone was about to bring on the lions. Before us was the five-point screening test:

1. A 500-yard swim, breaststroke or sidestroke, in 12 minutes, 30 seconds

2. A minimum of 42 push-ups in 2 minutes

3. A minimum of 50 sit-ups in 2 minutes

4. A minimum of 6 dead-hang pull-ups
5. A 1.5-mile run in 11 minutes, 30 seconds, done while wearing boots and long pants

Only one guy failed to complete. In fact, most of us did markedly better than we had the first time. I recall I managed close to eighty push-ups and a hundred sit-ups. I guess the apparition of Billy Shelton was standing hard by my shoulder, trying to frighten the life out of me and ready to throw me out of the navy if I blew it.

More important, Instructor Reno was watching us with eyes like a fighter jet's radar. He told me several months later he knew I was putting out for him. Made up his mind about me right then and there. Told me he'd never changed it either. Good decision. I give it everything. On time. Every time. Might not always be good enough, but it's always my very best shot.

Looking back, I'm not sure that early test showed very much. There were a lot of heavily muscled, bodybuilding types who looked pretty ferocious. I remember they were among the very first to go, because they just couldn't hack it. Their legs and upper bodies were just too heavy.

The SEALs do place a premium on brute strength, but there's an even bigger premium on speed. That's speed through the water, speed over the ground, and speed of thought. There's no prizes for a gleaming set of well-oiled muscles in Coronado. Bulk just makes you slow, especially in soft sand, and that's what we had to tackle every day of our lives, mile after mile.

On this first morning of Class 226, we immediately learned another value peculiar to BUD/S. We don't stroll, walk, or even jog. We run. We actually run like hell. Everywhere. All day. Remember that great Tom Hanks line in *A League of Their Own,*

"There's no crying in baseball"? Well, we have a line in Coronado: There's no walking in BUD/S.

Our first encounter with this cruel and heartless rule came when it was time for breakfast. The chow hall was a mile away, so we had to run two miles—there and back—for a plate of toast, eggs, and bacon. Same for lunch. Same for dinner. For anyone mathematically challenged, that's six miles every day just to find something to eat, nothing to do with our regular daily training runs, which often added up to another eight miles.

That morning we ran in formation all the way across the naval amphibious base to the Special Warfare Center. And there Instructor Reno, after about a thousand push-ups and God knows what else, finally had us seated and paying attention in a manner which satisfied him. This was not easy, because he had eyes like a sea eagle and some kind of a high-flying business degree from USC. He knew precisely what was required, and he missed nothing.

And right here I needed to remember a lesson drummed into me from an early age by Billy Shelton: when a special forces commander makes even a slight reference to an issue that may be helpful, listen and then *do it*. Even if it was an aside, not a proper command, maybe even starting with *I think it might be a good idea* . . .

Always pay attention and then carry out the task, no matter how minor it may seem. Billy's point was that these SF instructors were looking for the best, and it might be only small things that separate guys who are very good from guys who are absolutely excellent, outstanding. "Listen, Marcus," Billy told me, "always listen, and always jump all over anything your instructor tells you. Get out in front. Fast. Then make sure you stay there."

Well, that morning, Instructor Reno pulled himself up to his full height of about fifteen feet, in my eyes, and told us he wanted to talk to us briefly, and we better pay attention. "Better yet, take notes."

I was into my zipper bag instantly, getting hold of a dry notebook and a couple of pencils, the lesson of Billy Shelton ringing in my ears: even an aside, even a suggestion, *do it*.

I looked around the room, and a few others were doing the same as I was, but not everyone, by no means everyone. Some of them just sat there gazing at Instructor Reno, who suddenly said, mildly, "How many of you have pencil and paper?"

I stuck my hand up, along with the other guys who had them. And suddenly there was a look like a storm cloud on Reno's face.

"Drop! All of you!" he bellowed. And there was an unbelievable commotion as chairs were scraped back and we all hit the floor in the straight-arm rest position. *"Push 'em out!"* he snapped. And we made the twenty then were left in the rest position.

He stared at us and said, "Listen. You were told to have a pencil and paper with you at all times. *So why don't you? Why the hell don't you!"*

The room went stone silent. Reno glared. And since I was not able to write while I was prostrate on the floor supporting myself with the palms of my hands, I can't say verbatim the exact words he said, but I bet I can come damn close.

"This is a school for warriors, understand? This is the most serious business there is. And if you don't want to do it, then get the hell out right now."

Christ. He was not joking, and I just hoped to hell he knew who had pencil and paper and who didn't. Months later I reminded him of that day and asked him. "Of course I knew," he said, adjusting his sunglasses. "It was your first test. I had the names of the guys who paid attention written down before you'd done your first twenty. And I still remember you were on that list."

Anyway, that first morning, we did another couple of sets of push-ups and somehow gasped out a loud *Hooyah, Instructor Reno!* And then he let us sit down again.

What followed was probably the most stern lecture in SEAL ethos and ethics I've ever attended. I did take notes, and I recall everything he told us, and I'll try to relate it as I believe Reno would wish.

"This is high-risk training. And we define that as anywhere there is potential for serious injury or loss of life. Any of you see anything unsafe, or any situation where you may be in unnecessary danger, speak up immediately. We do not like mistakes, understand me?"

"Hooyah!"

"Always remember your own accountability, to yourselves, your superiors, and your teammates. The chain of command is sacred. Use it. Keep your boat-crew leaders and your class leaders informed of any digression from the normal. And stay with your swim buddy. I don't care if you're going to the head, you stay right with him. Understood?"

"Hooyah!"

"Respect. I expect you to show complete respect for the instructor staff, the class officers, and the senior petty officers. You are in the military. You will be courteous at all times. Understood?"

"Hooyah!"

"Integrity, gentlemen. You don't lie, cheat, or steal. Ever. You lose an item of gear, you put in a chit and report it. You do not take someone else's gear. I won't pretend that has not happened here in the past. Because it has. But those guys were instantly finished. Their feet never touched the ground. They were gone. That day. You will respect your classmate. And his gear. You do not take what is not yours. Understood?"

"Hooyah!"

"I'm your class proctor for the next two weeks. And I'll help you, if you need help, over matters of pay, family, and personal concerns. If you get injured, go to medical and get it fixed and get back into training. I'm your proctor. Not your mother. I'm here to teach you. You stay in the box, I'll help you. You get outside the box, I'll hammer you. Understood?"

"Hooyah!"

"Finally, reputation. And your reputation begins right here. And so does the reputation of Class Two-two-six. And that's a reflection on me. It's a responsibility I take very personally. Because reputation is everything. In life, and especially right here in Coronado. So stay focused. Keep your head right in the game. Put out a hundred percent at all times, because we'll know if you don't. And never, ever, leave your swim buddy. Any questions?"

"Negative!"

Who could ever forget that? Not me. I can still hear in my mind the sharp crack as Instructor Reno snapped shut his notebook. It sounded to me like Moses, hammering together the granite slabs which held the 10 Commandments. That Reno was a five-foot-six-inch giant. He was some presence in our lives.

That day we bailed out of the classroom and went for a four-mile run along the beach. Three times he stopped us and told us to get in the surf and "get wet and sandy."

Our boots were waterlogged and each passing mile was murder. We never could get the sand out of our shorts. Our skin was chafing, and Reno didn't give a damn. At the end of the run, he ordered us to drop and start pushing 'em out. He gave us two sets of twenty, and right toward the end of the first set, I noticed he was doing the exercise with us. Except he was using only one arm, and he didn't even look like he was breathing hard.

That guy could have arm wrestled a half-ton gorilla. And just the sight of him cruising through the push-ups alongside us gave us a fair idea of the standard of fitness and strength required for us to make it through BUD/S.

As we prepared to make the mile run to the chow hall around noon, Reno told us calmly, "Remember, there's just a few of you here who we'd probably have to kill before you'd quit. We know that, and I've already identified some of you. That's what I am here to find out. Which of you can take the pain and the cold and the misery. We're here to find out who wants it most. Nothing more. Some of you won't, some of you can't and never will. No hard feelings. Just don't waste our time any longer than necessary."

Thanks a bunch, Reno. Just can't understand why you have to sugarcoat everything. Why not just tell it like it is? I didn't say that, of course. Four hours with the pocket battleship of Coronado had slammed a very hefty lid on my personal well of smart-ass remarks. Besides, he'd probably have broken my pelvis, since he couldn't possibly have reached my chin.

We had a new instructor for the pool, and we were all driven through the ice-cold jets of the decontamination unit to get rid of the sand on our skin. That damn thing would have blasted the scales off a fresh haddock. After that, we piled into the water, split into teams, and began swimming the first of about ten million lengths we would complete before our years of service to the navy were complete.

They concentrated on buoyancy control and surface swimming for the first few days, made us stretch our bodies, made us longer in the water, timing us, stressing the golden rule for all young SEALs—you must be good in the water, no matter what. And right here the attrition began. One guy couldn't swim at all! Another swore to God he had been told by physicians that he should not put his head underwater under any circumstances whatsoever!

That was two down. They made us swim without putting our heads up, taught us to roll our heads smoothly in the water and breathe that way, keeping the surface calm, instead of sticking our mouths up for a gulp of air. They showed us the standard SEAL swim method, a kind of sidestroke that is ultra-efficient with flippers. They taught us the technique of kick, stroke, and glide, the beginning of the fantastic SEAL underwater system that enables us to gauge distances and swim beneath the surface with astounding accuracy.

They taught us to swim like fish, not humans, and they made us swim laps of the pool using our feet only. They kept telling us that for other branches of the military, water is a pain in the ass. For us, it's a haven. They were relentless about times, always trying to make us faster, hitting the stopwatches a few seconds sooner every day. They insisted brute strength was never the answer. The only way to find speed was technique, and then more technique. Nothing else would work. And that was just the first week.

In the second, they switched us to training almost entirely underwater throughout the rest of the course. Nothing serious. They just bound our ankles together and then bound our wrists together behind our backs and shoved us into the deep end. This caused a certain amount of panic, but our instructions were clear:

Take a huge gulp of air and drop to the bottom of the pool in the standing position. Hold it there for at least a minute, bob up for new air, then drop back down for another minute, or more if you could.

The instructors swam alongside us wearing fins and masks, looking like porpoises, kind of friendly, in the end, but at first glance a lot like sharks. The issue was panic. If a man was prone to losing it under the water when he was bound hand and foot, then he was probably never going to be a frogman; the fear is too deeply instilled.

This was a huge advantage for me. I'd been operating underwater with Morgan since I was about ten years old. I'd always been able to swim on or below the surface. And I'd been taught to hold my breath for two minutes, minimum. I worked hard, gave it all I could, and never strayed more than about a foot from my swim buddy. Unless it was a race, when he remained on shore.

I was leader in the fifty-yard underwater swim without fins. I already knew the secret to underwater swimming: get real deep, real early. You can't get paid for finding the car keys if you can't get down there and stay down. At the end, they graded us underwater. I was up there.

Throughout this week we took ropes with us underwater. There was a series of naval knots that had to be completed deep below the surface. I can't actually remember how many guys we lost during that drownproofing part of the Indoc training, but it was several.

That second week was very hard for a lot of guys, and my memory is clear: the instructors preached competence in all techniques and exercises. Because the next week, when phase one of the BUD/S course began, we were expected to carry it all out. The BUD/S instructors would assume we could accomplish everything from Indoc with ease. Anyone who couldn't was gone. The Indoc chiefs would not be thanked for sending up substandard guys for the toughest military training in the world.

And while we were jumping in and out of the pool and the Pacific, we were also subjected to a stringent regime of physical training, high-pressure calisthenics. Not for us the relatively smooth surface of the grinder, the blacktop square in the middle of the BUD/S compound. The Indoc boys, not yet qualified even to join the hallowed ranks of the BUD/S students, were banished to the beach out behind the compound.

And there Instructor Reno and his men did their level best to level us. Oh, for the good old days of twenty arm-tearing push-ups. Not anymore. Out here it was usually fifty at a time, all interspersed with exercises designed to balance and hone various muscle groups, especially arms and abs. The instructors were consumed with abdominal strength, the reasons for which are now obvious: the abdomen is the bedrock of a warrior's strength for climbing rocks and ropes, rowing, lifting, swimming, fighting, and running.

Back there in Indoc, we did not really get that. All we knew was the SEAL instructors were putting us through hell on a daily basis. My personal hell was the flutter kick: lie on your back, legs dead straight and six inches off the sand, point your toes, and then kick as if you were doing the backstroke in the pool. And don't even consider putting your legs down, because there were instructors walking past at all times, like they were members of a firing squad under the orders of the Prince of Darkness.

One time early on, the pain in the nerves and tendons behind my thighs and back was so intense, I let my feet drop. Actually, I dropped them three times, and you'd have thought I'd committed murder. The first time, there was a roar of anguish from an instructor; the second time, someone called me a faggot; and the third time, there was a roar of anguish and someone else called me a faggot. Each time, I was ordered to go straight into the ice-cold Pacific then come out and roll in the sand.

It wasn't until the third time I realized that nearly everyone was in the Pacific and then rolling in the sand. We all looked like creatures from the Black Lagoon. And still they drove us forward, making us complete those exercises. It was funny really, but within four or five days, those flutter kicks were no problem at all. And we were all a whole lot fitter for them. All? Well, most. Two or three guys just could not take it and fluttered their way right out of there with smiles on their faces.

Me? I hung in there, calling out the exercise count, doing the best I could, cursing the hell out of Billy Shelton for getting me into this nuthouse in the first place, even though it was plainly not his fault.

I completed the exercises with obvious motivation, not because I was trying to make a favorable impression but because I would do nearly anything to avoid running into the freezing ocean and then rolling in the sand. And that was the consequence of not trying. Those instructors never missed a slacker. Every couple of minutes some poor bastard was told, "Get wet and sandy."

Wasn't that bad, though. Right after we finished the PT class and staggered to our feet, Instructor Reno, god of all the mercies, would send us on a four-mile run through the soft sand, running alongside us at half speed (for him), exhorting us to greater effort, barking instructions, harassing, cajoling. Those runs were unbelievably hard, especially for me, and I labored in the second half of the field trying to force my long legs to go faster.

Reno knew damn well I was trying my best, but in those early days he'd call out my name and tell me to get going. Then he'd tell me to get wet and sandy, and I'd run into the ocean, boots and all. Then I'd have to try and catch up with boots full of water. I guess he knew I could take it, but I cannot believe he was not laughing his ass off behind those black sunglasses.

Still, eventually it would be lunchtime, and it was only another mile to get something to eat. And all the time they were telling us about diet, what to eat, what never to eat, how often to eat. Jesus. It was a miracle any of us ever made it to the chow hall, never mind study our diets.

There was also the obstacle course, known to us as the O-course, and a place of such barbaric intensity that real live SEALs, veteran combat warriors from the teams, came over to supplement their training, often preparing for overseas deployment to a theater of war: jungle, mountain, ocean, or desert.

The Coronado O-course was world famous. And if it tested the blooded warriors of the teams, imagine what it was like for us, ten-day wonders, fresh out of boot camp, soft as babies compared to these guys.

I stared at the O-course, first day we went there. We were shown around, the rope climbs, the sixty-foot cargo net, the walls, the vaults, the parallel bars, the barbed wire, the rope bridges, the Weaver, the Burma Bridge.

For the first time I wished to hell I'd been a foot shorter. It was obvious to me this was a game for little guys. Instructor Reno gave a couple of demonstrations. It was like he'd been born on the rope bridge. It would be more difficult for me. All climbing is, because, in the end, I have to haul 230 pounds upward. Which is why all the world's great climbers are tiny guys with nicknames like the Fly, or the Flea, or Spider, all of them 118 pounds soaking wet.

I assessed rightly this would be a major test for me. But there were a lot of very big SEALs, and they'd all done it. That meant I could do it. Anyway, my mindset was the same old, same old. I'm either going to do this right, or I'll die trying. That last part was closer to the reality.

There were fifteen separate sections of the course, and you needed to go through, past, over, or under all of them. Naturally they timed us right from the get-go, when guys were tripping up, falling off, falling down, getting stuck, or generally screwing up. As I suspected, the bigger guys were instantly in the most trouble, because the key elements were balance and agility. Those Olympic gymnasts are mostly four feet tall. And when did you last see a six-foot-five, 230-pound ice dancer?

It was the climbing which put the big guys at the most disadvantage. One of our tests was called slide for life, a thick eighty-foot nylon rope attached to a tower and looped down to a vertical pole about ten feet high. You had to climb up the tower hanging on to the rope then slide all the way back down or pull yourself, whichever was easier.

For the record, on the subject of Instructor Reno, when we had to climb various ropes, he would amuse himself by climbing to the same height as us while using *two* ropes, one in each hand, never losing his grip and never letting go of either one. To this day, I believe that was impossible and that Reno was some kind of a mirage in sunglasses on the sand.

I struggled through the rope loop, making the top and sliding down, but one guy lost his grip and fell down, straight onto the sand, and broke his arm and, I think, his leg. He was a pretty big guy, and there was another one gone. The other discipline that sticks in my memory was that cargo net. You know the type of thing, heavy-duty rope knotted together in squares, the kind of stuff that has come straight from a shipyard. It was plainly imperative we all got damn good at this, since SEALs use such nets to board and disembark submarines and ships and to get in and out of inflatable boats.

But it was hard for me. It seemed when I shoved my boot in and reached upward, the foothold slipped downward, and my intended handhold got higher. Obviously, if I'd weighed 118 pounds soaking wet, this would not have been the case. First time I climbed the net, ramming my feet into the holes, I got kind of stuck about forty-five feet off the ground, arms and legs spreadeagled. I guess I looked like Captain Ahab trapped in the harpoon lines after a trip to the ocean floor with Moby Dick.

But like all the rest of our exercises, this one was completely about technique. And Instructor Reno was there to put me straight. Four days later, I could zip up that net like a circus acrobat. Well...okay, more like an orangutan. Then I'd grab the huge log at the top, clear that, and climb down the other side like Spider-Man. Okay, okay...like an orangutan.

I had similar struggles on the rope bridge, which seemed always to be out of kilter for me, swinging too far left or too far right. But Instructor Reno was always there, personally, to help me regain my equilibrium by sending me on a quick rush into the ocean, which was so cold it almost stopped my heart. This was followed by a roll in the sand, just to make the rest of the day an absolute itching, chafing hell until I hit the decontamination unit to get power washed down, same way you deal with a mud-caked tractor.

Naturally, the newly clean tractor had it all over us because no one then dumps it into the deep end of a swimming pool and more or less leaves it there until it starts to sprout fins. It was just another happy day in the life of a fledgling student going through Indoc. Understandably, Class 226 shrank daily, and we had not even started BUD/S.

And you think it was a great relief finally to get through the day and retire to our rooms for peace and perhaps sleep? Dream on. There's no such thing as peace in Coronado. The place is a living, breathing testimony to that Roman strategist who first told the world, "Let him who desires peace prepare for war" (that's translated from the Latin *Qui desiderat pacem, praeparet bellum*—Flavius Vegetius Renatus, fourth century). Or, as a SEAL might say, *You want things to remain cool, pal? Better get your ass in gear.* I knew I was close.

That old Roman knew a thing or two. His military treatise *De Rei Militari* was the bible of European warfare for more than 1,200 years, and it still applies in Coronado, stressing constant drilling, training, and severe discipline. He advised the Roman commanders to gather intelligence assiduously, use the terrain, and then drive the legionnaires forward to encircle their objective. That's more or less how we operate in overseas deployment against terrorists today. *Hooyah*, Flavius Vegetius.

Coronado, like New York, is a city that never sleeps. Those instructors are out there patrolling the corridors of our barracks by night into the small hours. One of them once came into my room after I'd hot mopped it and high polished the floor till you could almost see your face in it. He dropped a trickle of sand onto the floor and chewed me out for living in a dust bowl! Then he sent me down to the Pacific, in the company of my swim buddy and of course himself, to "get wet and sandy." Then we had to go through the decontamination unit, and the shrieking of those cold hydraulic pipes and the ferocious jets of water awakened half the barracks and nearly sent us into shock. Never mind the fact that it was 0200 and we were due back under those showers again in another couple of hours.

I think it was that time. I can't be absolutely sure. But my roommate quit that night. He went weak at the knees just watching what was happening to me. I don't know how the hell he thought I felt.

One time during Indoc while we were out on night run, one of the instructors actually climbed up the outside of a building, came through an open window, and absolutely trashed a guy's room, threw everything everywhere, emptied detergent over his bed gear. He went back out the way he'd come in, waited for everyone to return, and then tapped on the poor guy's door and demanded a room inspection. The guy couldn't work out whether to be furious or heartbroken, but he spent most of the night cleaning up and still had to be in the showers at 0430 with the rest of us.

I asked Reno about this weeks later, and he told me, "Marcus, the body can take damn near anything. It's the mind that needs training. The question that guy was being asked involved mental strength. Can you handle such injustice? Can you cope with that kind of unfairness, that much of a setback? And still come back with your jaw set, still determined, swearing to God you will never quit? That's what we're looking for."

As ever, I do not claim to quote Instructor Reno word for word. But I do know what he said, and how I remember it. No one talks to him and comes away bemused. Trust me.

Thus far I've only dealt with that first two weeks of training on the land and in the pool, and I may not have explained how much emphasis the instructors put on the correct balanced diet for everyone. They ran classes on this, drilling into us how much fruit and vegetables we needed, the necessity for tons of carbohydrates and water.

The mantra was simple—you take care of your body like the rest of your gear. Keep it well fed and watered, between one and two gallons a day. Start no discipline without a full canteen. That way your body will take care of you when you begin to ask serious questions of it. Because there's no doubt in the coming months you will be asking those questions.

This was an area, I remember, where there were a lot of questions, because even after those first few days here, guys were feeling the effects: muscle soreness, aches and pains in shoulders, thighs, and backs where there had been none before.

The instructor who dealt with this part of our training warned us against very strong drugs like Tylenol, except for a fever, but he understood we would need ibuprofen. He conceded it was difficult to get through the coming Hell Week without ibuprofen, and he told us the medical department would make sure we received a sufficient amount to ease the pain, though not too much of it.

I remember he said flatly, "You're going to hurt while you're here. That's our job, to induce pain; not permanent injury, of course, but we need to make you hurt. That's a big part of becoming a SEAL. We need proof you can take the punishment. And the way out of that is mental, in your mind. Don't buckle under to the hurt, rev up your spirit and your motivation, attack the courses. Tell yourself precisely how much you want to be here."

The final part of Indoc involved boats—the fabled IBS (inflatable boat, small) or, colloquially, itty-bitty ship. These boats are thirteen feet long and weigh a little under 180 pounds. They are unwieldy and cumbersome, and for generations the craft has been used to teach BUD/S students to pull a paddle as a tight-knit crew, blast their way through the incoming surf, rig properly, and drag the thing into place in a regimented line for inspection on the sandy beach about every seven minutes. At least that's how it seemed to us.

At that point we lined up in full life jackets right next to our boats. Inside the boat, the paddles were stowed with geometric precision, bow and stern lines coiled carefully on the rubber floor. Inch perfect.

We started with a series of races. But before that, each of our teams had a crew leader, selected from the most experienced navy personnel among us. And they lined up with their paddles at the military slope-arms position, the paddles resting on their shoulders. Then they saluted the instructors and announced their boat was correctly rigged and the crew was ready for the sea.

Meanwhile, other instructors were checking each boat. If a paddle was incorrectly stowed, an instructor seized it and hurled it down the beach. That happened on my first day, and one of the guys standing very near to me raced off after it, anxious to retrieve it and make amends. Unhappily, his swim buddy forgot to go with him, and the instructor was furious.

"Drop!" he yelled. And every one of us hit the sand and began to execute the worst kind of push-up, our feet up on the rubber gunwales of the boats, pushing 'em out in our life jackets. The distant words of Reno sung in my ears: "Someone screws it up, the consequences affect everyone."

We raced each other in the boats out beyond the surf. We raced until our arms felt as if they might fall off. We pulled, each crew against the rest, hauling our grotesquely unstreamlined little boats along. And this was not Yale versus Harvard on the

Thames River in Connecticut, all pulling together. This was the closest thing to a floating nuthouse you've ever seen. But it was my kind of stuff.

Boat drill is a game for big, strong guys who can pull. Pull like hell. It's also a game for heavy lifters who can haul that boat up and run with their team.

Let me take you through one of these races. First, we got the boat balanced in the shallows and watched the surf roll in toward us. The crew leader had issued a one-minute briefing, and we all watched the pattern of those five- to six-foot breakers. This part is called surf passage, and on the command, we were watching for our chance. Plainly, we didn't want to charge into the biggest incoming wave, but we didn't have much time.

The water was only a fraction above sixty degrees. We all knew we had to take that first wave bow on, but we didn't want the biggest, so we waited. Then the crew leader spotted a slacker one, and he bellowed, *"Now! Now! Now!"* We charged forward, praying to God we wouldn't get swept sideways and capsize. One by one we scrambled aboard, digging deep, trying to get through the overhanging crest, which was being whipped by an offshore breeze.

"Dig! Dig! Dig!" he roared as we headed for two more incoming walls of water. This was the Pacific Ocean, not some Texas lake. Close to us, one of the nine boats capsized, and there were paddles and students all in the water. You could hear nothing except the crash of the surf and shouts of *"Dig! Stroke! Portside . . . starboard . . . straighten up! Let's go! Go! Go!"*

I pulled that paddle until I thought my lungs would burst, until we had driven out beyond the breakers. And then our class leader yelled, *"Dump the boat!"* The bow-side men slipped overboard, the others (including me) grabbed the strap handles fixed on the rubber hull, stood up, and jumped over the same side, dragging the boat over on top of us.

As the boat hit the water, three of us grabbed the same handles and climbed back on the upturned hull of the boat. I was first up, I remember. Weightless in the water, right? Just give me a chance.

We backed to the other side of the hull and pulled, dragging the IBS upright, flipping it back on its lines. Everyone was aware that the tide was sweeping us back into the breakers. Feeling something between panic and frenzy, we battled back, grabbed our paddles and hauled out into flatter water and took a bead on the finish line. We paddled like hell, racing toward the mark, some tower on the beach. Then we dumped the boat again, grabbed the handles, carried it through the shallows onto the beach, and hauled it into a head carry.

We ran up the dunes around some truck, still with the boat on our heads, and then, as fast as we could, back along the beach to the point where we had started, and the instructors awaited us, logging the positions we finished and the times we clocked. They thoughtfully gave the winning crew a break to sit down and recover. The losers were told to push 'em out. It was not unusual to complete six of these races in one afternoon. By the end of Indoc week two, we had lost twenty-five guys.

The rest of us, somehow, had managed to show Instructor Reno and his colleagues we were indeed fit and qualified enough to attempt BUD/S training. Which would begin the next week. There would be just one final briefing from Reno before we attacked BUD/S first phase.

I saw him outside the classroom, and, still with his sunglasses on, he offered his hand and smiled quietly. "Nice job, Marcus," said Reno. He had a grip like a crane. His hand might have been bolted onto blue twisted steel, but I shook it as hard as I could, and I replied, "Thank you, sir."

We all knew he'd changed us drastically in those two weeks in Indoc. He'd showed us the depth of what we must achieve, guided us to the brink of the forthcoming unknown abyss of BUD/S. He'd knocked away whatever cocksure edges we might still have possessed.

We were a lot tougher now, and I still towered over him. Nonetheless, Reno Alberto still seemed fifteen feet tall to me. And he always will.

4

Welcome to Hell, Gentlemen

Battlefield whistle drills were conducted in the midst of high-pressure water jets, total chaos, deafening explosions, and shouting instructors... *"Crawl to the whistle, men! Crawl to the whistle! And keep your goddamned heads down!"*

We assembled in the classroom soon after 1300 that last afternoon of Indoc. Instructor Reno made his entry like a Roman caesar, head held high, and immediately ordered us to push 'em out. As ever, chairs scraped back and we hit the floor, counting out the push-ups.

At twenty, Reno left us in the rest position and then said crisply, "Recover."

"Hooyah, Instructor Ree-no!"

"Give me a muster, Mr. Ismay."

"One hundred and thirteen men assigned, Instructor Reno. All present except two men at medical."

"Close, Mr. Ismay. Two men quit a few minutes ago."

All of us wondered who they were. My boat's crew members? Heads whipped around. I had no idea who had crashed at the final hurdle.

"Not your fault, Mr. Ismay. You were in the classroom when

they quit. Two-two-six will class up in BUD/S first phase with a hundred and eleven men."

Hooyah!

I realized we had been losing guys fairly steadily. But according to these numbers, Class 226 had had 164 men assigned on the first day, and we'd lost more than fifty of them. I know a few never showed up at all, mostly through sheer intimidation. But the rest had somehow vanished into the void. I never saw any of them leave, not even my roommate.

And I still cannot work out quite how it happened. I guess they just reached some type of breaking point, or maybe they anguished for days over their own inability to cut the mustard. But gone is gone in this man's navy. I did not entirely comprehend it at the time, but me and my 110 cohorts were witnessing the ruthless elimination process of a U.S. fighting force that cannot tolerate a suspect component.

Instructor Reno now spoke formally. "You're on your way to first phase BUD/S. And I want each and every one of you to make me proud. Those of you who survive Hell Week will still have to face the pool competency test—that's in second phase—and then the weapons practicals in third phase. But I want to be at your graduation. And right there I want to shake your hand. I want to think of you as one of Reno's warriors."

The *Hooyah, Instructor Ree-no!* with our clenched fists in the air could have lifted the roof off the classroom. We loved him, all of us, because we all sensed he truly wanted the best for us. There was not a shred of malice in the guy. Neither was there a shred of weakness.

He repeated the orders he had been giving us for two weeks. "Stay alert. Be on time. And be accountable for your actions at all times, in and out of uniform. Remember, your reputation is everything. And you all have a chance to build on that reputation, beginning right here on Monday morning, zero five hundred. First phase.

"For those of you who make the teams, remember you're joining a brotherhood. You'll be closer to those guys than you ever were to friends in school or college. You'll live with them . . . and, in combat, some of you may die with them. Your family must always come first, but the brotherhood is a privileged place. And I don't want you ever to forget it."

And with that, he left us, walked away and slipped out of a back entrance, leaving behind a very long shadow: a bunch of guys who were revved up, gung ho, and ready to give everything to pass the challenging tests ahead. Just the way Reno wanted it.

Enter Instructor Sean Mruk (pronounced *MUR-rock*), ex-SEAL from Team 2, veteran of three overseas deployments, native of Ohio, a cheerful-looking character we had not encountered during Indoc. He was assistant to our new proctor. We heard him before we saw him, his quiet command, "Drop and push 'em out," before he had even made his way to the front of the classroom.

In the following few minutes he ran through the myriad of tasks we must complete after hours in first phase. Stuff like preparing the boats and vehicles, making sure we had the right supplies. He told us he expected 100 percent at all times, because if we did not put out, we'd surely pay for it.

He made sure we had all moved from our Indoc barracks, behind the grinder, over to the naval special warfare barracks a couple of hundred yards north of the center. Prime real estate on the sandy beach, and it's all yours—just as long as you can stay on the BUD/S bandwagon and remain in Class 226, the numbers of which will shortly be blocked in stark white on either side of your new green phase one helmet. Those numbers stay with you as long as you serve in the Navy SEALs. My class's three white-painted numbers would one day become the sweetest sounds I ever heard.

Instructor Mruk nodded agreeably and told us he would be over to the new barracks at 1000 Sunday to make sure we knew how to get our rooms ready for inspection. He gave us one last warning: "You're an official class now. First phase owns you."

And so to the cloudless Monday morning of June 18, all of us assembled outside the barracks two hours before sunrise. It was 0500 and the temperature not much above fifty degrees. Our new instructor, a stranger, stood there silently. Lieutenant Ismay reported, formally, "Class Two-two-six is formed, Chief. Ninety-eight men present."

David Ismay saluted. Chief Stephen Schulz returned the salute without so much as a "Good morning" or "How y'doing?" Instead, he just snapped, "Hit the surf, sir. All of you. Then get into the classroom."

Here we went again. Class 226 charged out of the compound and across the beach to the ocean. We floundered into the icecold water, got wet, and then squelched our way back to the classroom, freezing, dripping, already full of apprehension.

"Drop!" ordered the instructor. Then again. Then again. Finally, Ensign Joe Burns, a grim-looking SEAL commander, took his place in front of us and informed us he was the first phase officer. A few of us flinched. Burns's reputation as a hard man had preceded him. He later proved to be one of the toughest men I ever met.

"I understand you all want to be frogmen?"

Hooyah!

"I guess we'll see about that," said Ensign Burns. "Find out how bad you really want it. This is my phase, and these are my staff instructors."

Each of the fourteen introduced himself to us by name. And then Chief Schulz, presumably terrified we'd all go soft on him after an entire two minutes of talk, commanded, "Drop and push 'em out." And again. And again.

Then he ordered us out to the grinder for physical training. *"Move! Move! Move!"*

And finally we formed up, for the first time, on the most notorious square of black tarmac in the entire United States Armed Forces. It was 0515, and our places were marked by little frog flippers painted on the ground. It was hardly worth the visit.

"Hit the surf. Get wet and sandy!" yelled Schulz. "Fast!"

Our adrenaline pumped, our legs pumped, our arms pumped, our hearts pumped. Every goddamn thing there was pumped as we thundered off the blacktop, still dressed in our squelching boots and fatigue pants, went back down to the beach, and hurled ourselves into the surf.

Jesus, it was cold. The waves broke over me as I struggled back into the shallows, flung myself onto the sand, rolled over a couple of times, and came up looking like Mr. Sandman, except I wasn't bringing anyone a dream. I could hear the others all around me, but I'd heard Schulz's last word. *Fast.* And I remembered what Billy Shelton had taught: pay attention to even the merest suggestion...and I ran for my goddamned life straight back to the grinder, right up with the leaders.

"Too slow!" bellowed Schulz. "Much too slow...*drop!*"

Schulz's instructors roamed among us, berating us, yelling, harassing us as we sweated and strained to make the push-ups...*"Like a goddamned fairy." "Get a grip on yourself." "For*

Christ's sake, look as if you mean it." "C'mon, let's go! Go! Go!" "You sure you wanna be here? You wanna quit right now?"

I learned in the next few minutes there was a sharp difference between "get wet and sandy" and just plain "get wet." Parked at the side of the grinder were two of the inflatable boats, laden to the gunwales with ice and water. "Get wet" meant plunge over the bow, under the water, under the rubber seat struts, and out to the other side. Five seconds, in the dark, in the ice, under the water. A killer whale would have begged for mercy.

Now, I'd been cold before, in the freakin' Pacific, right? But the water in that little boat would have frozen the balls off a brass monkey. I came out of there almost blue with the cold, ice in my hair, and blundered my way to my little frogman's marker. At least I'd gotten rid of the sand, and so had everyone else. Two instructors were going down the lines with freezing cold power hoses, spraying everyone from the head down.

By 0600 I had counted out more than 450 push-ups. And there were more, I just couldn't count anymore. I'd also done more than fifty sit-ups. We were ordered from one exercise to another. Guys who were judged to be slacking were ordered to throw in a set of flutter kicks.

The result of this was pure chaos. Some guys couldn't keep up, others were doing push-ups when they'd been ordered to do sit-ups, men were falling, hitting the ground facedown. In the end, half of us didn't know where the hell we were or what we were supposed to be doing. I just kept going, doing my absolute best, through the roars of abuse and the flying spray of the power hoses: push-ups, sit-ups, screwups. It was now all the same to me. Every muscle in my body ached to hell, especially those in my stomach and arms.

And finally Schulz offered us mercy and a quiet drink. *"Hydrate!"* he yelled with that Old World charm that came so naturally to him, and we all reached for our canteens and chugged away.

"Canteens down!" bellowed Schulz, a tone of pained outrage in his voice. *"Now push 'em out!"*

Oh, yes. Of course. I'd forgotten all about that. I'd just had a nine-second break. Down we all dropped again and went back to work with the last remnants of our strength, counting the push-ups. We only did twenty that time. Schulz must have been seized by an attack of conscience.

"Get in the surf!" he bawled. *"Right now!"*

We floundered to the beach and darn near fell into the surf. We were now so hot, the cold didn't even matter. Much. And when we splashed back to the beach, Chief Schulz was there, ranting and yelling for us to form up and run the mile to the chow hall.

"Get moving," he added. "We don't have much time."

When we arrived, I was just about dead on my feet. I didn't think I had the energy to chew a soft-boiled egg. We walked into that chow hall like Napoleon's army on the retreat from Moscow, wet, bedraggled, exhausted, out of breath, too hungry to eat, too battered to care.

It was, of course, all by design. This was not some kind of crazed Chinese fire drill arranged by the instructors. This was a deadly serious assessment of their charges, a method used to find out, in the hardest possible way, who really wanted to do this, who really cared enough to go through with it, who could face the next four weeks before Hell Week, when things got seriously tough.

It was designed to compel us to reassess our commitment. Could we really take this punishment? Ninety-eight of us had formed up on the grinder two hours earlier. Only sixty-six of us made it through breakfast.

And when that ended, we were still soaked, boots, long pants, and T-shirts. And once more we set off for the beach, accompanied by an instructor who showed up from nowhere, running alongside us, shouting for us to get moving. We had been told what awaited us. A four-mile run along the beach, going south, two down and two back. Thirty-two minutes on the stopwatch was allowed, and God help anyone who could not run eight-minute miles through the sand.

I was afraid of this, because I knew I was not a real fast runner, and I psyched myself up for a maximum effort. I seem to have spent my whole life doing that. And when we arrived at the beach, I knew I would need that effort. There could not have been a worse time to make the run. The tide was almost full, still running in, so there was no appreciable width of drying hard sand. This meant running in either shallow water or very soft sand, both of which were a complete nuisance to a runner.

Our instructor Chief Ken Taylor lined us up and warned us darkly of the horrors to come if thirty-two minutes proved to be beyond some of us. And sent us away, with the sun now climbing out of the Pacific to our right. I picked the line I would run, right along the high point of the tide, where the waters first receded and left a slim strip of hard sand. This meant I'd be splashing some of the time, but only in the shallowest surf foam, and that was a whole lot better than the deep sand that stretched to my left.

Trouble was, I had to stick to this line, because my boots would be permanently wet and if I strayed up the beach, I'd have half a pound of sand stuck to each one. I did not think I could lay up with the leaders, but I thought I could hang in there in the group right behind them. So I put my head down, watched the tide line stretching in front of me, and pounded my way forward, staying right on the hardest wet sand.

The first two miles were not that awful. I was up there in the first half of the class, and I was not feeling too bad. On the way back, though, I was flagging. I glanced around and I could see everyone else was also looking really tired. And right then I decided to hit it. I turned up the gas and thumped my way forward.

The tide had turned during the first twenty minutes and there was just a slight width of wet sand that was no longer being washed by the ocean. I hit this with every stride, running until I thought I'd drop. Every time I caught a guy, I treated it as a personal challenge and pulled past him, finally clocking a time well inside thirty minutes, which wasn't half bad for a packhorse.

I forget who the winner was, probably some hickory-tough farm boy petty officer, but he was a couple of minutes better than I was. Anyway, the guys who made the time were sent up into the soft sand to rest and recover.

There were about eighteen guys outside thirty-two minutes, and one by one they were told, *"Drop!"* Then start pushing 'em out. Most of them were on their knees with exhaustion, and that kinda saved them a step in the next evolution, which was a bear crawl straight into the Pacific, directly into the incoming surf. Instructor Taylor had them go in deep, until the freezing cold water was up to their necks.

They were kept there for twenty minutes, very carefully timed, I now know, to make sure no one developed hypothermia. Taylor and his men even had a pinpoint-accurate chart that showed precisely how long a man could stand that degree of cold. And one by one they were called out and given the most stupendous hard time for failing to achieve the thirty-two-minute deadline.

I understand some of them may have just given up, and others just could not go any faster. But those instructors had a fair idea of what was going on, and on this, the first day of BUD/S training, they were ruthless.

As those poor guys came out of the surf, the rest of us were now doing regular push-ups, and since this was now second nature to me, I looked up to see the fate of the slow guys. Chief Taylor, the Genghis Khan of the beach gods, ordered these half-dead, half-drowned, half-frozen guys to lie on their backs, their heads and shoulders in and under the water with the rhythm of the waves. And he made them do flutter kicks. There were guys choking and spluttering and coughing and kicking and God knows what else.

And then, only then, did Chief Taylor release them, and I remember, vividly, him yelling out to them that we, dry and doing our push-ups up the beach, were winners, whereas they, the slowpokes, were *losers!* Then he told them they better start taking this seriously or they would be out of here. "Those guys up there, taking it easy, they paid the full price," he yelled. "Right up front. You did not. You failed. And for guys like you there's a bigger price to pay, understand me?"

He knew this was shockingly unfair, because some of them had been doing their genuine best. But he had to find out for certain. Who believed they could improve? Who was determined to stay? And who was halfway out the door already?

Next evolution: log PT, brand-new to all of us. We lined up wearing fatigues and soft hats, seven-man boat crews, standing right by our logs, each of which was eight feet long and a foot in diameter. I can't remember the weight, but it equaled that of a small guy, say 150 to 160 pounds. Heavy, right? I was just moving into packhorse mode when the instructor called out, "Go get wet and sandy." All in our nice dry clothes, we charged once more toward the surf, up and over a sand dune, and down into the water. We rushed out of the waves and back up the sand dune, rolled down the other side, then stood up like the lost company from the U.S. Navy's Sandcastle Platoon.

Then he told us to get our logs wet and sandy. So we heaved them up, waist high, and hauled them up the sand dune. We ran down the other side, dumped the goddamned log in the ocean, pulled it out, went back up the sand dune, and rolled it down the other side.

The crew next to us somehow managed to drop their log on the downward slope.

"You ever, ever drop one of my logs again," the instructor bellowed, *"I can't even describe what will happen to you. All of you!"* He used the enraged, vengeance-seeking tone of voice that might have been specially reserved for *"You guys ever, ever gang-rape my mother again..."* Rather than just dropping the stupid log.

We all stood there in a line, holding our logs straight-arm, above our heads. They try to make the teams a uniform height, but my six foot five inches means I'll always be carrying at least my fair share of the burden.

More and more guys were accused of slacking, and more and more of them were on the ground doing push-ups while me and a couple of other big guys on the far end were bearing the weight. We must have looked like the three pillars of Coronado, sandstone towers holding up the temple, eyes peering grittily out at a sandscape full of weird, sandy, burrowing creatures fighting for breath.

Right after this they taught us all the physical training moves we would need: squats, tossing the log overhead, and a whole lot of others. Then, still in formation, we were told, "Fall in on your logs," and we charged forward.

"Slow! Too slow! Get wet and sandy!"

Back down to the surf, into the waves, into the sand. By this time, guys really were on their last legs, and the instructors knew it. They didn't really want anyone to collapse, and they spent a while teaching us the finer points of log teamwork. To our total amazement, they concluded the morning by telling us we'd done a damn nice job, made a great start, and to head off now for chow.

A lot of us thought this was encouraging. Seven of our number, however, were not to be consoled by these sudden, calming words uttered by guys who should have been riding with Satan's cavalry in *Lord of the Rings*. They went straight back to the grinder, rang the hanging bell outside the first phase office, and handed in their helmets, placing them in a line outside the CO's door. That's the way it's done in first phase: the exit ritual. There were now a dozen helmets signifying resignation, and we hadn't even had lunch on day one.

Most of us thought they were a bit hasty, because we knew a certain part of the afternoon was taken up by the weekly room inspection. Most of us had spent all day Sunday getting into order, cleaning the floor with a mop and then high polishing it. Somehow I had found myself way down the waiting list to use one of the two electric buffers.

I had had to wait my turn and did not get finished before about 0200. But the time had not been wasted. I'd fixed my bed gear, pressed my starched fatigues, and spit-shined my boots. I looked better, not like some darned sand-encrusted beachcomber, the way I had most of the day.

The instructors arrived. I cannot remember which of them walked into my room. But he gazed upon it, this picture of military order and precision, and at me with an expression of undiluted disgust. Carefully he opened my chest of drawers and hurled everything all over the room. He heaved the mattress off the bed and cast it aside. He emptied the contents of my locker into a pile and informed me that he was unused to meeting trainees who were happy to live in a garbage dump. Actually, his words were a bit more colorful than that, more...well...earthy.

Beyond the confines of my room, there was absolute bedlam; stuff was hurled all over the place in room after room. I just stood there gaping as the entire barracks was ransacked by our own instructors. Outside in the corridor, I could hear someone bawling out Lieutenant David Ismay, the class leader. The soft, dulcet tones of Chief Schulz were unmistakable.

"What kind of rathole are you running here, Mr. Ismay? I've never seen rooms like these in my life. Your uniforms are a disgrace. *Hit the surf...all of you!*"

There were, by my count, thirty rooms. Only three of them had passed muster. And even those guys were not exempt from our first ocean plunge of the afternoon. In our shiny boots and pressed fatigues, we pounded back down to the beach, leaving a scene of total chaos behind us.

We raced into the water, deep, right into the waves. Then we turned and floundered back to the beach, formed up, and headed back to the BUD/S area. Chief Taylor was back in our lives with a major rush, obviously preparing for the last evolution of the day, on the beach or in the water. We did not know which.

All day long we had been wondering precisely who he was, but our inquiries had yielded little save that the chief was a true veteran of the teams who had seen combat in overseas deployment four times, including the Gulf War. He was a medium-sized man but immensely muscular; he looked like he could walk straight through a wall without breaking stride. But you could see he had a sense of humor, and he was not averse to telling us we were doing okay. Sweet of him, right? Half of us were hanging in there by willpower alone.

And we needed all the willpower we had, because in a few moments we were preparing to take the boats into the water again. I have never forgotten that surf drill on that first day because Chief Taylor made us paddle the boats out backward, facing aft. When we returned through the surf to the beach, we faced aft again, but now we were paddling forward.

When we first started, the journey out beyond the breakers seemed impossible to do while facing the beach and holding the oar so awkwardly, but we got better. And somehow we got it done. But not before all kinds of chaos had broken out. We capsized, flipped over, crashed backward trying to drive head-on into a big wave. And there was a lot of spluttering and coughing when we attempted Chief Taylor's finale, which was to dump boat, right it again, stow the oars correctly, and then swim the boat back in through the surf and onto the beach.

Before we left, we were taken through an exercise called surf observation, in which two-man teams observe the condition of the sea and make a report. I paid strict attention to this, which was good, since from now on, every morning at 0430, two of our number would go down to the water's edge and come back to make that report. Chief Taylor, smiling, as he was prone to do, dismissed us with the words "And don't screw up that report. I want no discrepancies about sea conditions, or there'll be hell to pay."

We sharpened up our rooms that evening, and on day two were under way with the normal morning grind of push-ups, running, and getting wet and sandy. Our first classroom involved meeting our leading petty officer instructor, Chief Bob Nielsen, another Gulf War veteran of several overseas deployments. He was tall, slim for a SEAL, and, I thought, a bit sardonic. His words to us were packed with meaning, edged with menace, but nonetheless optimistic.

He introduced himself and told us what he expected. As if we didn't know. Everything, right? Or die in the attempt. He gave us a slide presentation of every aspect of first phase. Before the first picture had been taken off the screen, he told us to forget all about trying to put one over on the instructors.

"Guys," he said, "we've seen it all. You can try it on, if you like, but it won't do anyone any good. We'll catch you, and when we do, watch out!"

I think everyone in the room made a mental note not to "try it on." We all listened carefully while Chief Nielsen ran quickly through the first four weeks and what we could expect—more running, log PT boats, and swimming, the full catastrophe. Purely to find out how tough we really were.

"Conditioning," he said. "Conditioning and a whole lot of cold water. Get used to it. The next month represents a hard kick in the crotch. Because we're going to hammer you." I still have my notes of Bob Nielsen's speech.

"You fail to meet those standards, you're out. Of course most of you will end up being dropped. And most of you will not be back. You must make that four-mile thirty-two-minute run, and you must make the two-mile swims in an hour and a half. You'll get a tough written test. There's pool standards, there's drown-proofing. With and without the fins—kick, stroke, and glide.

"You may be thinking, What does it take? What must I do to make it through? The cold truth is, two-thirds of you sitting right here will quit."

I remember him standing next to my row and saying, "There's seven rows of you sitting here. Only two rows will succeed." He seemed to look straight at me when he said, "The rest of you will be gonzo, history, back to the fleet. That's the way it is. The way it's always been. So try your best to prove me wrong."

He issued one further warning. "This training does not suit everyone. We get a lot of very good guys through here who just decide this is not for them. And that's their right. But they will walk away from here with dignity, understand? We catch one of you laughing or making fun of a man who has requested DOR (dropped on request), we'll hammer you without mercy. *Big time.* You will regret those moments of ridicule for a long time. I advise you not even to consider it."

He closed by telling us the real battle is won in the mind. It's won by guys who understand their areas of weakness, who sit and think about it, plotting and planning to improve. Attending to the detail. Work on their weaknesses and overcome them. Because they can.

"Your reputation is built right here in first phase. And you don't want people to think you're a guy who does just enough to scrape through. You want people to understand you always try to excel, to be better, to be completely reliable, always giving it your best shot. That's the way we do business here.

"And remember this one last thing. There's only one guy here in this room who knows whether you're going to make it, or fail. And that's you. Go to it, gentlemen. And always give it everything."

Chief Nielsen left, and five minutes later we stood by for the commanding officer's report. Six instructors filed into the room, surrounding a navy captain. And we all knew who he was. This was Captain Joe Maguire, the near-legendary Brooklyn-born Honor Man of Class 93 and onetime commanding officer of SEAL Team 2. He was also the future Rear Admiral Maguire, Commander, SPECWARCOM, a supreme SEAL warrior. He had served all over the world and was beloved throughout Coronado, a big guy who never forgot a fellow SEAL's name, no matter how junior.

He talked to us calmly. And he gave us two pieces of priceless advice. He said he was addressing those who really wanted this kind of life, those who could put up with every kind of harassment those instructors at the back of the room could possibly dish out.

"First of all, I do not want you to give in to the pressure of the moment. Whenever you're hurting bad, just hang in there. Finish the day. Then, if you're still feeling bad, think about it long and hard before you decide to quit. Second, take it one day at a time. One evolution at a time.

"Don't let your thoughts run away with you, don't start planning to bail out because you're worried about the future and how much you can take. Don't look ahead to the pain. Just get through the day, and there's a wonderful career ahead of you."

This was Captain Maguire, a man who would one day serve as deputy commander of the U.S. Special Operations in Pacific Command (COMPAC). With his twin-eagles insignia glinting on his collar, Captain Maguire instilled in us the knowledge of what really counted.

I stood there reflecting for a few moments, and then the roof fell in. One of the instructors was up and yelling. *"Drop!"* he shouted and proceeded to lay into us for the sins of one man.

"I saw one of you nodding off, right here in the middle of the captain's briefing. How dare you! How dare you fall asleep in the presence of a man of that caliber? You guys are going to pay for this. *Now push 'em out!*"

He drilled us, gave us probably a hundred push-ups and sit-ups, and he drove us up and down the big sand dune in front of the compound. He raved at us because our times over the O-course were down, which was mostly due to the fact that we were paralyzed with tiredness before we got there.

And so it went on, all week. There was a swim across the bay, one mile with a guy of comparable swimming ability. There were evolutions in the pool, in masks, wearing flippers and without. There was one where we had to lie on our backs, masks full of water, flippers on, trying to do flutter kicks with our heads out over the water. This was murder. So was the log PT and our four-mile runs. The surf work in the boats was also a strength-sapping experience, running the boats out through the waves, dumping boat, righting boat, paddling in, backward, forward, boat being dragged, boat on our heads.

It never ended, and by the close of that first week we had lost more than twenty men, one of them in tears because he could not go on. His hopes, his dreams, even his intentions had been dashed to bits on that Coronado beach.

That was more than sixty rings on the big bell right outside the office door. And every time we heard it, without exception, we knew we'd lost an essentially good guy. There weren't any bad guys who made it through Indoc. And as the days wore on and we heard that bell over and over, it became a very melancholy sound.

Could I be standing there outside the office door, a broken man, a few days from now? It was not impossible, because many of these men had had no intention of quitting a few hours or even minutes before they did. Something just gave way deep inside them. They could no longer go on, and they had no idea why.

Ask not for whom the bell tolls, Marcus. Because the sonofabitch might toll for thee. Or for any one of the sixty-odd others still standing after the brutal reality of week one, first phase. Every time we crossed the grinder, we could see the evidence right there before our eyes, a total of twenty helmets on the ground, lined up next to the bell. Each one of those helmets had been owned by a friend, or an acquaintance, or even a rival, but a guy whom we had suffered alongside.

That line of lonely hard hats was a stark reminder not only of what this place could do to a man but also of the special private glory it could bestow on those who would not give in. It drove me onward. Every time I looked at that line, I gritted my teeth and put some extra purpose into my stride. I still felt the same as I had on my very first day. I'd rather die than surrender.

The third week of first phase brought us into a new aspect of BUD/S training, called rock portage. This was dangerous and difficult, but basically we had to paddle the IBS along to an outcrop of rocks opposite the world-famous Hotel del Coronado and land it there. I don't mean moor it, I mean land it, get it up there on dry land with the surf crashing all around you, the ocean swell trying to suck that boat right back out again.

I had to figure pretty big in this because of my size and ability to heave. But none of my crew was quite ready for this desperate test. It was something we just had to learn how to do. And so we went at it, paddling hard in from the sea, driving into those huge rocks, straight into waves which were breaking every which way.

The bow of our boat slammed into the rocks, and the bowline

man, not me, jumped forward and hung on, making the painter firm around his waist. His job was to get secure and then act like a human capstan and stop the boat being swept backward. Our man was pretty sharp; he jammed himself between a couple of big boulders and yelled back to us, *"Bowline man secure!"*

We repeated his call just so everyone knew where they were. But the boat was now jammed bow-on against the rocks. It had no rhythm with the waves and was vulnerable to every swell that broke over the stern. In this static position, it cannot ride with the waves.

Our crew leader's cries of *"Water!"* were little help. The surf was crashing straight at us and then through the boat and up and over the rocks. We had on our life jackets, but the smallest man among us had to hop over the bow, carry out all of the paddles, and get them safely onto dry ground.

Then we all had to disembark, one by one, clambering onto the rocks, with the poor old bowline man hanging on for his life, jammed between the rocks with the boat still lashed to his torso. By now we were all on the rope, trying to grab the handles, but the bowline man had to move first, heading upward into a new position, with us now taking the weight.

He set off. *Bowline man moving!* I hauled ass down in the engine room, pulling with all my strength. A wave slammed into the boat and nearly took us all into the water, but we hung tough.

Bowline man secure! And then we gave it everything, knowing our crewmate could not come catapulting backward right into us. Somehow we heaved that baby onward and upward, dragged it clean out of the Pacific, cheated the Grim Reaper, and manhandled it right up there onto the rocks, high and dry.

"Too slow," said our instructor. And then he went into a litany of details as to what we'd done wrong. Too long in the opening stages, bowline man not quick enough up the rocks, too long on the initial pulls, too long being battered by the waves.

He ordered us onto the sand with the boat, gave us a set of twenty push-ups, then ordered us straight back the way we'd come—up and over the rocks, boat into the water, bowline man making us secure while we damn near drowned...get in, get going, shut up and paddle. Simple really.

That first month ended much like it had begun, with a soaking wet, cold, tired, and depleted class. At the conclusion of the four weeks, the instructors made some harsh decisions, assessing the weakest among us, guys who had failed the tests, perhaps one test, maybe two. They looked hard at very determined young men who would rather die than quit but simply could not swim well enough, run fast enough, lift heavy enough, guys who lacked endurance, underwater confidence, skills in a boat.

These were the hardest to dismiss from the program, because these were guys who had given their all and would go on doing so. They just lacked some form of God-given talent to carry out the work of a U.S. Navy SEAL. Years later I knew several instructors quite well, and they all said the same about that fourth week first phase assessment, the week before Hell Week—"We all agonized over it. No one wants to be in the business of breaking a kid's heart."

But neither could they allow the weak and the hopeless to go forward into the most demanding six days of training in any fighting force in the world. That's not the free world, by the way, that's the whole world. Only Great Britain's legendary SAS has anything even comparable.

The results of the four-week assessment meant there were just fifty-four of us left; fifty-four of the ninety-eight who had started first phase. And Class 226 would start early, as all Hell Week classes do, Sunday at noon.

Late that last Friday, we assembled in the classroom to be formally addressed once more by Captain Maguire, who was accompanied by several instructors and class officers.

"Everyone ready for Hell Week?" he asked us cheerfully.

Hooyah!

"Excellent," he replied. "Because you are about to experience a very searching and painful test. Each one of you is going to find out what you are really made of. And every step of the way, you will be faced with a choice. Do I give in to the pain and the cold, or do I go on? It will always be up to you. There's no quotas, no numbers. We don't decide who passes. You do. But I'll be there on Friday when Hell Week ends, and I hope to shake the hand of each and every one of you."

We all stood in some awe for the exit of Captain Maguire, the quintessential Coronado man, who understood the pride of achievement at having scaled the heights and who knew what really counted, in the SEALs and beyond. He was the everlasting chief.

They briefed us about what to bring to class on Sunday—our gear, equipment, change of clothes, dry clothes, and some off-duty clothes, which would be placed in a paper bag so the successful guys would have something to wear when it was all over. Guys who went DOR (dropped on request) would also have dry clothes available anytime during the week when they prepared to leave.

Our instructor told us to eat plenty, right through the weekend, but not to worry about sleep gear on Sunday afternoon, during which time we would be incarcerated in the classroom.

"You'll be too keyed up to sleep," he added brightly. "So just get in here and relax, watch movies, and get ready."

On the notice board was the official doctrine of the U.S. Navy SEALs, week five, first phase: "Students will demonstrate the qualities and personal characteristics of determination, courage, self-sacrifice, teamwork, leadership, and a never-quit attitude, under adverse environmental conditions, fatigue, and stress throughout Hell Week."

That's laying it on the line, right? Almost. Hell Week turned out to be a lot worse than that.

We spent the weekend organizing ourselves, and we assembled in the classroom at noon on Sunday, July 18. Two dozen instructors from all over the compound, guys we'd never even met before, were in attendance. It takes that many to get a class through Hell Week, plus attending medics and support and logistics guys. I guess you need a full staff to march men into the ultimate physical tests of the navy's warrior elite.

This is known as the Hell Week Lockdown. No one leaves; we sit and wait all afternoon; we have our seabags; and the paper bags with our dry clothes are lined up, our names written on the outside in black marker. They served us pizza, a whole stack of it, in the late afternoon.

And outside you could sense it was quiet. No one passed by, no patrols, no wandering students. Everyone on the base knew that Hell Week for 226 was about to begin. It was not exactly respect for the dead, but I guess you understand by now more or less what I mean.

I remember how hot it was, must have been ninety degrees in the room. We'd all been goofing off, wearing Sunday casuals most of the day, and we all knew something was going to happen as the evening wore on. Some movie was running, and the hours ticked by. There was an atmosphere of heightened tension as we waited for the starter's pistol. Hell Week begins with a frenzy of activity known as Breakout. And when it came for us, there were a lot more guns than the starter's.

I can't remember the precise time, but it was after 2030 and before 2100. Suddenly there was a loud shout, and someone literally kicked open the side door. *Bam!* And a guy carrying a machine gun, followed by two others, came charging in, firing from the hip. The lights went off, and then all three gunmen opened fire, spraying the room with bullets (blanks, I hoped).

There were piercing blasts from whistles, and the other door was kicked open and three more men came crashing into the room. The only thing we knew for sure right now was when the whistles blew, we hit the floor and took up a defensive position, prostrate, legs crossed, ears covered with the palms of the hands.

Hit the deck! Heads down! Incoming!

Then a new voice, loud and stentorian. It was pitch dark save for the nonstop flashes of the machine guns, but the voice sounded a lot like Instructor Mruk's to me — *"Welcome to hell, gentlemen."*

For the next couple of minutes there was nothing but gunfire, deafening gunfire. They were certainly blanks, otherwise half of us would have been dead, but believe me, they sounded just like the real thing, SEAL instructors firing our M43s. The shouting was drowned by the whistles, and everything was drowned by the gunfire.

By now the air in the room was awful, hanging with the smell of cordite, lit only by the muzzle flashes. I kept my head well down on the floor as the gunmen moved among us, taking care not to let hot spent cartridges land on our skin.

I sensed a lull. And then a roar, plainly meant for everyone. *"All of you, out! Move, you guys! Move! Move! Move! Let's go!"*

I struggled to my feet and joined the stampede to the door. We rushed out to the grinder, where it was absolute bedlam. More gunfire, endless yelling, and then, again, the whistles, and once more we all hit the deck in the correct position. In barrels around the grinder's edge, artillery simulators blasted away. I didn't know where Captain Maguire was, but if he'd been here he'd have thought he was back in some foreign battle zone. At least, if he'd shut his eyes, he would have.

Then the instructors opened fire for real, this time with high-pressure hoses aimed straight at us, knocking us down if we tried to get up. The place was awash with water, and we couldn't see a thing and we couldn't hear anything above the small-arms and artillery fire.

Battlefield whistle drills were conducted in the midst of high-pressure water jets, total chaos, deafening explosions, and shouting instructors... *"Crawl to the whistle, men! Crawl to the whistle! And keep your goddamned heads down!"*

Some of the guys were suffering from mass confusion. One of 'em ran for his life, straight over the beach and into the ocean. He was a guy I knew really well, and he'd lost it completely. This was a simulated scene from the Normandy beaches, and it did induce a degree of panic, because no one knew what was happening or what we were supposed to be doing besides hitting the deck.

The instructors knew this. They understood many of us would be at a low ebb. Not me. I'm always up for this kind of stuff, and anyway I knew they weren't really trying to kill us. But the instructors understood this would not be true of everyone, and they moved among us, imploring us to quit now while there was still time.

"All you gotta do is ring that little bell up there."

Lying there in the dark and confusion, freezing cold, soaked to the skin, scared to stand up, I told one of them he could stick that little bell straight up his ass, and I heard a loud roar of laughter. But I never said it again, and I never let on it was me. Until now, that is. See that? Even in the chaos, I could still manage the smart-ass remark.

By now we were in a state of maximum disorientation, just trying to stay on the grinder with the others. The teamwork mantra had set in. I didn't want to be by myself. I wanted to be with my soaking wet teammates, whatever the hell it was we were supposed to be doing.

Then I heard a voice announcing we were a man short. Then I heard another voice, sharp and demanding. I don't know who it was, but it was close to me and it sounded like the Biggest Bossman, Joe Maguire, with a lot of authority. "What do you mean? A man short? Get a count right now."

They ordered us to our feet instantly, and we counted off one by one, stopping at fifty-three. We were a man short. Holy shit! That's bad, and very serious. Even I understood that. A party was dispatched immediately to the beach, and that's where they found the missing trainee, splashing around out in the surf.

Someone reported back to the grinder. And I heard our instructor snap, "Send 'em all into the surf. We'll sort 'em out later." And off we went again, running hard to the beach, away from the gunfire, away from this madhouse, into the freezing Pacific in what felt like the middle of the night. As so often, we were too wet to worry, too cold to care.

But when we were finally summoned out of the surf, something new happened. The whistles began blasting again, and this meant we had to crawl toward the whistles all over again, but this time not on the smooth blacktop. This time on the soft sand.

In moments we looked like sand beetles groping around the dunes. The whistles kept blowing, one blast, then two, and we kept right on crawling, and by now my elbows were really getting hot and sore, and my knees were not doing that great either. All four joints felt red-raw. But I kept moving. Then the instructors ordered us back into the surf, deep, so we could stay there for fifteen minutes, maximum immersion time in water hovering just under sixty degrees. We linked arms until we were ordered out to more whistles and more crawling.

Then they sent us down to the surf for flutter kicks, heads in the waves. Then more whistles, more crawling, and back into the water for another fifteen minutes. Right next to me, one of the top guys in the class, an officer and a boat-crew leader, great runner, good swimmer, quit unconditionally.

This was a real shaker. Another officer in his crew went running up the beach after him, imploring him not to go, telling the attending instructor, on his behalf, the guy did not mean it. No, sir. The instructor gave him another chance, told him it wasn't too late and if he wished he could go right back into the water.

But the man's mind was made up, closed to all entreaties. He kept walking, and the instructor told him to get in the truck right next to the ambulance. Then he asked the guy doing the pleading if he wanted to quit too, and we all heard the sharp *"Negative,"* and we saw the guy running like a scalded cat down the beach to join us in the water.

The temperature seemed to grow colder as we jogged around in the freezing surf. And finally they called us out and the whistles blew again. We all dived back onto the sand. Crawling, itching, and burning. Five guys quit instantly and were sent up to the truck. I didn't understand any of that, because we had done this before. It was bad, but not *that* bad, for chrissakes. I guess those guys were just thinking ahead, dreading the forthcoming five days of Hell Week, the precise way Captain Maguire had told us not to.

Anyway, right now we were ordered to grab the boats and get them in the surf, which we did without much trouble. But they made us paddle hundreds of yards, dig and row, lift and carry, dump boat and right boat, swim the boat, walk the boat, run the boat, crawl, live, die. We were so exhausted it didn't matter. We hardly knew where we were. We just floundered on with bloody knees and elbows until they ordered us out of the water.

I think it was just before midnight, but it could have been Christmas morning. We switched to log PT in the surf. No piece of wood in all of history, except possibly the massive wooden Cross carried to Calvary by Jesus Christ, was ever heavier than our eight-foot hunk of wood that we manhandled in the Pacific surf. After all of our exertions, it was a pure backbreaker. Three more men quit.

Then the instructors came up with something new and improved. They made us carry the boats over the O-course and manhandle them over the goddamned obstacles. Another man quit. We were down to forty-six.

Right then we switched to rock portage and charged back down the beach to get the IBS into the water. We crashed through the light incoming waves like professionals and paddled like hell, using the remnants of our strength, to the rocks opposite the Hotel del Coronado. My swim buddy, Matt McGraw, was calling the shots in our boat by now, and we drove forward, crashed straight into the rocks, and the bowline man leaped for his life and grabbed on to the painter. We steadied the boat with the oars, and I thought we were doing real good.

Suddenly the instructor, standing up on the top of the rocks right there at damned near two o'clock in the morning, bellowed at our crew officer, *"You! You, sir. You just killed your entire squad! Stop getting between the boat and the rocks!"*

We hauled the boat out of the water, over the rocks, and onto the sand. The instructor gave us two sets of push-ups and sent us back the way we came. Twice more we assaulted the rocks, slowly and clumsily, I suppose, and the instructor never stopped yelling his freakin' head off at us. In the end we had to run the boat back along the beach, drop it, and get right back into the surf for flutter kicks with heads and shoulders in the water, then push-ups in the surf. Then sit-ups. Two more men quit.

These DORs happened right next to me. And I distinctly heard the instructor give them another chance, asking them if they wanted to reconsider. If so, they were welcome to press on and get back in the water.

One of them wavered. Said he might, if the other guy would join him. But the other guy wasn't having it. "I'm done with this shit," he said, "and I'm outta here."

They both quit together. And the instructor looked like he could not give a flying fuck. I later learned that when a man quits and is given another chance and takes it, he never makes it through. All the instructors know that. If the thought of DOR enters a man's head, he is not a Navy SEAL.

I guess that element of doubt forever pollutes his mind. And puffing, sweating, and steaming down there on that beach on the first night of Hell Week, I understood it.

I understood it, because that thought could never have occurred to me. Not while the sun still rises in the east. All the pain in Coronado could not have inserted that poison into my mind. I might have passed out, had a heart attack, or been shot before a firing squad. But I never would have quit.

Soon as the quitters had gone, we were put right back to work. Lifting the boats into a head carry for the run over to the chow hall, only another mile. When I got there I was as close to collapse as I'd ever been. But they still made us push 'em out, lift the boat, to work up an appetite, I suppose.

Eventually they freed us to get breakfast. We had lost ten men during the nine hours that had passed since Hell Week began; nine hours since those yelling, shooting gunmen had driven Class 226 out of their classroom, nine hours since we had been dry and felt more or less human.

They were nine hours that had changed the lives and perceptions of those who could stand it no more. I doubt the rest of us would ever be quite the same again.

Inside the chow hall some of the guys were shell-shocked. They just sat staring at their plates, unable to function normally. I was not one of them. I felt like I was on the edge of starvation, and I steamed into those eggs, toast, and sausages, relishing the food, relishing the freedom from the shouts and commands of the instructors.

Just as well I made the most of it. Seven minutes on the clock after I finished my breakfast, the new shift of instructors was up and yelling.

"That's it, children — up and out of here. Let's get going. Outside! Right now! Move! Move! Move! Let's start the day right."

Start the day! Was this guy out of his mind? We were still soaked, covered in sand, and we'd been up half killing ourselves all night.

Right then I knew for certain: there was indeed no mercy in Hell Week. Everything we'd heard was true. *You think you're tough, kid? Then you go right ahead and prove it to us.*

5

Like the Remnants
of a Ravaged Army

We helped one another back over the sand dunes, picking up those who fell, supporting those who could barely walk... The baptism of fire that had reduced Class 226 by more than half was over... No one had ever dreamed it would be this bad.

We lined up outside the chow hall and hoisted the boats onto our heads. It was now apparent we would go nowhere without them. As bankers carry their briefcases, as fashion models walk around with their photograph portfolios, we travel around with our boats on our heads. It's a Hell Week thing.

I have to admit that after the first straight thirty hours, my memory of those five days begins to grow a little hazy. Not of the actual events, but of the sequence. When you're moving on toward forty hours without sleep, the mind starts playing tricks, causing fleeting thoughts suddenly to become reality. You jerk yourself awake and wonder where the hell you are and why your mom, holding a big, juicy New York sirloin, is not pulling the paddle right next to you.

It's the forerunner to outright hallucination. Kind of semi-hallucinations. They start slowly and get progressively worse. Mind you, the instructors do their level best to keep you awake. We were given fifteen minutes of hard physical training both when we reached the chow hall and when we left. We were sent into the surf fast and often. The water was freezing, and every time we carried out boat drills, racing through the breakers with the four remaining teams, we were ordered to dump boat, pull that sucker over on top of us, then right it, get back in, and carry on paddling to our destination.

The reward for the winners was always rest. That's why we all kept trying so hard. Same for the four-mile run, during which we got slower, times slipped below the thirty-two-minute standard, and the instructors feigned outrage as if they didn't know we were slowly being battered to hell. By that first Monday evening, we'd been up for thirty-six hours plus and were still going.

Most of us ate an early dinner, looking like a group of zombies. And right afterward we were marched outside to await further orders. I remember that three guys had just quit. Simultaneously. Which put us down to six officers out of the original twelve.

Judging by the one guy I knew, I didn't think any of the ones who quit were in much worse shape than they had been twelve hours before. They might have been a bit more tired, but we had done nothing new, it was all part of our tried-and-tested routines. And in my view, they had acted in total defiance of the advice handed to us by Captain Maguire.

They weren't completing each task as it came, living for the day. They had allowed themselves to live in dread of the pain and anguish to come. And he'd told us never to do that, just to take it hour by hour and forget the future. Keep going until you're secured. You get a guy like that, a legendary U.S. Navy SEAL and war hero, I think you ought to pay attention to his words. He earned the right to say them, and he's giving you his experience. Like Billy Shelton told me, even the merest suggestion.

But we had no time to mourn the departure of friends. The instructors marched us down to an area known as the steel pier, which used to be the training area for SDV Team 1 before they decamped for Hawaii. It was dark now and the water was very cold, but they ordered us to jump straight in and kept us treading water for fifteen minutes.

Then they let us out back onto dry land and gave us a fierce period of calisthenics. This warmed us a bit. But my teeth were chattering almost uncontrollably, and they still ordered us straight back into the water for another fifteen minutes, the very limit of the time when guys start to suffer from hypothermia. That next fifteen minutes were almost scary. I was so cold, I thought I might pass out. There was an ambulance right there in case someone did.

But I held on. So did most of us, but another officer climbed out of the water early and quit. He was the best swimmer in the class. This was a stunning blow, both to him and the rest of us. The instructor let him go immediately and just carried on counting off the minutes the rest of us were submerged.

When we were finally back on shore, I was not really able to speak and neither was anyone else, but we did some more PT, and then they ordered us back into the water for another period, I forget how long. Maybe five, ten minutes. But time had ceased to matter, and now the instructors knew we were right on the edge, and they came around with mugs of hot chicken broth. I was shaking so much I could hardly hold the cup.

But nothing ever tasted better. I seem to remember someone else quit, but hell, I was almost out of it. I wouldn't have known if Captain Maguire had quit. All I knew was, there were half as many still going as there had been at the start of Hell Week. The hour was growing later, and this thing was not over yet. We still had five boats in action, and the instructors reshuffled the crews and ordered us to paddle over to Turners Field, the eastern extension of the base.

There they made us run around a long loop, carrying the boat on our heads, and then they made us race without it. This was followed by another long period in the water, at the end of which this member of the crew of boat one, a tough-as-nails Texan (I thought), cracked up with what felt like appendicitis. Whatever it was, I was absolutely unreachable. I didn't even know my name, and I had to be taken away by ambulance and revived at the medical center.

When I regained consciousness, I got straight out of bed and came back. I would not discuss quitting. I remember the instructors congratulating me on my new warm, dry clothes and then sending me straight back into the surf. "Better get wet and sandy. Just in case you forget what we're doing here."

Starting at around 0200, we spent the rest of the night running around the base with the goddamned boat on our heads. They released us for breakfast at 0500, and Tuesday proceeded much like Monday. No sleep, freezing cold, and tired to distraction. We completed a three-mile paddle up to North Island and back, at which time it was late in the evening and we'd been up for more than sixty hours.

The injury list grew longer: cuts, sprains, blisters, bruises, pulled muscles, and maybe three cases of pneumonia. We worked through the night, making one long six-mile paddle, and reported for breakfast again at 0500 on Wednesday. We'd had no sleep for three days, but no one else quit.

And all through the morning we kept going, swim-paddle-swim, then a run along the beach. We carried the boat to chow at noon, and then they sent us to go sleep. We'd have one hour and forty-five minutes in the tent. We had thirty-six guys left.

Trouble was, some of them could not sleep. I was one. The medical staff tried to help the wounded get back into the fray. Tendons and hips seemed to be the main problems, but guys needed muscle-stretching exercises to keep them supple for the day ahead.

The new shift of instructors turned up and started yelling for everyone to wake up and get back out there. It was like standing in the middle of a graveyard and trying to wake the dead. Slowly it dawned on the sleepers: their worst nightmare was happening. Someone was driving them forward again.

They ordered us into the surf, and somehow we fell, crawled, or stumbled over that sand dune and into the freezing water. They gave us fifteen minutes of surf torture, exercises in the waves, then ordered us out and told us to hoist the boats back on our heads and make the elephant walk to chow.

They worked us all night, in and out of the surf; they walked us up and down the beach for God knows how many miles. Finally, they let us sleep again. I guess it was about 0400 on the Thursday morning. Against many pessimistic forecasts, we all woke up and carried the boats to breakfast. Then they worked us without mercy, had us racing the boats in the gigantic pool without paddles, just hands, and then swimming them, one crew against the other.

Wednesday had run into Thursday, but we were in the final stages of Hell Week, and before us was the fabled around-the-world paddle, the last of the major evolutions of the week. We boarded the boats at around 1930 and set off, rushing into the surf off the special warfare center and paddling right around the north end of the island and back down San Diego Bay to the amphibious base. No night in my experience has ever lasted longer.

Some of the guys really were hallucinating now, and all three of the boats had a system where one could sleep while the others paddled. I cannot explain how tired we were; every light looked like a building dead in our path, every thought turned into reality. If you thought of home, like I did, you thought you were rowing straight into the ranch. The only saving grace was, we were dry.

But one guy in our boat was so close to breakdown, he simply toppled into the water, still holding his paddle, still stroking, kicking automatically, and continuing to row the boat. We dragged him out, and he did not seem to understand he'd just spent five minutes in San Diego Bay. In the end, I think we were all paddling in our sleep.

After three hours, they summoned us to shore for medical checks and gave us hot soup. After that we just kept going, until almost 0200 on Friday, when they called us in from the beach with a bullhorn. No one will ever forget that. One of those bastards actually yelled, *"Dump boat!"*

It was like taking a kick at a dying man. But we kept quiet. Not like an earlier response from a student, who had earned everlasting notoriety by yelling back the most insubordinate reply anyone had ever given one of the instructors. Never mind *"Hooyah, Instructor Pat-stone!"* (Because Terry Patstone was normally a super guy, always harsh but fair.) That particular half-crazed paddler bellowed, *"Ass-h-o-o-ole!"* It echoed across the moonlit water and was greeted by a howl of laughter from the night-shift instructors. They understood, and never mentioned it.

So we crashed over the side of the boat into the freezing water, flipped the hull over and then back, climbed back in, soaking wet, of course, and kept paddling. I locked one thought into my brain and kept it there: everyone else who ever became a U.S. Navy SEAL completed this, and that's what we're going to do.

We finally hauled up on our home beach at around 0500 on Friday. Instructor Patstone knew we just wanted to hoist boats and get over to the chow hall. But he was not having that. He made us lift and then lower. Then he had us push 'em out, feet on the boat. He kept us on the beach for another half hour before we were loosed to make the elephant walk to breakfast.

Breakfast was rushed. Just a few minutes, and then they had us right out of there. And the morning was filled with long boat races and a series of terrible workouts in the demo pits—that's a scum-laden seawater slime, which we had to traverse on a couple of ropes, invariably falling straight in. To make everything worse, they kept telling us it was Thursday, not Friday, and the entire exercise was conducted under battle conditions— explosions, smoke, barbed wire—while we were crawling, falling into the slime.

Finally, Mr. Burns sent us into the surf, all the time telling us how slow we were, how much more there was to accomplish this day, and how deeply he regretted there was as yet no end in sight for Class 226. The water almost froze us to death, but it cleaned us off from the slime pits, and after ten minutes, Chief Taylor ordered us back to the beach.

We now didn't know whether it was Thursday or Friday. Guys collapsed onto the sand, others just stood there, betraying nothing but in dread of the next few hours, too many of them wondering how they could possibly go on. Including me. Knees were buckling, joints throbbing. I don't think anyone could stand up without hurting.

Mr. Burns stepped forward and shouted, "Okay, guys, let's get right on to the next evolution. A tough one, right? But I think you're up for it."

We gave out the world's weakest *hooyah*. Hoarse voices, disembodied sounds. I didn't know who was speaking for me; it sure as hell sounded like someone else.

Joe Burns nodded curtly and said, "Actually, guys, there is no other evolution. All of you. Back to the grinder."

No one believed him. But Joe wouldn't lie. He might fool around, but he would not lie. It slowly dawned on us that Hell Week was over. We just stood there, zonked out with pure disbelief. And Lieutenant Ismay, who was really hurting, croaked, "We made it, guys. Sonofabitch. We made it."

I turned to Matt McGraw, and I remember saying, "How the hell did you get here, kid? You're supposed to be in school."

But Matt was on the verge of exhaustion. He just shook his head and said, "Thank God, thank God, Marcus."

I know this sounds crazy if you haven't gone through what we went through. But this was an unforgettable moment. Two guys fell to their knees and wept. Then we all began to hug one another. Someone was saying, "It's over."

Like the remnants of a ravaged army, we helped one another back over the sand dunes, picking up those who fell, supporting those who could barely walk. We reached the bus that would take us back to base. And there, waiting for us, was Captain Joe Maguire, the SEAL commanding officers, and the senior chiefs. Also in attendance was the ex-SEAL governor of Minnesota, Jesse Ventura, who would perform the official ceremony when we returned to the grinder.

But right now, all we knew was the baptism of fire that had reduced Class 226 by more than half was over. It hadn't beaten thirty-two of us. And now the torture was completed. In our wildest imaginations, no one had ever dreamed it would be this bad. God had given us justice.

We lined up on that sacred blacktop, and Governor Ventura formally pronounced the official words that proclaimed we never had to tackle another Hell Week: "Class Two-two-six, you're secured." We gave him a rousing *"Hooyah! Governor Ventura!"*

Then Instructor Burns called us to order and said, "Gentlemen, for the rest of your lives there will be setbacks. But they won't affect you like they will affect other people. Because you have done something very few are ever called upon to achieve. This week will live with you for all of your lives. Not one of you will ever forget it. And it means one thing above all else. If you can take Hell Week and beat it, you can do any damn thing in the world."

I can't pretend the actual words are accurate in my memory. But the sentiment is precise. Those words signify exactly what Instructor Joe Burns meant, and how he said it.

And it affected us all, deeply. We raised our tired voices, and the shout split the noontime air above that beach in Coronado.

"Hooyah, Instructor Burns!" we bellowed. And did we ever mean it.

The SEAL commanders and chiefs stepped forward and took each one of us by the hand, saying, "Congratulations," and offering words of encouragement about the future, telling us to be sure and contact their personal teams once we were through.

Tell the truth, it was all a bit of a blur for me. I can't really recall who invited me to join what. But one thing remains very clear in my mind. I shook the hand of the great SEAL warrior Joe Maguire, and he had a warm word for me. And thus far in my life, there had been no greater honor than that.

* * *

We probably devoured a world-record amount of food that weekend. Appetites returned and then accelerated as our stomachs grew more used to big-sized meals. We still had three weeks to go in first phase, but nothing compared to Hell Week. We were perfecting techniques in hydrology, learning tide levels and demographics of the ocean floor. That's real SEAL stuff, priceless to the Marines. While they're planning a landing, we're in there early, moving fast, checking out the place in secret, telling 'em what to expect.

There were only thirty-two members of the original class left now, mostly because of injury or illness sustained during Hell Week. But they'd been joined by others, rollbacks from other classes who'd been permitted another go.

This applied to me, because I had been on an enforced break when I had my broken femur. And so when I rejoined for phase two, I was in Class 228. We began in the diving phase, conducted in the water, mostly under it. We learned how to use scuba tanks, how to dump them and get 'em back on again, how to swap them over with a buddy without coming to the surface. This is difficult, but we had to master it before we could take the major pool competency test.

I failed my pool competency, like a whole lot of others. This test is a royal bastard. You swim down to the bottom of the pool with twin eighty-pound scuba tanks on your back, a couple of instructors harassing you. You are not allowed to put a foot down and kick to the surface. If you do, you've failed, and that's the end of it.

First thing these guys do is rip off your mask, then your mouthpiece, and you have to hold your breath real quick. You fight to get the mouthpiece back in, then they unhook your air-line intake, and you have to get that back in real fast, groping around over your shoulder, behind your back.

Somehow you find yourself able to breathe in pure oxygen, but the only way you can breathe out is through your nose. A lot of guys find the cascade of bubbles across their faces extremely disconcerting. Then the instructors disconnect your airline completely and put a knot in it. And you *must* try to get your inhalation and exhalation lines reconnected. If you don't or can't even try, you're gone. You need a good lungful of air before this starts, then you need to feel your way blind to the knot in the line behind your back and start unraveling it. You can more or less tell by the feel if it's going to be impossible, what the instructors call a whammy. Then you run the flat edge of your hand across your throat and give the instructor the thumbs-up. That means "I'm never going to get that knot undone, permission to go to the surface." At that point, they cease holding you down and let you go up. But you better be right in your assessment of that knot.

In my case, I decided too hastily that the knot in my line was impossible, gave them the signal, ditched my tanks over my shoulder, and floated up to the surface. But the instructors decided the knot was nothing like impossible and that I had bailed out of a dangerous situation. Failed.

I had to go and sit in a line in front of the poolside wall. It would have been a line of shame, except there were so many of us. I was instructed to take the test again, and I did not make the mistake the second time. Undid the sonofabitch knot and passed pool comp.

Several of my longtime comrades failed, and I felt quite sad. Except you can't be a SEAL if you can't keep your nerve underwater. As one of the instructors said to me that week, "See that guy in some kind of a panic over there? There's confusion written all over him. You might have your life in his hands one day, Marcus, and we cannot, will not, allow that to happen."

Pool comp is the hardest one of all to pass, just because we all spent so much time in the water and right now had to prove we had the potential to be true SEALs, guys to whom the water was always a sanctuary.

It must not be a threat or an obstacle but a place where we alone could survive. Some of the instructors had known many of us for a long time and desperately wanted us to pass. But the slightest sign of weakness in pool competency, and they wouldn't take the chance.

Those of us who did stay moved on to phase three. With a few rollbacks coming in, we were twenty-one in number. It was winter now in the Northern Hemisphere, early February, and we prepared for the hard slog of the land warfare course. That's where they turn us into navy commandos.

This is formally called Demolitions and Tactics, and the training is as strict and unrelenting as anything we had so far encountered. It's a known fact that phase three instructors are the fittest men in Coronado, and it took us little time to find out why. Even the opening speech by our new proctor was edged with dire warnings.

His name was Instructor Eric Hall, a veteran of six SEAL combat platoons, and before we even started on Friday afternoon, he laid it right on the line. "We don't put up with people who feel sorry for themselves. Any problems with drugs or alcohol, you're gone. There's four bars around here that guys from the teams sometimes visit. Stay the hell out of all of 'em, hear me? Anyone lies, cheats, or steals, you're done, because that's not tolerated here. Just so we're clear, gentlemen."

He reminded us it was a ten-week course and we weren't that far from graduation. He told us where we'd be. Five weeks right here at the center, with days at the land navigation training area in La Posta. There would be four days at Camp Pendleton on the shooting ranges. That's the 125,000-acre Marine Corps base between Los Angeles and San Diego. We would finish at San Clemente Island, known to SEALs as the Rock and the main site for more advanced shooting and tactics, demolitions, and field training.

Eric Hall finished with a characteristic flourish. "Give me a hundred and ten percent at all times—and don't blow it by doing something stupid."

Thus we went at it again for another two and a half months, heading first for the group one mountain training facility, three thousand feet up in the rough, jagged Laguna Mountains at La Posta, eighty miles east of San Diego. That's where they taught us stealth, camouflage, and patrolling, the essential field craft of the commando. The terrain was really rough, hard to climb, steep, and demanding. Sometimes we didn't make it back to barracks at night and had to sleep outside in the wild country.

They taught us how to navigate across the land with maps and compass. At the end of the week, we all passed the basic courses, three-mile journeys conducted in pairs across the mountains. Then we headed back to the center to prepare for Camp Pendleton, where we would undergo our first intensive courses in weaponry.

No time was lost. We were out there with submachine guns, rifles, and pistols, training for the not-too-distant days when we would go into combat armed with the M4 rifle, the principal SEAL weapon of war.

First thing was safety. And we all had to learn by heart the four critical rules:

1. Consider all weapons to be loaded at all times.
2. Never point a weapon at anything you do not want to put a bullet through.
3. Never put your finger on the trigger unless you want to shoot.
4. Know your target and what's behind it.

They kept us out on the shooting range for hours. In between times we had to dismantle and assemble machine guns and the M4, all under the eyes of instructors who timed us with stopwatches. And the brutal regime of fitness never wavered. It was harder than second phase, because now we had to run carrying heavy packs, ammunition, and guns.

We also had a couple of weeks at the center to study high explosives and demolition. This mostly involved straightforward TNT and plastic, with various firing assemblies. The practical work happened only on the island of San Clemente. And before we got to do that, we had another rigorous training schedule to complete, including one fourteen-mile run along the beach and back.

This was the first time we had run any race without being wet and probably sandy. Just imagine, dry shorts and running shoes. We floated along, not a care in the world.

It was mid-March before we decamped to San Clemente for four weeks of training, long hours, seven days a week until we finished. This rugged moonscape of an island is situated off the California coast, sixty miles west of San Diego, across the Gulf of Santa Catalina.

For almost fifty years, the U.S. Navy has been in command here, using the place as an extensive training area. There are no civilians, but parts of the island are an important wildlife sanctuary. There are lots of rare birds and California sea lions, who don't seem to care about violent explosions, shells, and naval air landings. Up in the northeast, right on the coast, you find SEALs.

And there we learned the rudiments of fast and accurate combat shooting, the swift changing of magazines, expert marksmanship. We were introduced to the deadly serious business of assaulting an enemy position and taught how to lay down covering fire. Slowly, then faster, first in daylight, then through the night. We were schooled in all the aspects of modern warfare we would one day need in Iraq or Afghanistan—ambushes, structure searches, handling prisoners, planning raids. This is where we got down to all the serious techniques of reconnaissance.

We moved on to really heavy demolition, setting off charges on a grand scale, then hand grenades, then rockets, and generally causing major explosions and practicing until we demonstrated a modicum of expertise.

Our field training tasks were tough, combat mission simulations. We paddled the boats to within a few hundred yards of the shore and dropped anchor. From that holding area, we sent in the scout recon guys, who swam to the beach, checked the place out, and signaled the boats to bring us in. This was strict OTB (over the beach), and we hit the sand running, burrowing into hides just beyond the high-water mark. This is where SEALs are traditionally at their most vulnerable, and the instructors watch like hawks for mistakes, signs that will betray the squad.

We practiced these beach landings all through the nights, fighting our way out of the water with full combat gear and weapons. And at the end of the fourth week we all passed, every one of the twenty trainees who had arrived on the island. We would all graduate from BUD/S.

I asked one of our instructors if this was in any way unusual. His reply was simple. "Marcus," he said, "when you're training the best of the best, nothing's unusual. And all the BUD/S instructors want the very best for you."

They gave us a couple of weeks' leave after graduation, and thereafter for me it was high-density education. First jump school at Fort Benning, Georgia, where they turned me into a paratrooper. I spent three weeks jumping out of towers and then out of a C-130, from which we all had to make five jumps.

That aircraft is a hell of a noisy place, and the first jump can be a bit unnerving. But the person in front of me was a girl from West Point, and she dived out of that door like Superwoman. I remember thinking, *Christ! If she can do it, I'm definitely gonna do it,* and I launched myself into the clear skies above Fort Benning.

Next stop for me was the Eighteenth Delta Force medical program, conducted at Fort Bragg, North Carolina. That's where they turned me into a battlefield doctor. I suppose it was more like a paramedic, but the learning curve was huge: medicine, injections, IV training, chest tubes, combat trauma, wounds, burns, stitches, morphine. It covered just about everything a wounded warrior might need under battle conditions. On the first day I had to memorize 315 examples of medical terminology. And they never took their foot off the high-discipline accelerator. Here I was, working all day and half the night, and there was *still* an instructor telling me to get wet and sandy during training runs.

I went straight from North Carolina to SEAL qualification training, three more months of hard labor in Coronado, diving, parachute jumping, shooting, explosives, detonation, a long, intensive recap of everything I had learned. Right after that, I was sent to join the SDV school (submarines) at Panama City,

Florida. I was there on 9/11, and little did I realize the massive impact those terrible events in New York City would have on my own life.

I remember the pure indignation we all felt. Someone had just attacked the United States of America, the beloved country we were sworn to defend. We watched the television with mounting fury, the fury of young, inexperienced, but supremely fit and highly trained combat troops who could not wait to get at the enemy. We wished we could get at Osama bin Laden's al Qaeda mob in Iraq, Iran, Afghanistan, or wherever the hell these lunatics lived. But be careful what you wish for. You might get it.

A lot of guys passed SEAL qualification training and received their Tridents on Wednesday afternoon, November 7, 2001. They pinned it right on in a short ceremony out there on the grinder. You could see it meant all the world to the graduates. There were in fact only around thirty left from the original 180 who had signed up on that long-ago first day of Indoc. For myself, because of various educational commitments, I had to wait until January 31, 2002, for my Trident.

But the training never stopped. Right after I formally joined what our commanders call the brotherhood, I went to communication school to study and learn satellite comms, high-frequency radio links, antenna wavelength probability, in-depth computers, global positioning systems, and the rest.

Then I went to Sniper School back at Camp Pendleton, where, unsurprisingly, they made sure you could shoot straight before you did anything else. This entailed two very tough exams involving the M4 rifle; the SR-25 semiautomatic sniper rifle, accurate to nine hundred yards; and the heavy, powerful 300 Win Mag bolt-action .308-caliber rifle. You needed to be expert with all of them if you were planning to be a Navy SEAL sniper.

Then the real test started, the ultimate examination of a man's ability to move stealthily, unseen and undetected, across rough, enemy-held ground where the slightest mistake might mean instant death or, worse, letting your team down.

Our instructor was a veteran of the first wave of U.S. troops who had gone in after Osama. He was Brendan Webb, a terrific man. Stalking was his game, and his standards were so high they would have made an Apache scout gasp. Working right alongside him was Eric Davis, another brilliant SEAL sniper, who was completely ruthless in his examination of our abilities to stay concealed.

The final "battleground" was a vast area out near the border of Pendleton. There was not much vegetation, mostly low, flat bushes, but the rough rocks-boulders-and-shale terrain was full of undulations, valleys, and gullies. Trees, the sniper's nearest and dearest friends, were damn sparse, obviously by design. Before they let us loose in this barren, dusty no-man's-land, they subjected us to long lectures stressing the importance of paying attention to every detail.

They retaught us the noble art of camouflage, the brown and green creams, the way to arrange branches in your hat, the dangers of a gust of wind, which might ruffle your branches alone if they weren't set tight, betraying your position. We practiced all the hours God made, and then they sent us out onto the range.

It's a vast sweep of ground, and the instructors survey it from a high platform. Our stalk began a thousand yards from that platform, upon which the gimlet-eyed Webb and Davis stood, scanning the acres like a pair of revolving radars.

The idea was to get within two hundred yards of them and then fire through the crosshairs at the target. We had practiced doing this alone and with a partner, and boy, does this ever teach you patience. It can take hours just to move a few yards, but if the instructors catch you as they sweep the area with high-powered binoculars, you fail the course.

For the final test I was working with a partner, and this meant we both had to stay well concealed. In the end, he finds the range and calls the shot, and I adhere to his command. At this stage the instructors have installed walkers all over the place, and they're communicating by radios with the platform. If the walker gets within two steps of you, you've failed.

Even if you get your shot off unseen *and* hit the target, if they find you afterward, you *still* fail. It's a hard, tough, thinking man's game, and the test is exhaustive. In training, an instructor stands behind both of you while you're crossing the forbidden ground. They're writing a constant critique, observing, for example, that my spotter has made a wrong call, either incorrect distance or direction. If I then miss with the shot, they know the mistake was not mine. As ever, you must operate as a team. The instructor knows full well you cannot position, aim, and fire the rifle without a spotter calling down the range, and Jesus, he better be right.

There was just one day during training where they walked on me, which I thought was pretty damned nervy. But it taught me something. Our enemy had a damn good idea where we might head before we even started, a kind of instinct based on long experience of rookie snipers looking for cover. They had me in their sights before I even got moving, because they knew where to look, the highest probability area.

That's a lifetime lesson for the sniper: never, ever go where your enemy might expect you to be. My only solace on that rueful occasion was that the instructors walked on every single one of us that day.

In the final test, I faced that thousand-yard barren desert once again and began my journey, wriggling and scuffling through the dusty ground, my head well down, camouflage branches firm in my hat, groveling my way between the boulders. It took me hours to make the halfway point and even longer to ease my way over the last three hundred yards to my chosen spot for the shot. I was not seen, and I moved dead slowly through the rocks, from gully to gully, staying low, pressing into the ground. When I arrived at my final point, I scuffled together a little hide of dirt and sticks, and tucked down behind it, my rifle carefully aimed. I squeezed the trigger slowly and deliberately, and my shot pinged into the metal target, right in the middle. If that had been a man's head, he'd have been history.

I saw the instructors swing around and start looking for the place my shot had come from. But they were obviously guessing. I pressed my face into the dirt and never moved an inch for a half hour. Then I made my slow and careful retreat, still lying flat, disturbing not a twig nor a rock. An unknown marksman, just the way we like it.

It had taken three months, and I passed Sniper School with excellent marks. SEALs don't look for personal credit, and thus I cannot say who the class voted their Honor Man.

The last major school I attended was joint tactical air control. It lasted one month, out in the Fallon Naval Airbase, Nevada. They taught us the basics of airborne ordnance, five-hundred-pound bombs and missiles, what they can hit and what they can't. We also learned to communicate directly with aircraft from the ground—getting them to see what we can see, relaying information through the satellites to the controllers.

I realize it has taken me some time to explain precisely what a Navy SEAL is and what it takes to be one. But as we are always told, you have to earn that Trident every day. We never stop learning, never stop training. To state that a man is a Navy SEAL communicates about a ten thousandth of what it really means. It would be as if General Dwight D. Eisenhower mentioned he'd once served in the army.

But now you know: what it took, what it meant to all of us, and, perhaps, why we did it. Okay, okay, we do have our own little brand of arrogance. But we paid for every last drop of that sin in sweat, blood, and brutally hard work.

Because above all, we're patriots. We will willingly carry the fight to whoever may be the enemies of the United States of America. We're your front line, unafraid and ready to go in against al Qaeda, jihadists, terrorists, or whoever the hell else threatens this nation.

Every Navy SEAL is supremely confident, because we're indoctrinated with a belief in victory at all costs; a conviction that no earthly force can withstand our thunderous assault on the battlefield. We're invincible, right? Unstoppable. That's what I believed to the depths of my spirit on the day they pinned the Trident on my chest. I still believe it. And I always will.

6

'Bye, Dudes, Give 'Em Hell

The final call came—"Redwing is a go!" The landing
controller was calling the shots..."One minute...Thirty
seconds!...*Let's go!*" The ramp was down...the gunner
was ready with the M60 machine gun...No moon...
Danny went first, out into the dark.

As day broke over the mighty sprawl of the U.S. base at Bagram
in Afghanistan on that morning in March 2005, we checked
into our bee hut and slept for a few hours before attending a
general briefing. Dan Healy, Shane, James, Axe, Mikey, and I,
the new arrivals from SDV Team 1, were immediately seconded
to SEAL Team 10 out of Virginia Beach, led right now by the
teak-hard Lieutenant Commander Eric Kristensen, standing in
for the absent CO, who was on duty elsewhere.

Eric was funny as hell, always one of the boys, so much so it
might have impeded his progress through the higher ranks in
later years. These days 75 percent of all SEALs have college degrees, and the line between officers and enlisted men is more
blurred than it has ever been. But Eric was thirty-two and the
son of an admiral from Virginia. Despite his sense of humor and
his often wry look at higher authority, he was a very fine SEAL
commander, and he presided over one of the best fighting pla-

toons in the entire U.S. Navy. Team 10 was brilliantly trained for the kind of warfare we were now entering. Lieutenant Commander Kristensen had a couple of right-hand men, Luke Newbold and Master Chief Walters, very special guys. I can only say it was a pleasure to work with them.

Our briefing, like everything associated with Team 10, was top of the line, a kind of grim educational lecture on what was happening up on the northwest frontier, which divides Afghanistan and Pakistan. The steep, stony mountain crevasses and cliffs, dust-colored, sinister places, were now alive with the burgeoning armies of the Taliban. Angry, resentful men, regrouping all along the unmarked high border, preparing to take back the holy Muslim country they believed the infidel Americans had stolen from them and then presented to a new, elected government.

Up there, complex paths emerge and then disappear behind huge boulders and rocks. Every footstep that dislodges anything, a small rock, a pile of shale, seems like it might cause an earth-shaking avalanche. Stealth, we were told, must be our watchword on the high, quiet slopes of the Hindu Kush.

These paths, trodden down for centuries by warring tribesmen, were the very routes taken by the defeated Taliban and al Qaeda after the withering U.S. bombardment had all but annihilated them in 2001. We would find out all about them soon enough.

Within literally hours, we began our first mission. No one regarded us as rookies; we were all fully trained SEALs, ready for action, ready to get up there into those mountain passes and help slow the tide of armed warrior tribesmen moving back across the border from Pakistan.

We flew by helicopter up into those passes, into the hills above a deep valley. We arrived, maybe twenty of us, including Dan,

Shane, Axe, and Mikey, and fanned out around the mountain. Axe, Mikey, and James Suh (call sign Irish One) were positioned about one and a half miles from Chief Healy, Shane, and me (call sign Irish Three).

This was a border hot spot, where multiple Taliban troop movements were taking place on a weekly, or even daily, basis. We expected to observe the Taliban way below us on that narrow, treacherous path through the mountains, moving along with their swaying camels, many of them loaded up with explosives, grenades, and God knows what else.

I was walking with great caution. We had all been warned these glowering Afghanistan tribesmen would fight, and none of them were likely to be pushovers. I also knew that one false step, a dislodged rock, however small, would betray our positions. Those tribesmen had lived up here for centuries, and they had eyes like falcons. If they heard us or saw us, they would attack immediately. Our high command had left no doubt in our minds. This was dangerous stuff, but we had to stop the influx of armed terrorists.

Carefully I moved along the ridge, occasionally stopping to scan the mountain pass with my binos. I was walking silently. Everything was clear in my mind. If a troop of wild tribesmen with camels and missiles came rolling into the pass, I must instantly whistle up reinforcements on the radio. If it was a lesser force, something we could deal with right here, we'd swoop and try to capture the leaders and take care of the rest by whatever means were necessary.

Anyway, I continued my silent patrol, hunkered down behind a couple of huge boulders, and again scanned the pass. Nothing. I stepped out once more, into steep, barren, open country, and below me I suddenly saw three armed Afghanistan tribesmen. My brain raced. There was seventy yards between me and Shane. Do I open fire? How many more of them were there?

Too late. They opened fire first, shooting uphill, and a volley of bullets from their AK-47s slammed into the rocks all around me. I hurled myself back behind the rocks, knowing Shane must have heard something. Then I stepped out and let 'em have it. I saw them retreat into cover. At least I'd pinned them down.

But they came at me again, and again I returned fire. But right then, they unleashed two rocket-propelled grenades (RPGs), and thank God I saw them coming. I dived for cover, but they blew out one of the boulders which had given me shelter. Now there were ricocheting bullets, dust, shrapnel, and flying rock particles everywhere.

It felt like I was fighting a one-man war, and Christ knows how I avoided being hit. But suddenly, the echoes of the blast died away, and I could hear sporadic gunfire from these three maniacs. I waited quietly until I believed they had broken cover, and then I stepped out and hit the trigger again. I don't know what or who I hit, but it suddenly went very quiet again. As if nothing had happened. Welcome to Afghanistan, Marcus.

This was one type of patrol, standing guard up there over the passes and trying to remain concealed. The other kind was a straight surveillance and reconnaissance mission (SR), where we were tasked with observing and photographing a village, looking for our target. It was always expected we would locate him since our intel was excellent, often with good photographs. And we were always in search of some sonofabitch in a turban who had for too long been indulging in his favorite pastime of blowing up U.S. Marines.

On these sorties into the mountains, we were expected to pick out our quarry, either with high-powered binoculars or the photo lens of one of our cameras, and then swoop down into the village and take him. If he was alone, that was always the primary plan of the SEALs: grab the target, get him back to base, and make him talk, tell us where the Taliban were gathered, locate for us the huge ammunition piles they had hidden in the mountains.

That high explosive had only one use, to kill and maim U.S. troops, up there in support of the elected government. We found it well to remember those Taliban insurgents were the very same guys who sheltered and supported Osama bin Laden. We were also told, no ifs, ands, or buts, that particular mass murderer was right where we were going, somewhere.

Generally speaking, we were to grab our man in the village if he was protected by, say, only four bodyguards. No problem. But if there were more of them, some kind of Taliban garrison crawling with armed men, we were to call for a proper fighting force to fly in and take care of the problem. Either way, when we arrived, things ceased to look great for young Abdul the Bomb-maker measuring out his dynamite down there in Main Street, Mud Hut Central, Northeast Afghanistan.

Our next mission was a huge operation, around fifty guys dropped into the mountains, in the worst terrain you've ever seen. Well, maybe not if there are any mountain goats or mountain lions among my readers, but it sure as hell was the worst I'd ever seen. There were steep cliff faces, loose footing, sheer drops, hardly any bushes or trees, nothing to grab, nowhere to take cover if necessary.

I have explained how supremely fit we were. We could all climb anything, go anywhere. But—you're not going to believe this—we took *eight hours* to walk one and a half miles. Guys were falling down the goddamned mountain, getting hurt, bad.

It was hotter than a Texas griddle, and one of my buddies told me later, "I'd have quit the teams just to get out of there."

I know he didn't mean it. But we all knew the feeling. We were tired, frustrated, roped together in teams, crawling across the face of this dangerous mountain with full rucksacks and rifles. To this day it remains the worst journey of my life. And we weren't even facing the enemy. It was so bad we made up a song about it, which our resident expert banjo player put to the music of the Johnny Cash song "Ring of Fire":

I fell into a hundred-foot ravine,
We went down, down, down, and busted up my spleen,
And it burned, burned, burned — that Ring of Fire...

Our dual targets on that next mission were two Afghan villages set into the mountainside, one above the other. We had no clues which one harbored the most Taliban forces, and it had been decided we needed to take them both at gunpoint. No bullshit. The reason for this was a very young guy. We had terrific intel on him, from both satellites and the FBI. We did not, however, have photographs.

I never knew where he was educated, but this young Taliban kid was a scientist, a master of explosives. We call them IED guys (improvised explosive devices), and in this part of the mountains, this kid was King IED. And he and his men had been wreaking havoc on U.S. troops, blowing stuff up all over the place. He'd recently blown up a couple of U.S. Marine convoys and killed a lot of guys.

Foxtrot Platoon regrouped in the small hours of the morning after the trek across the mountains and positioned ourselves high above the upper village. As the sun came up, we moved swiftly down the hillside and charged into the village, crashing down the doors to the houses, arresting anyone and everyone. We were not shooting, but we were very intimidating, no doubt about that. And no one resisted. But the kid wasn't there.

Meanwhile the main force, SEAL Team 10, was in and playing hell in the bigger, lower village. It took them a while, because this required interrogation, a skill at which we were all very competent. In these circumstances, we were grilling everyone, looking for the liar, the guy who changed his story, the guy who was somehow different. We wanted the guy who was obviously not a goatherd, as the rest of them were; a young guy who lacked the gnarled, rough look of the native mountain farmer.

We got our man. It was my first close-up encounter with a fanatical Taliban fighter. I'll never forget him. He was only just old enough to have a decent beard, but he had wild, crazy eyes, and he stared at me like I'd just rejected the entire teachings of the Koran.

I knew in that instant that if he could have killed me, he would have. No one had ever looked at me before, or has since, with that much hatred.

That second operation in Afghanistan, the snatch-and-grab of Abdul the Bombmaker or whatever the hell his name was, brought home two aspects of this conflict to us newly arrived SEALs. First, the rabid hatred these Muslim extremists had for all of us; second, the awkwardness of complying with our rules of engagement (ROE) in this type of warfare.

SEALs, by our nature, training, and education, are not very stupid. And along with everyone else, we read the newspaper headlines from all over the world about serving members of the armed forces who have been charged with murder in civilian courts for doing what they thought was their duty, attacking their enemy.

Our rules of engagement in Afghanistan specified that we could not shoot, kill, or injure unarmed civilians. But what about the unarmed civilian who was a skilled spy for the illegal forces we were trying to remove? What about an entire secret army, diverse, fragmented, and lethal, creeping through the mountains in Afghanistan *pretending* to be civilians? What about those guys? How about the innocent-looking camel drovers making their way through the mountain passes with enough high explosive strapped to the backs of their beasts to blow up Yankee Stadium? How about those guys?

We all knew that we'd chosen to do what 999 Americans out of every thousand would not even think about doing. And we were taught that we were necessary for the security of our nation. We were sent to Afghanistan to carry out hugely dangerous missions. But we were also told that we could not shoot that camel drover before he blew up all of us, because he might be an unarmed civilian just taking his dynamite for a walk.

And how about his buddy? The younger guy with the stick, running along behind, prodding the freakin' camels? How about him? How about if he can't wait to scamper up those mountains and find his brother and the rest of the Taliban hard men? The ones with the RPGs, waiting in the hidden cave?

We wouldn't hear him reveal our position, and neither would the politicians who drafted those ROEs. And those men in suits won't be on that mountainside when the first grenade explodes among us and takes off someone's leg, or head.

Should we have shot that little son of a gun right off the bat, before he had a chance to run? Or was he just an unarmed civilian, doing no harm to anyone? Just taking his TNT for a walk, right?

These terrorist/insurgents know the rules as well as they did in Iraq. They're not their rules. They're *our* rules, the rules of the Western countries, the civilized side of the world. And every terrorist knows how to manipulate them in their own favor. Otherwise the camel drovers would be carrying guns.

But they don't. Because they know we are probably scared to shoot them, because we might get charged with murder, which I actually know they consider to be on the hysterical side of laughable.

And if we did shoot a couple of them, they would be on their cell phones with the speed of ten thousand gigabytes, direct to the Arab television station al-Jazeera:

BRUTAL US TROOPS GUN DOWN
PEACE-LOVING AFGHAN FARMERS
US Military Promises SEALs
Will Be Charged

Well, something like that. I'm sure you get my drift. The media in the United States of America would crucify us. These days, they always do. Was there ever a greater uproar than the one that broke out over Abu Ghraib? In the bigger scheme of things, in the context of all the death and destruction that Muslim extremists have visited upon this world, a bunch of Iraqi prisoners being humiliated does not ring my personal alarm bell. And it would not ring yours either if you ever saw firsthand what these guys are capable of. I mean, Jesus, they cut off people's heads, American heads, aid workers' heads. They think nothing of slaughtering thousands of people; they've stabbed and mutilated young American soldiers, like something out of the Middle Ages.

The truth is, in this kind of terrorist/insurgent warfare, no one can tell who's a civilian and who's not. So what's the point of framing rules that cannot be comprehensively carried out by anyone? Rules that are unworkable, because half the time no one knows who the goddamned enemy is, and by the time you find out, it might be too late to save your own life. Making sense of the ROEs in real-time situations is almost impossible.

Also, no one seems clear on what we should be called in Afghanistan. Are we a peace-keeping force? Are we fighting a war against insurgents on behalf of the Afghan government, or are we fighting it on behalf of the U.S.A.? Are we trying to hunt down the master terrorist bin Laden, or are we just trying to prevent the Taliban from regaining control of the country, because they were the protectors of bin Laden and all who fought for him?

Search me. But everything's cool with us. Tell us what you want, and we'll do it. We're loyal servants of the U.S. government. But Afghanistan involves fighting behind enemy lines. Never mind we were invited into a democratic country by its own government. Never mind there's no shooting across the border in Pakistan, the illegality of the Taliban army, the Geneva Convention, yada, yada, yada.

When we're patrolling those mountains, trying everything we know to stop the Taliban regrouping, striving to find and arrest the top commanders and explosive experts, we are always surrounded by a well-armed, hostile enemy whose avowed intention is to kill us all. That's behind enemy lines. Trust me.

And we'll go there. All day. Every day. We'll do what we're supposed to do, to the letter, or die in the attempt. On behalf of the U.S.A. But don't tell us who we can attack. That ought to be up to us, the military. And if the liberal media and political community cannot accept that sometimes the wrong people get killed in war, then I can only suggest they first grow up and then serve a short stint up in the Hindu Kush. They probably would not survive.

The truth is, any government that thinks war is somehow fair and subject to rules like a baseball game probably should not get into one. Because nothing's fair in war, and occasionally the wrong people do get killed. It's been happening for about a million years. Faced with the murderous cutthroats of the Taliban, we are not fighting under the rules of Geneva IV Article 4. We are fighting under the rules of Article 223.556mm—that's the caliber and bullet gauge of our M4 rifle. And if those numbers don't look good, try Article .762mm, that's what the stolen Russian Kalashnikovs fire at us, usually in deadly, heavy volleys.

In the global war on terror, we have rules, and our opponents use them against us. We try to be reasonable; they will stop at nothing. They will stoop to any form of base warfare: torture, beheading, mutilation. Attacks on innocent civilians, women and children, car bombs, suicide bombers, anything the hell they can think of. They're right up there with the monsters of history.

And I ask myself, Who's prepared to go furthest to win this war? Answer: they are. They'll willingly die to get their enemy. They will take it to the limit, any time, any place, whatever it takes. And they don't have rules of engagement.

Thus we have an extra element of fear and danger when we go into combat against the Taliban or al Qaeda—the fear of our own, the fear of what our own navy judge advocate general might rule against us, the fear of the American media and their unfortunate effect on American politicians. We all harbor fears about untrained, half-educated journalists who only want a good story to justify their salaries and expense accounts. Don't think it's just me. We all detest them, partly for their lack of judgment, mostly because of their ignorance and toe-curling opportunism. The first minute an armed conflict turns into a media war, the news becomes someone's opinion, not hard truths. When the media gets involved, in the United States, that's a war you've got a damned good chance of losing, because the restrictions on us are immediately amplified, and that's sensationally good news for our enemy.

Every now and then, a news reporter or a photographer gets in the way sufficiently to stop a bullet. And without missing a beat, those highly paid newspeople become national heroes, lauded back home in the press and on television. SEALs are not churlish, but I cannot describe how irksome this is to the highly trained but not very well paid guys who are doing the actual fighting. These are superb professionals who say nothing and place themselves in harm's way every day, too often being killed or wounded. They are silent heroes, unknown soldiers, except in equally unknown, heartbroken little home communities.

We did one early mission up there in the passes at checkpoint 6 that was worse than lethal. We'd just managed to get into position, about twenty of us, when these Afghan wild men hidden in the mountains unleashed a barrage of rockets at us, hundreds and hundreds of them, flying over our heads, slamming into the mountainside.

We couldn't tell whether they were classified as armed combatants against the United States or unarmed civilians. It took us three days to subdue them, and even then we had to call in heavy air support to enable us to get out. Three days later, the satellite pictures showed us the Taliban had sent in twelve cutthroats by night, armed with Kalashnikovs and tribal knives, who crept through the darkness intent on murder, directly to our old position.

But you can't prove their intentions! I hear the liberals squeal. No. Of course not. They were just headed up there for a cup of coffee.

Those Taliban night attacks were the very same tactics the mujahideen used against the Russians, sliding through the darkness and cutting the throats of guards and sentries until the Soviet military, and the parents of young soldiers, could stand it no more. The mujahideen has now emerged as the Taliban or al Qaeda. And their intentions against us are just as bloodthirsty as they were against the Russians.

The Navy SEALs can deal with that, as we can deal with any enemy. But not if someone wants to put us in jail for it back home in the U.S.A. And we sure as hell don't want to hang around in the mountains waiting for someone to cut our throats, unable to fight back just in case he might be classified as an unarmed Afghan farmer.

But these are the problems of the modern U.S. combat soldier, the constant worry about overstepping the mark and an American media that delights in trying to knock us down. Which we have done nothing to deserve. Except, perhaps, love our country and everything it stands for.

In the early weeks of our duties in Afghanistan, the fight went on. Platoons of us went out night after night, trying to halt the insurgents creeping through the mountain passes. Every time there was a full moon, we launched operations, because that was really the only time we could get a sweep of light over the dark mountains.

Following this lunar cycle, we'd send the helicopters up there to watch these bearded fanatics squirting over the border into Afghanistan, and then we'd round them up, the helos driving them like sheepdogs, watching them run for their lives, straight toward us and the rest of the waiting U.S. troops for capture and interrogation.

I realize it might seem strange that underwater specialists from SDV Team 1 should be groping around nine thousand feet above sea level. It is generally accepted in the navy that the swimmer delivery vehicle (SDV), the minisubmarine that brings us into our ops area, is the stealthiest vehicle in the world. And it follows that the troops manning the world's stealthiest vehicle are the world's sneakiest guys. That's us, operating deep behind enemy lines, observing and reporting, unnoticed, living on the edge of our nerves. And our principal task is always to find the target and then call in the direct action guys. That's really what everyone wants to do, direct action, but it can't be done without the deadly business we conduct up there in those lonely peaks of the Hindu Kush.

Lieutenant Commander Eric Kristensen was always aware of our value, and in fact was a very good friend of mine. He used to name the operations for me. I was a Texan, which, being as he was a Virginia gentleman, somehow amused the life out of him. He thought I was some kind of cross between Billy the Kid and Buffalo Bill, quick on the draw and *Dang mah breeches!* Never mind both those cowboys were from way north of me, Kansas or somewhere. So far as Eric was concerned, Texas and all points west and north of it represented the badlands, lawless frontiers, Colt .44s, cattlemen and Red Indians.

Thus we were always flying out on Operation Longhorn or Operation Lone Star. Naming the ops for his Texas boy really broke him up. The vast majority of our missions were very quiet and involved strict surveillance of mountain passes or villages. We were always trying to avoid gunfire as we photographed and then swooped on our target. Invariably we were looking for the misfit, the one man in the village who did not fit in, the hit man of the Taliban who was plainly not a farmer.

Sometimes we'd run across a group of these guys sitting around a campfire, bearded, sullen, drinking coffee, their AK-47s at the ready. Our first task was to identify them. Were they Pashtuns? Peaceable shepherds, goatherds? Or armed warriors of the Taliban, the ferocious mountain men who'd slit your throat as soon as look at you? It took only a few days to work out that Taliban fighters were nothing like so rough and dirty as Afghan mountain peasants. Many of them had been educated in America, and here they were, carefully cleaning their AK-47s, getting ready to kill us.

And it did not take us much longer to realize how impressive they could be in action up here on their home ground. I always thought they would turn and run for it when we discovered them. But they did nothing of the kind. If they held or could reach the high ground, they would stand and fight. If we came down on them they'd usually either give up or head right back to the border and into Pakistan, where we could not follow them. But close up you could always see the defiance in their eyes, that hatred of America, the fire of the revolutionary that burned in their souls.

It was pretty damn creepy for us, because this was the heartland of terror, the place where the destruction of the World Trade Center was born and nourished, perfected by men such as these. I'll be honest, it seemed kind of unreal, not possible. But we all knew that it had happened. Right here in this remote dust bowl was the root of it all, the homeland of bin Laden's fighters, the place where they still plot and scheme to smash the United States. The place where the loathing of Uncle Sam is so ingrained, a brand of evil flourishes that is beyond the understanding of most Westerners. Mostly because it belongs to a different, more barbaric century.

And here stood Mikey, Shane, Axe, me, and the rest, ready for a face-off anytime against these silent, sure-footed warriors, masters of the mountains, deadly with rifle and tribal knife.

To meet these guys in these remote Pashtun villages only made the conundrum more difficult. Because right here we're talking Primitive with a big *P*. Adobe huts made out of sundried clay bricks with dirt floors and an awful smell of urine and mule dung. Downstairs they have goats and chickens living in the house. And yet here, in these caveman conditions, they planned and then carried out the most shocking atrocity on a twenty-first-century city.

Sanitation in the villages is as rudimentary as it gets. They have a communal head, a kind of a pit, out on the edge of the houses. And we are all warned to watch out for them, particularly on night patrols. I misjudged it one night, slipped, and got my foot in there. That caused huge laughter up there in the dead of night, everyone trying not to explode. Wasn't funny to me, however.

The next week it was much worse. We were all in the pitch dark, creeping through this very rough ground, trying to set up a surveillance point above a very small cluster of huts and goats. We could not see a thing without NVGs (night-vision goggles), and suddenly I slipped into a gaping hole.

I dared not yell. But I knew I was on my way down, and I shuddered to think where I was going to land. I just rammed my right arm rigid straight up, holding on tight to the rifle, and crashed straight into the village head. I went right under, vaguely hearing my teammates hiss, "Look out! Luttrell just found the shitter again!"

Never has there been that much suppressed laughter on an Afghan mission. But it was one of the worst experiences of my life. I could have given typhoid to the entire Bagram base. I was freezing cold but I cheerfully jumped into a river in full combat gear just to get washed off.

Sometimes there was real trouble on those border post checkpoints, and we occasionally had to load up the Humvees and transport about eighteen guys out there and then walk for miles. The problem was, the Pakistani government has obvious sympathy with the Taliban, and as a result leaves the border area in the northeast uncontrolled. Pakistan has decreed its authorities can operate on tarmac roads and then for twenty meters on either side of the road. Beyond that, anything goes, so the Taliban fighters simply swerve off the road and enter Afghanistan over the ancient pathways. They come and go as they please, the way they always have, unless we prevent them. Many of them only want to come in and rustle cattle, which we do not bother with. However, the Taliban know this, and they move around disguised as cattle farmers, and we most certainly do bother with that. And those little camel trains laden with high explosive, they really get our attention.

And every single time, we came under attack. The slightest noise, any betrayal of our position, someone would open fire on us, often from the Pakistan side of the border, where we could not go. So we moved stealthily, gathered our photographs, grabbed the ringleaders, stayed in touch with base, and whistled up reinforcements whenever we needed help.

It was the considered opinion of our commanders that the key to winning was intel, identifying the bombmakers, finding their supplies, and smashing the Taliban arsenal before they could use it. But it was never easy. Our enemy was brutal, implacable, with no discernible concern about time or life. As long as it takes, was their obvious belief. In the end they assume they will rid their holy Muslim soil of the infidel invaders. After all, they always have, right? Sorry, *nyet?*

Sometimes, while the head sheds (that's SEAL vernacular for our senior commanders) were studying a specific target, we were kept on hold. I volunteered my spare time working in the Bagram hospital, mostly in the emergency room, helping with the wounded guys and trying to become a better medic for my team.

And that hospital was a real eye-opener, because we were happy to treat Afghans as well as our own military personnel. And they showed up at the emergency room with every kind of wound, mostly bullets, but occasionally stabbings. That's one of the real problems in that country—everyone has a gun. There seems to be an AK-47 in every living room. And there were a lot of injuries. Afghan civilians would show up at the main gates so badly shot we had to send out Humvees to bring them into the ER. We treated anyone who came, at the American taxpayer's expense, and we gave everyone as good care as we could.

Bagram was an excellent place for me to improve my skills, and I hoped I was doing some good at the same time. I was, of course, unpaid for this work. But medicine has always been a vocation for me, and those long hours in that hospital were priceless to the doctor I hoped one day to be.

And while I tended the sick and injured, the never-ending work of the commanders continued, filtering the intel reports, checking the CIA reports, trying to identify the Taliban leaders so we could cut the head off their operation.

There was always a very big list of potential targets, some more advanced than others. By that I mean certain communities where the really dangerous guys had been located, identified, and pinpointed by the satellites or by us. It was work that required immense perseverance and the ability to assess the likelihood of actually finding the guy who mattered.

The teams in Bagram were prepared to go out there and conduct this very dangerous work, but no one likes going on a series of wild-goose chases where the chances of finding a top Taliban terrorist are remote. And of course the intel guys have to be aware at all times that nothing is static up there in the mountains. Those Taliban guys are very mobile and very smart. They know a lot but not all there is to know about American capability. And they surely understand the merit of keeping it moving, from village to village, cave to cave, never remaining in one place long enough to get caught with their stockpiles of high explosive.

Our senior chief, Dan Healy, was outstanding at seeking out and finding the good jobs for us, ones where we had a better than average chance of finding our quarry. He spent hours poring over those lists, checking out a certain known terrorist, where he spent his time, where he was last seen.

Chief Healy would comb through the photographic evidence, checking maps, charts, working out the places we had a real chance of victory, of grabbing the main man without fighting an all-out street battle. He had a personal short list of the prime suspects and where to find them. And by June, he had a lot of records, the various methods used by these kingpin Taliban guys and their approximate access to TNT.

And one man's name popped right out at him. For security reasons, I'm going to call him Ben Sharmak, and suffice to say he's a leader of a serious Taliban force, a sinister mountain man known to make forays into the cities and known also to have been directly responsible for several lethal attacks on U.S. Marines, always with bombs. Sharmak was a shadowy figure of around forty. He commanded maybe 140 to 150 armed fighters, but he was an educated man, trained in military tactics and able to speak five languages. He was also known to be one of Osama bin Laden's closest associates.

He kept his troops mobile, moving into or camping on the outskirts of friendly Pashtun villages, accepting hospitality and then traveling on to the next rendezvous, recruiting all the way. These mountain men were unbelievably difficult to trace, but even they need to rest, eat and drink, and perhaps even wash, and they need village communities to do all of that.

Almost every morning Chief Healy would run the main list of potential targets past Mikey, our team officer, and me. He usually gave us papers with a list of maybe twenty names and possible locations, and we made a short list of the guys we considered we should go after. We thus created a rogues' gallery, and we made our mission choices depending on the amount of intel we had. The name Ben Sharmak kept on showing up, and the estimates of his force size kept going up just as often.

Finally there was a tentative briefing about a possible Operation Redwing, which involved the capture or killing of this highly dangerous character. But he was always elusive. First he was here, then there, like the freakin' Scarlet Pimpernel. And the photos available were just head and shoulders, not great quality and very grainy. Still, we knew approximately what the sonofabitch looked like, and on the face of it, this was stacking up to be like any other SR operation — get above the target, stalk him, photograph him, and, if at all possible, grab him.

We had very decent intel on him, which suggested the CIA

and probably the FBI were also extremely interested in his capture or death. And as the various briefings went on, Ben Sharmak seemed to get progressively more important. There were now reports of an eighty-troop minimum and a two-hundred-troop maximum in his army, and this constituted a very big operation. And Chief Healy decreed that me and my three buddies in Alfa Platoon were the precise guys to carry it out.

We were not expected to take on this large bunch of wild-eyed killers. Indeed, we were expected to stay quieter than we had ever been in our lives. "Just find this bastard, nail him down, his location and troop strength, then radio in for a direct action force to come in by air and take him down." Simple, right?

If we thought he might be preparing an immediate evacuation of the village in which he resided, then we would take him out forthwith. That would be me or Axe. The chances were I'd get only one shot at Sharmak, just one time when I could trap him in the crosshairs and squeeze that trigger, probably from hundreds of yards away. I knew only one thing: I better not miss, because the apparitions of Webb and Davis, not to mention every other serving SEAL, would surely rise up and tear my ass off. This was, after all, *precisely* what they had trained me for.

And in case anyone's wondering, I had absolutely no qualms about putting a bullet straight through this bastard's head. He was a fanatical sworn enemy of the United States of America who had already murdered many of my colleagues in the U.S. Marines. He was also the kind of terrorist who would like nothing better than to mastermind a new attack on the U.S. mainland. If I got a shot, he'd get no mercy from me. I knew what was expected of me. I knew the team boss wanted this character eliminated, and when I thought about it, I was damned proud they considered me and my buddies the men for the job. As ever, we would do everything possible not to let anyone down.

Every day we checked the intel office to see what further data there was on Sharmak. Chief Healy was right on the case, working with the ops officer and our skipper, Commander Pero. The problem was always the same: where was our target? He was worse than Saddam Hussein, disappearing, evading the prying eye of the satellites, keeping his identity and location secret even from the many CIA informers who were close to him.

There was of course no point in charging into the mountains armed to the teeth with weapons and cameras unless we were absolutely sure of his whereabouts. The Taliban were a serious threat to low-flying military aircraft, and the helo pilots knew they were in constant danger of being fired upon, even on night ops. These mountain men were as handy with missile launchers as they were with AK-47s.

There is a huge amount of backup required for any such operation: transportation, communications, available air support, not to mention ammunition, food, water, medical supplies, hand grenades, and weapons, all of which we would carry with us.

At one point, quite early on, we had a very definite "Redwing is a go." And preparations were well under way when the entire thing was suddenly called off. "Turn one!" They'd lost him again. They had data, and they had reason to believe they knew where he was. But nothing hard. The guys in intel studied the maps and the terrain, ringed probability areas, made estimates and guesstimates. They thought they had him pinned down but not sufficiently narrowly to place him in an actual village or a camp, never mind with the accuracy required for a sniper to get off a shot.

Intel was just waiting for a break, and meanwhile, me and the guys were out on other SR missions, probably Operation Goat Rope or something. We'd just come back from one of these when we heard there'd been a break in the hunt for Ben Sharmak. It was very sudden, and we guessed one of our sources had come up with something. Chief Healy had maps and studies of the terrain under way, and it looked like we were going straight out again.

We were called into a briefing: Lieutenant Mike Murphy, Petty Officer Matthew Axelson, Petty Officer Shane Patton, and I. We listened to the data and the requirements and still regarded it as just another op. But at the last minute there was a big change. They decided that Shane should be replaced by Petty Officer Danny Dietz, a thirty-four-year-old I had known well for years.

Danny was a short (well, compared with me), very muscular guy from Colorado, but he lived with his spectacularly beautiful wife, Maria, known to all of us as Patsy, just outside the base in Virginia Beach. They had no children but two dogs, both of them damn near as tough as he was, an English bulldog and a bullmastiff.

Danny was with me at the SDV school in Panama City, Florida. We were both there on 9/11. He was heavily into yoga and martial arts and was a very close friend of Shane's. Guess those beach gods and the mystic iron men have stuff in common. I was glad to have Danny on the team. He was a little reserved, but underneath he could be very funny and was a sweet-natured person. It was not a great plan to upset him, though. Danny Dietz was a caged tiger and a great Navy SEAL.

Now it seemed Redwing was again given the green light. The four-man team was nailed down. The two snipers would be Axe and me; the two spotters, Mikey and Danny. Command control,

Mikey. Communications, Danny and me. The final shoot-on-target, me or Axe, either one of us spotting, whichever way it fell on the terrain.

The plan was to sit up there and hide above the place we believed Sharmak was resident, if necessary for four days, probably not able to move more than a foot, remaining deadly still in a deadly place—high in the hills.

At no time would we be anything but carefully concealed, watching these heavily armed mountain men, who were lifelong experts on the local terrain, awaiting our chance to gun down their leader. It doesn't get a whole lot more dangerous than that.

We were actually in the helicopter, dressed and organized, ready to leave, "Redwing is a go," when the mission was called off again. "Turn two!" It was not so much that we'd lost track of Sharmak as the fact that the slippery little son of a gun had turned up somewhere else.

We disembarked and wandered back to our quarters. We shed our heavy packs and weapons, changed out of our combat gear, cleaned the camouflage cream off our faces, and rejoined the human race. The break lasted for two weeks, during which time we did a couple of minor missions up in the passes and nearly got our heads blown off at least twice.

I surpassed myself once by nailing down one of the most dangerous terrorists in northeast Afghanistan. I had POSIDENT, and I actually saw him make a break for it on his own, riding a freakin' bicycle along the track. I didn't shoot him because I did not wish to betray our position by opening fire or even moving. We were expecting his complete camel train of high explosive to move along this route anytime, and we wanted both him and his munitions. At least I didn't emulate the actions of a former colleague, who, according to SEAL folklore, fired up the direct link and advised a cruising U.S. fighter/bomber of the GPS position. Then he watched a five-hundred-pound bomb demolish the terrorist, his camel, and everything within fifty yards of him. On this mission, we halted the camel train and managed to capture the terrorist and unload the explosive without resorting to such wild-and-woolly action.

Sorry, lefties. But, like we say back home in Texas, a man's gotta do what a man's gotta do.

And so the days passed by, until on Monday morning, June 27, 2005, they located Sharmak again. This time it looked really good. By noon the detailed maps and photos of the terrain were spread out before us. The intel was excellent, the maps weren't bad, the photographs of the terrain passable. We still didn't have a decent picture of Sharmak, just the same old head and shoulders, grainy, indistinct. But we'd located other killers up here with a lot less, and there was no doubt this time. "Redwing is a go!"

Right after the briefing, Chief Dan Healy said to me, quietly, "This is it, Marcus. We're going. Go get the guys ready."

I gave the crisp reply expected from a team leader to a SEAL CPO. "Okay, Chief. We're outta here."

And I walked out of the briefing room and headed back to our quarters with a lot on my mind. I can't quite explain it, but I was assailed by doubts, and that feeling of disquiet never left me.

I'd seen the maps, and they were clear. What I couldn't see was a place to hide. We did not have good intel on the vegetation. It was obviously bad and barren way up there in the Hindu Kush, around ten thousand feet. You don't need to be a Fellow of the Royal Geographic Institute to know this is arid country above the tree line, not much growing. Great for climbers, a goddamned nightmare for us.

The village we were surveying had thirty-two houses. I counted them on the satellite picture. But we did not know which one Sharmak was in. Neither did we know if the houses were numbered in case we got better intel while we were up there.

We had some pictures of the layout but very little on the surrounding country. We had good GPS numbers, very accurate. And we had a short list of possible landing zones, unnecessary for the insert, because we'd fast-rope in, but critical for the extract.

I was certain we'd need to blow down a few trees on a lower level of the mountain in order to have cover when we left and to bring the helicopters in with the DA force if it was required. Barren, treeless mountainscapes are no place to conduct secretive landings and takeoffs, not with Taliban rocket men all around. Especially the highly trained group that surrounded Sharmak. He was goddamned lethal, and he'd proved it, more than once, blowing up the Marines.

The one aspect of the mission that dominated my thoughts as I walked back to meet the guys was that there was no place to hide, no place from which to watch. You simply cannot do effective reconnaissance if you can't get into good position. And if those mountain cliffs that surrounded the village were as rough and stony as I suspected, we'd stick out on those heights like a diamond in a goat's ass.

And there were likely to be between eighty and two hundred armed warriors keeping a very careful lookout on all the land around their boss. I was worried, not about the numbers of our enemy but about the problems of staying concealed in order to complete the mission. If there was a very limited selection of hiding places, we might have to compromise our angle on the village, not to mention our distance from it.

I met Mikey back at the bee hut. I told him we were going

in, showed him the maps and what photographs we had, and I remember his reply. "Beautiful. Just another three days of fun and sun." But I saw his expression change as he looked at the pictures, at the obviously very steep gradients, truly horrible terrain, a mountain we would have to clomp up and down in order to find cover.

By this time Axe and Danny had appeared. We briefed them and wandered, a bit apprehensively, over to the chow hall for lunch. I had a large bowl of spaghetti. Right afterward we went back to dress and get organized. I wore my desert bottoms and woodland top, mostly because intel had said the landing zone was fairly green and we would drop into an area of trees. I also had a sniper hood.

Mikey and Danny had their M4 rifles plus grenades; Axe had the Mark 12 .556-caliber rifle, and I had one as well. We all carried the SIG-Sauer 9mm pistol. We elected not to take a heavy weapon, the big twenty-one-pound machine gun M60, plus its ammunition. We were already loaded down with gear, and we thought it would be too heavy to haul up those cliffs.

I also took a couple of claymores, which are a kind of high-explosive device with a trip wire, to keep any intruder from walking up on us. I'd learned a hard lesson about that on my first day, when two Afghans got a lot closer than they should have and might easily have finished me.

We took a big roll of detonator cord to blow the trees for the incoming landing zone when the mission was complete or for the insert of a direct action force. At the last moment, still worried about this entire venture, I grabbed three extra magazines, which gave me a total of eleven, each holding thirty rounds. Eight was standard, but there was something about Operation

Redwing. It turned out everyone felt the same. We all took three extra magazines.

I also carried an ISLiD (an acronym for image stabilization and light distribution unit) for guiding in an incoming helo, plus the spotting scope, and spare batteries for everything. Danny had the radio, and Mikey and Axe had the cameras and computers.

We took packed MREs—beef jerky, chicken noodles, power bars, water—plus peanuts and raisins. The whole lot weighed about forty-five pounds, which we considered traveling light. Shane was there to see us away: "'Bye, dudes, give 'em hell."

All set, we were driven down to the special ops helicopter area, waiting to hear if there was a change. That would have been "Turn three!" The third time Redwing had been aborted. But this time there was only "Rolex, one hour," which meant we were going as soon as it was dark.

We put down our loads and lay on the runway to wait. I remember it was very cold, with snowcaps on the not-too-distant mountains. Mikey assured me he had remembered to pack his lucky rock, a sharp-pointed bit of granite which had jabbed into his backside for three days on a previous mission when we were in a precarious hide and none of us could move even an inch. "Just in case you need to stick it up your ass," he added. "Remind you of home."

And so we waited, in company with a couple of other groups also going out that night. The quick reaction force (QRF) was going to Asadabad at the same time. We had just done a full photo recon of Asadabad, which they carried with them. The deserted Russian base was still there, and Asadabad, the capital city of Kunar Province, remained a known dangerous area. It was of course where the Afghan mujahideen had almost totally surrounded the base and then proceeded to slaughter all of the Russian enlisted men. It was the beginning of the end for the Soviets in 1989, only one range of mountains over from the spot we were going.

Finally, the rotor blades began to howl on the helos. Apparently the many moving parts of Operation Redwing, so susceptible to change, were still in place. The call came through, "Redwing is a go!", and we hoisted up our gear and clambered on board the Chinook 47 for the insert, forty-five minutes away to the northeast. "Guess this fucker Ben Sharmak is still where we think he is," said Mikey.

We were joined by five other guys going in to Asadabad, and the other helo took off first. Then we lifted off the runway, following them out over the base and banking around to our correct course. It was dark now, and I spent the time looking at the floor rather than out of the window. Every one of the four of us, Mikey, Axe, Danny, and me, made it clear, each in his own way, that we did not have a good feeling about this. And I cannot describe how unusual that was. We go into ops areas full of gung ho bravado, the way we're trained — *Bring 'em on, we're ready!*

No SEAL would ever admit to being scared of anything. Even if we were, we would never say it. We open the door and go outside to face the enemy, whoever the hell he might be. Whatever we all felt that night, it was not fear of the enemy, although I recognize it might have been fear of the unknown, because we really were unsure about what we would encounter in the way of terrain.

When we reached the ops area, the helicopter made three false inserts, several miles apart, coming in very low and hovering over places we had no intention of going anywhere near. If the Afghans were watching, they must have been very confused — even we were confused! Going in, pulling out, going back in again, hovering, leaving. I'm damn sure, if Sharmak's guys were out there, they could not have had the slightest clue where we were, if we were, or how to locate us.

Finally, we were on the way into our real landing zone. The final call came—"Redwing is a go!" The landing controller was calling the shots: "Ten minutes out...Three minutes out...One minute...Thirty seconds!...*Let's go!*"

The ramp was down, we were open at the rear, the gunner was ready with the M60 machine gun in case of ambush. It was pitch black outside, no moon, and the rotor blades were making that familiar *bom-bom-bom-bom* on the wind. So far no one had fired anything at us.

The rope snaked from the rear of the aircraft to the ground, positioned expertly so our guns could not get caught as we left. Right now no one spoke. Loaded with our weapons and gear, we lined up. Danny went first, out into the dark, I followed him, then Mikey, then Axe. Each one of us grabbed the rope and slid down fast, wearing gloves to avoid the burn. It was a drop of about twenty feet, and there was a stiff, biting wind.

We hit the deck and spread, moving twenty yards away from one another. It was really cold up there, and the downward gale from the rotors, beating on us, whisking up the dust, made it much worse. We did not know if we were being watched by unseen tribesmen, but it was plainly a possibility, out here in this lawless rebel-held territory. We heard the howl of the helicopter's engines increase as it lifted off. And then it clattered away into the darkness, gaining speed and height rapidly as it left this godforsaken escarpment.

We froze into the landscape for fifteen minutes of total silence. There was not a movement, not a single communication among us. And there was not a sound on the mountain. This was beyond silence, a stillness beyond the concept of silence, like being in outer space. Way down below us we could see two fires, or perhaps lanterns, burning, probably about a mile away, goatherds, I hoped.

The fifteen minutes passed. To my left was the mountain, a great looming mass sweeping skyward. To my right was a group of huge, thick trees. All around us were low tree stumps and thick foliage.

We were way below the place where we would ultimately operate, and it was very unnerving, because right here anyone could hide out. We couldn't see a damn thing and had no idea if there was anyone around. Sixteen years ago, not too far away from here, I guess those Russian conscripts sensed something very similar before someone slashed their throats.

Finally, we climbed to our feet. I walked over to Danny and told him to get the comms up and let the controllers know we were down. Then I walked up the hill to where Mikey and Axe had the big rope which had, absurdly, been cut down and dropped from the helicopter.

This was definitely a mistake. That helo crew was supposed to have taken the rope away with them. God knows what they thought we were going to do with it, and I was just glad Mikey found it. If he hadn't and we'd left it lying on the ground, it might easily have been found by a wandering tribesman or farmer, especially if they had heard the helicopter come in. That rope might have rung our death knell, signifying, as it surely must, that the American eagle had landed.

We did not have a shovel, and Mikey and Axe had to cover the rope with trees, weeds, and foliage. While they were completing this, I opened up comms to the AC-130 Spectre gunship, which

I knew was way up there somewhere monitoring us. I passed my message succinctly:

"Sniper Two One, this is Glimmer Three—preparing to move."

"Roger that."

It was the last time I spoke to them. And now we were assembled for our journey—about four miles. Our route was preplanned, along a mountain ridge that stretched out into a long right-hand dogleg. Our waypoints were marked on our map, and the GPS numbers, detailing the precise position from the satellite, were clear, numbered 1, 2, and 3.

That was just about the only thing that was straightforward. Because the terrain was absolutely horrible, the moonless night was still pitch black, and our route was along a mountain face so steep, it was a goddamned miracle we didn't all fall off and break our necks. Also, it was raining like a bastard and freezing cold. Within about ten minutes we were absolutely soaked, like Hell Week.

It was really slow going, clambering and slipping, stumbling and looking for footholds, handholds, anything. All of us fell down the mountain in the first half hour. But it was worse for me, because the other three were all expert mountain climbers and much smaller and lighter than I was. I was slower over the ground because of my size, and I kept falling behind. They had a rest while I was catching up, and then when I got there, Mikey signaled to go straight on. No rest for Marcus. "Fuck you, Murphy," I said without even a pretense of good nature.

In fact, conditions were so bad it was a lousy idea to rest up. You could freeze up here, soaked to the skin as we were, in about five minutes. So we kept going, always upward, keeping our body heat as high as possible. But it was still miserable. We never stopped ducking down under the trees and hanging limbs, holding on if we could, trying not to fall off the mountain again.

In the end we reached the top of the cliff face and found a freshly used trail. It was obvious the Taliban had been through here recently in substantial numbers, and this was good news for us. It meant Sharmak and his men could not be far away, and right now we were hunting them.

At the top, we suddenly walked out into an enormous flat field of very high grass, and the moon came out briefly. The pasture stretched away in front of us like some kind of paradise lit up in the pale light. We all stopped in our tracks because it looked amazingly beautiful.

But an enemy could easily have been lurking in that grass, and an instant later we ducked down, staying silent. Axe tried to find a path through it, then tried to make his own path. But he simply could not. The pasture was too thick, and it nearly covered him. Before long he returned and told us, poetically, there in the southeast Asian moonlight, in these ancient storied lands right up near the roof of the world, "Guys, that was totally fucking hopeless."

To our right was the deep valley, somewhere down which our target village was located. We'd already hit waypoint 1, and our only option was to find another trail and keep moving along the flank of the escarpment. And then, very suddenly, a great fog bank rolled in and drifted off the mountaintop beneath us and across the valley.

I remember looking down at it, moonlit clouds, so white, so pure, it looked as if we could have walked right across it to another mountain. Through the NODS (night optic device) it was a spectacular sight, a vision perhaps of heaven, set in a land of hellish undercurrents and flaming hatreds.

While we stood up there, transfixed by our surroundings, Mikey worked out that we were just beyond waypoint 1, and we still somehow had to proceed on our northerly course, though not through the high grass. We fanned out and Danny found a trail that led around the mountain, more or less where we wanted to go. But it was not easy, because by now the moon had disappeared and it was again raining like hell.

We must have gone about another half mile across terrain that was just as bad as anything we had encountered all night. Then, unexpectedly, I could smell a house and goat manure, even through the rain; an Afghan farmhouse. We had nearly walked straight into the front yard. And now we had to be very careful. We ducked down, crawling on our hands and knees through thick undergrowth, staying out of sight, right on the escarpment.

Miserable as all this was, conditions were really perfect for a SEAL operation behind enemy lines. Without night-vision goggles like ours, people couldn't possibly see us. The rain and wind had certainly driven everyone else under cover, and anyone still awake probably thought only a raving lunatic could be out there in such weather. And they were right. All four of us had taken quite heavy falls, probably one in every five hundred yards we traveled. We were covered in mud and as wet as BUD/S phase two trainees. It was true. Only a lunatic, or a SEAL, could willingly walk around like this.

We could not see that much ourselves. Nothing except that farmhouse, really. And then, quite suddenly, the moon came out again, very bright, and we had to move swiftly into the shadows, our cover stolen by that pale, luminous light in the sky.

We kept going, moving away from the farm, still moving upward on the mountainside, through quite reasonable vegetation. But then all of my own personal dreads came out and whacked us. We walked straight out of the trees into a barren, harsh, sloping hillside, the main escarpment set steeply on a northern rise.

There was not a tree. Not a bush. Just wet shale, mud, small rocks, and boulders. The moon was directly in front of us, casting our long shadows onto the slope.

This was my nightmare, ever since I first stared at those plans back in the briefing room: the four of us starkly silhouetted against a treeless mountain above a Taliban-occupied village. We were an Afghan lookout's finest moment, unmissable. We were Webb and Davis's worst dream, snipers uncovered, out in the open, trapped in nature's spotlight with nowhere to hide.

"Holy shit," said Mikey.

7

An Avalanche of Gunfire

Down the mountain, from every angle. Axe flanked
left, trying to cut off the downward trail, firing nonstop.
Mikey was blasting away ... shouting, ... "Marcus, no
options now, buddy, *kill 'em all!*"

We edged back the way we had come, into the shadows cast
by the last of the trees. It was not far back to waypoint 2, and
we took a GPS reading right there. Mikey handed over naviga-
tional duties to Axe, and I groaned. Moving up and down these
steep cliffs was really tough for me, but the streamlined, expert
mountaineer Matthew Axelson could hop around like a fucking
antelope. I reminded him of those two correlating facts, and all
three of my teammates started laughing.

For some reason best known to our resident king of Trivial
Pursuit, he led us off the high mountain ridge and down toward
the valley which spread out from the elbow of the dogleg. It was
as if he had decided to eliminate the dogleg entirely and take the
straight line directly across to waypoint 3. Which was all fine
and dandy, except it meant a one-mile walk going steeply downward, followed, inevitably, by a one-mile walk going steeply upward. That was the part I was not built for.

Nonetheless that was our new route. After about fifty yards I was struggling. I couldn't keep up while going down, never mind up. They could hear me sliding and cursing in the rear, and I could hear Axe and Mikey laughing up front. And this was not a fitness problem. I was as fit as any of them, and I was not in any way out of breath. I was just too big to track a couple of mountain goats. Laws of nature, right?

Our path was inescapably zigzagged because Axe was always trying to find cover, stay out of the moonlight, as we grappled our way back up the cliff to waypoint 3. We reached the top approximately one hour before daylight. Our GPS numbers were correct, as planned back at home base. And right up there on top of this finger of pure granite, Mikey picked a spot where we could lay up.

He chose a position over the brow of the summit, maybe eighty feet down, right on the uppermost escarpment. There were trees, some of them close together, but directly beyond them was more barren land. We dropped our heavy loads, the four-mile journey complete, and tipped the grit and stones out of our boots. They always find a way in.

Medically, we were all okay, no injuries. But we were exhausted after our grueling seven-hour hike up and down this freakin' mountain. Especially Mikey and me, because we both suffered from insomnia, particularly prepping for an operation like this, and we hadn't slept the night before. Plus it was freezing cold, and we were still soaked to the skin even though the rain had stopped. So, for that matter, was everything we carried with us.

Danny had the radio up and he informed HQ, and any patrolling aircraft, that we were in position and good to go. But this was a little hasty, because right after that communication, the moon came out once more, and we swept the area with our NODs and couldn't see a damn thing. Not even the village we were supposed to be surveying in search of Sharmak. The trees were in the way. And we could not move out of the trees because that put us back on exposed barren ground, where there were a few very small tree stumps still in the ground but zero decent cover. Jesus Christ.

This was plainly a logging area, maybe abandoned, but a place where a lot of trees had been cut down. Away to our right, the night sky above the highest peaks was brightening. Dawn was near.

Danny and I sat on a rock in deep conversation, trying to work out how bad this really was and what to do. It was every frogman's dread, an operation where the terrain was essentially unknown and turned out to be as bad as or worse than anyone had ever dreamed. Danny and I reached identical conclusions. This really sucked.

Mikey came over to talk briefly. And we all stared at the brightness in the sky to the east. Lieutenant Murphy, as command controller, called the shot. "We're moving in five." And so we picked up our heavy loads once more and set off back the way we'd come. After a hundred yards we found a down trail on the other side of the ridge, walked below the waypoint, and selected a prime spot in the trees overlooking the village, which was more than a mile and a half away.

We settled in, jamming ourselves against trees and rocks, trying to get into a position where we could rest on this almost sheer escarpment. I glugged from my water canteen and, to tell the truth, I felt like a plant on the Hanging Gardens of Babylon. Danny was in his yoga position, sitting cross-legged like a goddamned snake charmer, his back against his tree.

Axe, ever alert, stood guard, blending into the mountain to my left, his rifle primed despite the quiet. He was probably doing a *New York Times* crossword which he'd memorized word for word in his head. He did not get much peace, though. My tree turned out to be some type of a mulberry, and since I could not even doze off, I spent the time hurling the berries at Axe on account of his shaky attitude during the climb back up the mountain.

Then another major fog bank rolled in and settled over all of us and the valley below. There was again no way to see the village, and the trouble with fog banks is they are likely to turn up in the same place often. It was plain we could not remain here in effective operational mode. Once more we had to leave.

Mikey and Axe were poring over the maps and scanning the mountain terrain above us, where there was less fog. Danny and I had to keep looking toward the village, trying to use the glass, peering at whatever there was to be seen. Which was nothing. Finally Mikey said he was leaving, alone, just taking his rifle, in search of a better spot. Then he changed his mind and took Axe with him. And I didn't blame him. This place was enough to give anyone the creeps, because you never knew who might be watching.

Danny and I waited, and the sun climbed high over the peaks and began to dry our wet clothes. The others came back after maybe an hour, and Mikey said they had found an excellent place for observing the village but that cover was sparse. I think he considered there would be some heightened risk in this operation, no matter what, because of the terrain. But if we did not take that risk we'd likely be up here till Christmas.

And once more we all hoisted our packs and set off to the new hiding place. It was only about a thousand yards, but it took us an hour, moving along, and then up, the mountain, right onto that granite finger at the end of the ridge. And when we got there, I had to agree it was perfect, offering a brilliant angle on the village for the lens, the spotting scope, and the bullet. It had sensational all-around vision. If Sharmak and his gang of villains were there, we'd get him. As Mikey observed, "That guy couldn't get to the goddamned communal shitter without us seeing him."

Danny's reply was not suitable for a family story such as this, entailing as it did the possible blasting of one of Sharmak's principal working parts.

I stood there gazing at our new mountain stronghold with its massive, sheer drops all around. It was perfect, but it was also highly dangerous. If an attacking force came up on us, especially at night, we'd have no choice but to fight our way out. If someone started firing RPGs at us, we'd all be blown to pieces. There was only one way out, the way we had come. A skilled strategist like Sharmak could have blockaded us out here on this barren, stony point, and we'd have needed to kill a lot of guys to get out. And there was the ever present, disquieting thought that Sharmak's buddy bin Laden might also be in the area—with probably the biggest al Qaeda force we'd ever faced.

But in its way, this place was perfect, with the most commanding views any surveillance team could wish for. We just somehow had to burrow into this loose, rocky shale, keep our heads down, stay camouflaged, and concentrate. We'd be okay as long as no one saw us. But I still had a very uneasy feeling. So did the others.

We all had something to eat, more water, and then we lay there facedown, quietly steaming as the sun dried our clothes. It was now hotter than hell, and I was lying under a felled log, jammed into the curve right against the wood, my feet out behind me. But unhappily, I was on top of a stinging nettle that was driving me mad. I could not, of course, move one muscle. Who knew if a pair of long-range binoculars was trained on us at this very moment?

I was on glass, silently using the scope and binos. Murph was fifty yards away, positioned higher than me among some rocks. Axe was to my right, perched in an old tree stump hollow. Danny was down to the left in the last of the trees with the radio, hunkered down, the only one of us with any shade from the burning sun. It was approaching noon, and the sun was directly in the south, high, really high, almost straight above us.

We could not be seen from below. And there was definitely no human being level with or above us. At least, not on this SEAL's mountain. We only had to wait, stay very still, shut up, and concentrate, four disciplines at which we were all expert.

It was deathly quiet up there, just as silent as the night. And the silence was broken only by the occasional terse exchange between one SEAL and another, usually aimed toward Danny's privileged position in the shade, out of the direct rays of the sweltering mountain sun. They were not particularly professional exchanges either, lacking grace and understanding.

"Hey, Danny, wanna switch places?"

"Fuck you!"

That type of thing. Nothing else. Not another sound to drift into the mountain air. But suddenly I did hear a sound, which carried directly to the southwest side of my felled tree. The unmistakable noise of soft footsteps right above me. Jesus Christ! I was lucky I didn't need to change my pants.

And just as suddenly, there was a guy, wearing a turban and carrying a fucking ax. He jumped off the log, right over the top of me. I damn near fainted with shock. I just wasn't expecting it. I wheeled around, grabbed my rifle, and pointed it straight at him, which I considered might at least discourage him from beheading me. He was plainly more startled than I was, and he dropped the ax.

And then I saw the other Axe, standing up and aiming his rifle right at the guy's turban. "You must have seen him," I snapped at him. "Why the hell didn't you tell me? He nearly gave me a heart attack."

"Just didn't want to make any noise," said Axe. "I drew a bead on him and kept him in my sights until he reached your log. One false move, I'd have killed him right there."

I told the guy to siddown, against the log. And then something ridiculous happened. About a hundred goats, all with little bells around their necks, came trotting up the mountain, swarming all around the spot where we were now standing. Then up over the hill came two more guys. All of us were now surrounded by goats. And I motioned for them to join their colleague on the ground against the log. That's the Afghans, not the goats.

Finally, Mikey and Danny made their way up through the bleating herd and saw immediately what was going on. Like me, they noted that one of the three was just a kid, around fourteen years old. I tried to ask them if they were Taliban, and they all shook their heads, the older men saying, in English, "No Taliban...no Taliban."

I gave the kid one of my power bars, and he scowled at me. Just put it down on a rock next to him, with no thanks or nod of appreciation. The two adults glared at us, making it obvious they disliked us intensely. Of course, they were probably wondering what the hell we were doing wandering about their farm with enough weapons and ammunition to conquer an entire Afghan province.

The question was, What did we do now? They were very obviously goatherds, farmers from the high country. Or, as it states in the pages of the Geneva Convention, unarmed civilians. The strictly correct military decision would still be to kill them without further discussion, because we could not know their intentions.

How could we know if they were affiliated with a Taliban militia group or sworn by some tribal blood pact to inform the Taliban leaders of anything suspicious-looking they found in the mountains? And, oh boy, were we suspicious-looking.

The hard fact was, if these three Afghan scarecrows ran off to find Sharmak and his men, we were going to be in serious trouble, trapped out here on this mountain ridge. The military decision was clear: these guys could not leave there alive. I just stood there, looking at their filthy beards, rough skin, gnarled hands, and hard, angry faces. These guys did not like us. They showed no aggression, but neither did they offer or want the hand of friendship.

Axelson was our resident academic as well as our Trivial Pursuit king. And Mikey asked him what he considered we should do. "I think we should kill them, because we can't let them go," he replied, with the pure, simple logic of the born intellect.

"And you, Danny?"

"I don't really give a shit what we do," he said. "You want me to kill 'em, I'll kill 'em. Just give me the word. I only work here."

"Marcus?"

"Well, until right now I'd assumed killing 'em was our only option. I'd like to hear what you think, Murph."

Mikey was thoughtful. "Listen, Marcus. If we kill them, someone will find their bodies real quick. For a start, these fucking goats are just going to hang around. And when these guys don't get home for their dinner, their friends and relatives are going to head straight out to look for them, especially for this fourteen-year-old. The main problem is the goats. Because they can't be hidden, and that's where people will look.

"When they find the bodies, the Taliban leaders will sing to the Afghan media. The media in the U.S.A. will latch on to it and write stuff about the brutish U.S. Armed Forces. Very shortly after that, we'll be charged with murder. The murder of innocent unarmed Afghan farmers."

I had to admit, I had not really thought about it quite like that. But there was a terrible reality about Mikey's words. Was I afraid of these guys? No. Was I afraid of their possible buddies in the Taliban? No. Was I afraid of the liberal media back in the U.S.A.? Yes. And I suddenly flashed on the prospect of many, many years in a U.S. civilian jail alongside murderers and rapists.

And yet...as a highly trained member of the U.S. Special Forces, deep in my warrior's soul I knew it was nuts to let these goatherds go. I tried to imagine what the great military figures of the past would have done. Napoleon? Patton? Omar Bradley? MacArthur? Would they have made the ice-cold military decision to execute these cats because they posed a clear and present danger to their men?

If these Afghans blew the whistle on us, we might all be killed, right out here on this rocky, burning-hot promontory, thousands and thousands of miles from home, light-years from help. The potential force against us was too great. To let these guys go on their way was military suicide.

All we knew was Sharmak had between 80 and 200 armed men. I remember taking the middle number, 140, and asking myself how I liked the odds of 140 to 4. That's 35 to 1. Not much. I looked at Mikey and told him, "Murph, we gotta get some advice."

We both turned to Danny, who had fired up the comms system and was valiantly trying to get through to HQ. We could see him becoming very frustrated, like all comms operators do when they cannot get a connection. He kept trying, and we were rapidly coming to the conclusion the goddamned radio was up the creek.

"That thing need new batteries?" I asked him.

"No. It's fine, but they won't fucking answer me."

The minutes went by. The goatherds sat still, Axe and Murph with their rifles aimed straight at them, Danny acting like he could have thrown the comms system over the goddamned cliff.

"They won't answer," he said through gritted teeth. "I don't know why. It's like no one's there."

"There must be someone there," said Murph, and I could hear the anxiety in his voice.

"Well, there isn't," said Danny.

"Murphy's god-awful law," I said. "Not you, Mikey, that other prick, the god of screwups."

No one laughed. Not even me. And the dull realization dawned on us: we were on our own and had to make our own decision.

Mike Murphy said quietly, "We've got three options. We plainly don't want to shoot these guys because of the noise. So, number one, we could just kill them quietly and hurl the bodies over the edge. That's probably a thousand-foot drop. Number two is we kill them right here, cover 'em up as best we can with rocks and dirt.

"Either way we get the hell out and say nothing. Not even when the story comes out about the murdered Afghan goatherds. And some fucking headline back home which reads, 'Navy SEALs Under Suspicion.'

"Number three, we turn 'em loose, and still get the hell out, in case the Taliban come looking."

He stared at us. I can remember it just like it was yesterday. Axe said firmly, "We're not murderers. No matter what we do. We're on active duty behind enemy lines, sent here by our senior commanders. We have a right to do everything we can to save our own lives. The military decision is obvious. To turn them loose would be wrong."

If this came to a vote, as it might, Axe was going to recommend the execution of the three Afghans. And in my soul, I knew he was right. We could not possibly turn them loose. But my trouble is, I have another soul. My Christian soul. And it was crowding in on me. Something kept whispering in the back of my mind, it would be wrong to execute these unarmed men in cold blood. And the idea of doing that and then covering our tracks and slinking away like criminals, denying everything, would make it more wrong.

To be honest, I'd have been happier to stand 'em up and shoot them right out in front. And then leave them. They'd just be three guys who'd found themselves in the wrong place at the wrong time. Casualties of war. And we'd just have to defend ourselves when our own media and politicians back in the U.S.A. tried to hang us on a murder charge.

None of us liked the sneaky options. I could tell that. I guess all four of us were Christians, and if we were thinking like ordinary law-abiding U.S. citizens, we would find it very hard to carry out the imperative military decision, the overriding one, the decision any great commander would have made: these guys can never leave this place alive. The possible consequences of that were unacceptable. Militarily.

Lieutenant Murphy said, "Axe?"

"No choice." We all knew what he meant.

"Danny?"

"As before. I don't give a shit what you decide. Just tell me what to do."

"Marcus?"

"I don't know, Mikey."

"Well, let me tell you one more time. If we kill these guys we have to be straight about it. Report what we did. We can't sneak around this. Just so you all understand, their bodies will be found, the Taliban will use it to the max. They'll get it in the papers, and the U.S. liberal media will attack us without mercy. We will almost certainly be charged with murder. I don't know how you guys feel about that...Marcus, I'll go with you. Call it."

I just stood there. I looked again at these sullen Afghan farmers. Not one of them tried to say a word to us. They didn't need to. Their glowering stares said plenty. We didn't have rope to bind them. Tying them up to give us more time to establish a new position wasn't an option.

I looked Mikey right in the eye, and I said, "We gotta let 'em go."

It was the stupidest, most southern-fried, lamebrained decision I ever made in my life. I must have been out of my mind. I had actually cast a vote which I knew could sign our death warrant. I'd turned into a fucking liberal, a half-assed, no-logic nitwit, all heart, no brain, and the judgment of a jackrabbit.

At least, that's how I look back on those moments now. Probably not then, but for nearly every waking hour of my life since. No night passes when I don't wake in a cold sweat thinking of those moments on that mountain. I'll never get over it. I cannot get over it. The deciding vote was mine, and it will haunt me till they rest me in an East Texas grave.

Mikey nodded. "Okay," he said, "I guess that's two votes to one, Danny abstains. We gotta let 'em go."

I remember no one said anything. We could just hear the short staccato sounds of the goats: *ba-aaaa...baaa...baaa*. And the tinkling of the little bells. It provided a fitting background chorus to a decision which had been made in fucking fairyland. Not on the battlefield where we, like it or not, most certainly were.

Axe said again, "We're not murderers. And we would not have been murderers, whatever we'd done."

Mikey was sympathetic to his view. He just said, "I know, Axe, I know, buddy. But we just took a vote."

I motioned for the three goatherds to get up, and I signaled them with my rifle to go on their way. They never gave one nod or smile of gratitude. And they surely knew we might very well have killed them. They turned toward the higher ground behind us.

I can see them now. They put their hands behind their backs in that peculiar Afghan way and broke into a very fast jog, up the steep gradient, the goats around us now trotting along to join them. From somewhere, a skinny, mangy brown dog appeared dolefully and joined the kid. That dog was a gruesome Afghan reminder of my own robust chocolate Labrador, Emma, back home on the ranch, always bursting with health and joy.

I guess that's when I woke up and stopped worrying about the goddamned American liberals. "This is bad," I said. "This is real bad. What the fuck are we doing?"

Axe shook his head. Danny shrugged. Mikey, to be fair, looked as if he had seen a ghost. Like me, he was a man who knew a massive mistake had just been made. More chilling than anything we had ever done together. Where were those guys headed? Were we crazy or what?

Thoughts raced through my mind. We'd had no comms, no one we could turn to for advice. Thus far we had no semblance of a target in the village. We were in a very exposed position, and we appeared to have no access to air support. We couldn't even report in. Worse yet, we had no clue as to where the goatherds were headed. When things go this bad, it's never one thing. It's every damn thing.

We watched them go, disappearing up the mountain, still running, still with their hands behind their backs. And the sense that we had done something terrible by letting them go was all-pervading. I could just tell. Not one of us was able to speak. We were like four zombies, hardly knowing whether to crash back into our former surveillance spots or leave right away.

"What now?" asked Danny.

Mikey began to gather his gear. "Move in five," he said.

We packed up our stuff, and right there in the noonday sun, we watched the goatherds, far on the high horizon, finally disappear from view. By my watch, it was precisely nineteen minutes after their departure, and the mood of sheer gloom enveloped us all.

We set off up the mountain, following in the hoofprints of the goats and their masters. We moved as fast as we could, but it took us between forty minutes and one hour to cover the same steep ground. At the top, we could no longer see them. Mountain goats, mountain herders. They were all the goddamned same, and they could move like rockets up in the passes.

We searched around for the trail we had arrived by, found it, and set off back toward the initial spot, the one we had pulled out of because of the poor angle on the village and then the dense fog bank. We tried the radio and still could not make a connection with home base.

Our offensive policy was in pieces. But we were headed for probably the best defensive position we had found since we got here, on the brink of the mountain wall, maybe forty yards from the summit, with tree cover and decent concealment. Right now we sensed we must remain in strictly defensive mode, lie low for a while and hope the Taliban had not been alerted or if they had that we would be too well hidden for them to locate us. We were excellent practitioners of lying low and hiding.

We walked on along the side of the mountain, and I have to say the place looked kind of different in broad daylight. But its virtues were still there. Even from the top of the escarpment we would be damn near impossible to see.

We climbed down and took up our precise old positions. We were still essentially carrying out our mission, but we remained on the highest possible alert for Taliban fighters. Below me, maybe thirty yards to my right, looking up the hill, Danny slipped neatly into his yoga tree, cross-legged, still looking like a snake charmer. I got myself wedged into the old mulberry tree, where I reapplied my camouflage cream and melted into the landscape.

Below me on the left, same distance as Danny, was Axe with our heaviest rifle. Mikey was right below me, maybe ten yards, jammed into the lee of a boulder. Above us the mountain was nearly sheer, then it went flat for a few yards, then it angled sharply up to the top. I'd tried looking down from there, so had Murph, and we were agreed, you could not really see anything over the small outward ridge which protected us.

For the moment, we were safe. Axe had the glass for twenty minutes, and then I took over for the next twenty minutes.

Nothing stirred in the village. It had now been more than an hour and a half since we turned the goatherds loose. And it was still quiet and peaceful, hardly a breath of wind. And by Christ it was hot.

Mikey was closest to me when he suddenly whispered, "Guys, I've got an idea."

"What is it, sir," I asked, suddenly formal, as if our situation demanded some respect for the man who must ultimately take command.

"I'm going down to the village, see if I can borrow a phone!"

"Beautiful," said Axe. "See if you can pick me up a sandwich."

"Sure," said Mikey. "What'll it be? Mule dung or goat's hoof?"

"Hold the mayo," growled Axe.

The jokes weren't that great, I know. But perched up there on this Afghan rock face, poised to fend off an attacking army, I thought they were only just shy of grade-one hilarity.

It was, I suppose, a sign of nerves, like cracking a one-liner on your deathbed. But it showed we all felt better now; not absolutely A-OK, but cheerful enough to get to our work and toss out the occasional light remark. More like our old selves, right? Anyhow, I said I was just going to close my eyes for a short while, and I pulled my camouflage hat down over my eyes and tried to nod off, despite my pounding heart, which I could not slow down.

Around ten minutes more passed. Suddenly I heard Mikey make a familiar alert sound... *Sssst! Sssst!* I lifted up my hat and instinctively looked left, over my portside quarter, to the spot where I knew Axe would be covering our flank. And he was right there, rigid, in firing position, his rifle aimed straight up the mountain.

I twisted around to look directly behind me. Mikey was staring wide-eyed up the hill, calling orders, instructing Danny to call in immediate backup from HQ if he could make the radio work. He saw I was on the case, looked hard at me, and pointed straight up the hill, urging me with hand signals to do the same.

I fixed my Mark 12 in firing position, pulled my head back a few inches, and looked up the hill. Lined along the top were between eighty and a hundred heavily armed Taliban warriors, each one of them with an AK-47 pointing downward. Some were carrying rocket-propelled grenades. To the right and to the left they were starting to move down our flanks. I knew they could see past me but not at me. They could not have seen Axe or Danny. I was unsure whether they had seen Mikey.

My heart dropped directly into my stomach. And I cursed those fucking goatherds to hell, and myself for not executing them when every military codebook ever written had taught me otherwise. Not to mention my own raging instincts, which had told me to go with Axe and execute them. And let the liberals go to hell in a mule cart, and take with them all of their fucking know-nothing rules of etiquette in war and human rights and whatever other bullshit makes 'em happy. You want to charge us with murder? Well, fucking do it. But at least we'll be alive to answer it. This way really sucks.

I pressed back against my tree. I was still sure they had not seen me, but their intention was to outflank us on both wings. I could see that. I scanned the ground directly above me. The hilltop still swarmed with armed men. I thought there were more than before. There was no escape by going straight up, and no possibility of moving left or right. Essentially they had us trapped, *if* they had spotted us. I still was unsure.

And so far not a shot had been fired. I looked up the hill again at one single tree above and to my left, maybe twenty yards away. And I thought I saw a movement. Then it was confirmed, first by a turban, then by an AK-47, its barrel pointed in my general direction though not directly at me.

I tightened my grip on the trusty rifle and moved it slightly in the direction of the tree. Whoever it was still could not see me because I was in a great spot, well hidden. I kept perfectly still, that's goddamned motionless, like a marble statue.

I checked with Mikey, who also had not moved. Then I checked the tree again, and this time that turban was around it. A hook-nosed Taliban warrior was peering straight at me through black eyes above a thick black beard. The barrel of his AK-47 was pointed right at my head. Had he seen me? Would he open fire? How did the liberals feel about my position? No time, I guess. I fired once, blew his head off.

And at that moment all hell broke loose. The Taliban unleashed an avalanche of gunfire at us, straight down the mountain, from every angle. Axe flanked left, trying to cut off the downward trail, firing nonstop. Mikey was blasting away straight over my head with everything he had. Danny was firing at them, trying to aim with one hand, desperately trying to rev up the radio with the other.

I could hear Mikey shouting, "Danny, Danny, for Christ's sake, get that fucking thing working...Marcus, no options now, buddy, *kill 'em all!*"

But now the enemy gunfire seemed to center on our two flank men. I could see the dust and rock shards kicking up all around us. The sound of AK-47s absolutely filled the air, deafening. I could see the Taliban guys falling all along the ridge. No one can shoot like us. I stayed right where I was, in my original position, and I still seemed to be taking less fire than the others. But in the next couple of minutes they had identified my position, and the volume of fire directly at me was increasing. This was bad. Very bad.

I could see Axe was acquiring his targets quicker than I was because he had an extra scope. I should have had one too, but for some reason I had not fitted it.

Right now all four of us were really amped up. We knew how to conduct a firefight like this, but we needed to cut down the enemy numbers, nail a few of these bastards real quick, give ourselves a better chance. It was hard for them to get us from directly above, which meant the flanks were our danger. I could see two of them making their way down, right and left.

Axe shot one of them, but it was bad to the right. They were shooting in a kind of frenzy but, thank Christ, missing. I guess we were too. And suddenly I was taking heavy fire myself. Bullets were slamming into the tree trunk, hitting rocks all around me. The bullets were somehow coming in from the sides.

I called down to Mikey, "We'll take 'em, but we might just need a new spot."

"Roger that," he yelled back. Like me, he could see the speed at which they were moving up into the attack. We'd been shooting them for all of five or six minutes, but every time we cleared that ridge high above us, it filled up again. It was as if they had reinforcements somewhere over the ridge, just waiting to come up to the front line. Whichever way we looked at it, they had a ton of guys trying to kill four SEALs.

At this point our options were nonexistent. We still could not charge the top of the mountain, because they'd cut us down like dogs. They had us left, and they had us right. We were boxed in on three sides, and there was never, not even for a couple of seconds, a lull in the gunfire. And we could not even see half of them or tell where the bullets were coming from. They had every angle on us.

All four of us just kept banging away, cutting 'em down, watching them fall, slamming a new magazine into the breech, somehow holding them at bay. But this was impossible. We had to give up this high ground, and I had to get close enough to Mikey to agree on a strategy, hopefully to save our lives.

I started to move, but Mikey, like the brilliant officer he was, had appreciated the situation and already called it. *"Fall back!"*

Fall back! More like *fall off*—the freakin' mountain, that is; a nearly sheer drop, right behind us, God knows how far down. But an order's an order. I grabbed my gear and took a sideways step, trying to zigzag down the gradient. But gravity made the decision for me, and I fell headlong down the mountain, completing a full forward flip and somehow landing on my back, still going fast, heels flailing for a foothold.

At least I thought I was going fast, but Murphy was right behind me. I could tell it was him because of the bright red New York City fireman's patch he'd worn since 9/11. That was actually all I saw.

"See you at the bottom!" I yelled. But right then I hit a tree, and Mikey went past me like a bullet. I was going slower now, and I tried to take a step, but I fell again, and on I went, catching up to Mikey now, crashing, tumbling over the ground like we were both bouncing through a pinball machine.

Ahead of us was a copse of trees on a slightly less steep gradient, and I knew this was our last hope before we plunged into the void. I had to grab something, anything. So did Mikey, and

I could see him up ahead, grabbing at tree limbs, snapping them off, and still plummeting downward.

In a split second I knew that nothing could save either of us, we'd surely break our backs or necks and then the Taliban would shoot us without mercy, as we would expect. But right now, entering the copse of trees at what felt like seventy miles an hour, my mind was in overdrive.

Almost everything had been ripped away from me in the fall, everything except my ammunition and grenades — all my packs, the medical stuff, food, water, comms, phone. I'd even lost my helmet with the flag of Texas painted on it. I was damned if I wanted some fucking terrorist wearing that.

I'd seen Mikey's radio aerial ripped off as we crashed downward. And that was not good. My gun strap had been ripped off me and my rifle whipped away. The trouble was, the terrain beyond the tree copse was completely unknown to us, because we could not see it from above. If we had, we might never have jumped; the ground just swept upward and then ducked away downward, inverted, like a goddamned ski jump.

I rocketed up the lip of that back slope making about eighty knots, on my back, feetfirst. In the air I made two complete backflips and I landed again feet first, on my back, still coming down the cliff face like a howitzer shell. And at that moment I knew there was a God.

First of all, I appeared not to be dead, which was right up there with Jesus walking on the water. But even more amazing was I could see my rifle not two feet from my right hand, as if God Himself had reached down to me and given me hope. *Marcus,* I heard Him say, *you're gonna need this.* At least, I think I heard Him. In fact, I swear to God I heard Him. Because this was a miracle, no doubt in my mind. And I had not even had time to say my prayers.

I didn't know how far down we'd fallen, but it must have been two or three hundred yards. And we were both still going very fast. I could see Mikey up ahead, and I honestly did not know whether he was dead or alive. It was just a person crashing through the dirt and boulders. If he had not broken every bone in his body, that too was a miracle.

Me? I was too battered to hurt, and I could still see my rifle tumbling down beside me. That rifle never strayed more than two feet from my hand throughout this death-defying fall. And I'll always know it was guided by the hand of God. Because there is no other explanation.

We hit the bottom, both of us landing with terrific impact, like we'd jumped off a goddamned skyscraper. It shook the wind out of me, and I gasped for breath, trying to work out how badly injured I was. My right shoulder hurt, my back hurt, and on one side of my face, the skin had been more or less scoured away. I was covered in blood and bruised to hell.

But I could stand, which was actually a really bad idea, because then the RPGs began to arrive, landing close, and I went down again. They exploded more or less harmlessly but sent up clouds of dust, shale, and wood shards from the trees. Mikey was next to me, maybe fifteen feet away, and we picked ourselves up from the ground.

He still had his rifle strapped on. Mine was resting at my feet. I grabbed it, and I heard Murphy shout through the din of explosions, "You good?"

I turned to him, and his entire face was black with dust. Even his goddamned teeth were black. "You look like shit, man," I told him. "Fix yourself up!"

Despite everything, Mikey laughed, and then I noticed he'd been shot during the fall. There was blood pumping out of his stomach. But just then there was a thunderous explosion from one of the grenades, too close, much too close. We both wheeled around in the swirling dust and smoke, and there behind us were two large logs, actually felled trees.

They were crossed over at the ends, like a pair of giant chopsticks, facing up the mountain, and we turned simultaneously and sprinted for cover. We cleared the logs and crashed down behind them, safe from gunfire attack for the moment. We were both still armed and ready to fight. I took the right-hand side, Mikey center left, guarding both the head-on approach and the flank.

We could see them plainly now, swarming down the flanks of the cliff we had just crashed down. They were moving very fast, though not nearly as fast as we had. Mikey had a pretty good line on them, and mine wasn't bad. We opened fire straight at them, picking them off one by one as they moved in on us. Trouble was, there were so many, and it didn't seem to matter how many we killed, they just kept coming. I remember thinking that the two hundred estimate was a lot closer than the eighty minimum we had been advised.

And this must have been Sharmak's work. Because these guys were not really marksmen, were using marginal rifles pretty recklessly, but nonetheless followed the military rules for this type of assault. They advanced down the side of the battlefield, trying to outflank their enemy, always attempting to get a 360-degree cover on their target. We were surely slowing their progress down, but we weren't stopping them.

The fire never slackened for five minutes. They had sustained, nonstop, that opening volley, the one fired way back up the mountain when they could not see their target. They had blasted away at us all the way down to these logs, and they had augmented their fire with aimed rocket-propelled grenades. These guys were not being led by some mad-eyed hysteric, they were being led by someone who understood the rudiments of what he was doing. Understood them well. Too well. The fucker. And now they had us pinned down behind the logs, and, as ever, the bullets were flying, but we were somehow getting the better of the exchanges.

Mikey was ignoring his wound and fighting like a SEAL officer should, uncompromising, steady, hard-eyed, and professional. I could see the guys on that left flank dropping down in their tracks as they raced toward us. On my side, over on the right, the ground was just a little flatter, with trees, and there did not seem to be so many of them. Every time they moved, I shot 'em.

It was probably clear to them that Mikey and I could not be dislodged as long as the big logs covered us. And that's when they went to their biggest barrage of RPGs yet. These damn things, trailing that familiar white smoke, were unleashed at us from farther up the mountain. They landed to the front and the side but not behind, and they caused a tidal wave of dirt, rocks, and smoke, showering us with the stuff, robbing us of our vision.

Our heads went down, and I asked Mikey where the hell were Axe and Danny, and of course neither of us knew. All we knew was they were up the mountain, not yet having jumped, as we had.

"Guess Axe must have dug in and kept fighting out on the left," he said. "Danny's got a better chance of radio contact high up than he would down here."

I'm sailing through calm harbor waters here. That's the American flag fluttering over the transom behind my right shoulder. I guess that's rare. Most people think I wear it on my heart. *Photo by Suzanne Robinson*

The guy in front is Billy Shelton, the local iron man who battered, trained, and half killed Morgan and me preparing us to be Navy SEALs. I'm with a good buddy, Army Ranger Tommy Richardson, another Shelton protégé. *Photo by Master Sergeant Daniel Marshall*

That boatload of SEAL students down there must somehow land the boat on these rocks and then drag it up to the beach. It's easy to identify the instructor — the dry one on the left, yelling his head off. "Too slow! Too clumsy! Too dangerous! Try harder!" *U.S. Navy photo by Photographer's Mate 2nd Class Eric S. Logsdon*

Taking the strain: This is a BUD/S training class starting work on the beach with the heavy log — hoisting it, hauling it, running with it. Easy, right? It only weighs about the same as a telephone pole. *U.S. Navy photo by Photographer's Mate 2nd Class Eric S. Logsdon*

This is SEAL training at the peak of its ruthlessness. It's known as getting wet and sandy. That water is freezing. That instructor is merciless. "You want to quit right now, boy, then go ahead — ring the goddamned bell." *U.S. Navy photo by Photographer's Mate 2nd Class Eric S. Logsdon*

Petty Officer Matthew Axelson in combat gear, ready to face the enemy. He held our left flank on the mountain for two hours, under murderous fire. He was shot twice, both times badly hurt, but he kept fighting. *Courtesy of Cindy Axelson*

Matthew Axelson with his wife, Cindy. His last words were of home: "Tell Cindy I love her." *Photo by Jarrett D. Broughton*

Lieutenant Michael Murphy. If they built a memorial to him as high as the Empire State Building, it would never be high enough for me. *Courtesy of Daniel J. Murphy, Esq.*

Lieutenant Murphy and his fiancée, Heather Duggan. They had planned to marry in November 2005. *Courtesy of Daniel J. Murphy, Esq.*

Petty Officer Danny Dietz provided our covering fire all afternoon. Desperately wounded, he once more opened fire at the enemy, blasting away up the hill. *Courtesy of Maria Dietz*

My close friend Danny Dietz at Virginia Beach with his powerful bullmastiff and English bulldog. They were damn near as tough as he was, but not quite. No one was tougher than Danny. *Courtesy of Maria Dietz*

Up in the mountains or down at sea level, Danny Dietz was the master of his environment. Rock climber, fisherman, warrior — he was the best. *Courtesy of Maria Dietz*

Erik Kristensen was a SEAL down to his fingertips, and he knew real trouble when he heard it. "They need every gun they can get!" he yelled. *"Move it, guys! Let's really move it!"* *Courtesy of Suzanne Kristensen*

Lieutenant Commander Erik Kristensen, SEAL Team 10's commanding officer. He did not have to go, but he dropped everything, picked up his rifle, and raced for the helicopter with the rest of them, answering our desperate cry for help. *Courtesy of Suzanne Kristensen*

Chief Petty Officer Dan Healy, the iron man SEAL strategist who died with his team when the rescue helicopter was hit by a rocket-propelled grenade fired by the Taliban in the Afghan mountains. *Courtesy of Navy Fleet Imaging, Pearl Harbor*

Shane Patton was replaced at the last moment in the SEAL team's Operation Redwing. He stood at the door and said goodbye to all of us, wishing us luck. But when we called in for help, Shane was the second man into the rescue helicopter. Less than two hours later, he was dead, killed when it crashed into the mountain. *Photo by DCI Photography, Randy Adger*

It's rough, arid ground up here. Often there's no cover for a watchful Navy SEAL — but we usually get in pretty close if we think the Taliban might be in residence. *U.S. Navy photo by PHCM(SW) Terry Cosgrove*

U.S. Special Forces move in single file through the snowcapped mountains of northeastern Afghanistan. *U.S. Navy photo by Photographer's Mate 1st Class Tim Turner*

The heavily armed Navy SEAL on the left is not me, but it might as well have been. I've often stood on a lonely Afghan mountainside staring through those passes, watching for an advancing Taliban convoy. *U.S. Navy photo by Photographer's Mate 1st Class Tim Turner*

Thankfully, not all Afghan villagers are hostile to us. Right here a couple of U.S. Special Forces question the locals, and a lot of them are happy to help. *U.S. Navy photo by Photographer's Mate 1st Class Tim Turner*

A small section of the crowd that held the vigil at our ranch. At lunchtime there were sometimes three hundred meals served. No one ever really knew where the food came from; it just kept arriving. "God knows, it was just like the loaves and fishes," according to my mom. *Courtesy of Holly Luttrell*

Night and day for one week these local people stayed, refusing to leave my mom and dad while everyone thought I was dead. A small group of them got together for this photograph five minutes after SEAL Command called from Coronado to announce that reports of my death were greatly exaggerated. *Photo by Master Sergeant Daniel Marshall*

Four Texans in the Oval Office: The president with my mom and dad and me. "Gosh," said President Bush, "it's great to start the day with Texans." *Courtesy of the White House*

I've taken it to the limit for my country on the battlefield, and I was honored to do it. Right here I'm still shoulder to shoulder with my commander in chief. *White House photo by Eric Draper*

The proudest moment of my life. My commander in chief pins the Navy Cross on my uniform, right below my SEAL Trident, in the Oval Office, July 18, 2006. *White House photo by Eric Draper*

We risked a look up through the gloom, and we saw a figure plummeting down the mountain, just to the left of where we had fallen. Axe, no doubt, but could he survive that fall? He was on the first slope before the trees, and a second later he hurtled over the ski jump, flipped, and crashed on down the almost sheer cliff face. The gradient saved him, as it had saved Mikey and me, the way the steep mountain saves a ski jumper, enabling him to continue down at high speed without a terminal collision with flat ground.

Axe arrived in one piece, stunned and disoriented. But the Taliban could see him now, and they opened fire on him as he lay on the ground. *"Run, Axe...right here, buddy, run!"* yelled Murph, top of his lungs.

And Axe recovered his senses real quick, bullets flying around him, and he cleared those logs and crashed into our hide, landing on his back. It's unbelievable what you can do when the threat to your own life is that bad.

He took the far left, slammed a new magazine into the breech, and started fighting, never missed a beat, hammering away at our most vulnerable point of enemy attack. The three of us just kept going, shooting them down, hoping and praying their numbers would lessen, that we had punched a hole in their assault. But it sure as hell never seemed like it. Those guys were still swarming, still firing. And the noise was still deafening.

The question was, Where was Danny? Was that little mountain lion still fighting, still trying to make contact, as he pounded away at Sharmak's troops? Was he still trying to get through to HQ? None of us knew, but the answer was not long in arriving. From high up on the right on the main cliff face there was a sudden, unusual movement. Someone was falling, and it had to be Danny.

The flailing body crashed through the high woods and flipped at the ski jump, tumbling, tumbling, all the way to the bottom, where it landed with a sickening thump. Just as we all had. But Danny never moved, just lay there, either stunned or dead. And the folklore of the brotherhood stood starkly before both Mikey and me: *No SEAL was ever left alone to die on the battlefield. No SEAL.*

I dropped my rifle and cleared the log in one bound. Mikey came right after me. Axe kept firing, trying to give us cover, as we ducked down and ran fast across the flat ground to the base of the cliff. Mikey was still pouring blood from his stomach, and I felt like I had a broken back, low down, base of my spine.

We reached Danny together, hoisted him up, and manhandled him back to the logs, dragging him into what passed for safety around here. They fired at us from the heights all the way across that lethal ground, but no one got hit, and somehow, against truly staggering odds, we were all still going, all in one piece, except for the shot Mikey took.

As the resident medic, I should have been able to help, but all my stuff had been ripped away in the fall, and there was no time to do anything except shoot these bastards who carried AK-47s and hope to Christ they'd give up. Or at least run out of those RPGs. They could hurt someone if they weren't careful. Fuckers.

Right then, I was confident we were going to make it. The ground fell away quite sharply behind us, but way below was our target village, and it was on flat ground, with sturdy-looking houses. Cover, that was all we needed, with our enemy caught flat-footed on flat ground. We'd be all right. We'd get 'em.

Danny fought back, cleared his head, and tried to get up. But his face was rigid. He was in terrible pain. And then I saw the blood pouring out of his hand.

"I've been shot, Marcus, can you help me?" he said.

"We've all been shot," replied Mikey. "Can you fight?"

I stared at Danny's right hand. His thumb had been blown right off. And I saw him grit his teeth and nod, sweat streaming down his blackened face. He adjusted his rifle, banged in a new magazine with the butt of his hand, and took his place in the center of our little gun line. Then he turned to face the enemy once more. He was a bullmastiff, glaring up the mountain, and he opened fire with everything he had.

Danny, Mikey, and Axe blasted that left flank while I held the right. The fire was still fierce on all sides, but we sensed there were more dead Afghans to the left than there were to the right. Murph shouted, "We're going for the higher ground, this side." And with all four barrels blazing, we tried to storm that left flank, get a foothold on the steep slope, maybe even fight our way back to the top if we could kill enough of them.

But they also wanted the higher ground, and they reinforced their right flank, driving down from the top, anything to stop us getting that upper hand. We must have killed fifty or more of them, and all four of us were still fighting. I guess they probably noticed that, because they were prepared to fight to the last man to hold our left, their right.

There were so many of them, and we found ourselves slipping inexorably back down the hill as the turbaned warriors closed in on us, driving us back by sheer weight of numbers, sheer volume of fire. When they loosed off another battery of RPGs, we had no other option but to retreat and dive back behind the crossed logs before they blew our heads off.

God only knew the size of whatever arms cache they were drawing ordnance from. But we were just finding out what a force Sharmak and his guys really were: trained, heavily armed, fearless, and strategically on the ball. Not quite what we expected when we first landed at Bagram.

Back behind the logs, we kept going, mowing them down on the flanks whenever we could get a clear shot. But again, the inflexible, unswerving progress of Sharmak's forces coming down the escarpment after us was simply too overwhelming. Not so much due to the volume of fire but because of their irresistible drive down the left and right of our position.

The logs gave us good cover from the front and not bad to ninety degrees. But once they got past that, firing from slightly behind us, on both sides—well, that was the reason we jumped from the heights in the first place, risking our necks, not knowing when or even if we would land on reasonable ground.

There were not enough of us to protect our flanks. We were too occupied defending our position against a head-on attack. I suppose the goatherds had told them we were only four, and Sharmak swiftly guessed we would be vulnerable on the wings.

I'm guessing a dozen SEALs could have held and then destroyed them, but that would have been odds of around ten or eleven to one. We were only four, and that was probably thirty-five to one. Which is known, in military vernacular, as a balls-to-the-wall situation. Especially as we now seemed incapable of calling up the cavalry from HQ.

Right here was a twenty-first-century version of General Custer's last stand, Little Bighorn with turbans. But they hadn't gotten us yet. And if I had my way, they were never going to. I know all four of us thought exactly that. Our only option, however, was to get to flatter ground. And there wasn't any of that up here. There was only one way for us to go, backward and down, straight down.

Mike Murphy called it. *"They'll kill us all if we stay here! Jump, guys, for fuck's sake, jump!"*

And once more all four of us clutched our rifles, stood up, braved the flying bullets, and headed for the precipice. We leaped into the void, Mikey first, me next, then Axe, then Danny. The drop must have been about thirty or forty feet, down into a thicket of shrubs alongside a little stream.

We were by no means at the base of this little escarpment, but at least we were once more on a flat bit and not clinging to some cliff face. I landed directly on top of Mikey, then Axe and Danny landed on both of us. There wasn't even time to let rip with a few curses.

We spread out and took up firing position again, preparing once more to blast the enemy away from our flanks, where they would be sure to begin their advance in the next stage of the battle. They were clambering down the rocks to our right, and I was trying to make sure none of them made it to the bottom. My rifle felt red-hot, and I just kept loading and shooting, aiming and firing, wishing to hell I still had my Texas helmet.

We were trying to move into a decent position, jumping between the rocks, working our way out into open ground. But we were picking up fire now. The Taliban had seen us and were raining bullets down, firing from a prime overhead spot. We moved back against the rocks, and Danny was shot again.

They hit him in his lower back, and the bullet blew out of his stomach. He was still firing, Christ knows how, but he was. Danny's mouth was open, and there was blood trickling out. There was blood absolutely everywhere. It was hot, and the stench of it was unmistakable, the cordite was heavy in the air, and the noise, which had not abated since they first opened fire, was deafening. Our ears were ringing from the blasts like we were wearing headphones.

And then they opened up with the grenades again. We saw the white smoke streaking through the air. We saw them coming, winging down that canyon right onto us. And when they blew, the blast was overpowering, echoing from the granite rocks that surrounded us on three sides.

It was like the world was blowing up around us, with the flying rock splinters, some of them pretty large, clattering off the cliff walls; the ricocheting bullets; the swirling dust cloud enveloping the shrapnel and covering us, choking us, obscuring everything.

Murph was trying to reassess the situation, desperately trying to make the right decision despite our limited options. And let's face it, the options had not changed very much since I first slammed a bullet between that guy's eyes from behind the tree. Right now we were not hemmed in on our flanks; our enemy was dead ahead. That, and straight up. Overhead. And that's bad.

I guess the oldest military strategy in the world is to gain the higher ground. In my experience, no Taliban commander had ever ordered his men to fight from anything other than the high ground. And did they ever have it now. If we'd been in a cornfield, it would have been nothing like so dangerous, because the bullets would have hit the earth and stayed there. But we were in a granite-walled corner, and everything bounced off at about a zillion miles per hour, which is more or less the definition of a ricochet. Everything, bullets, shrapnel, and fragments, came zinging off those rocks. It seemed to us like the Taliban were getting double value for every shot. If the bullet missed, watch the hell out for the ricochet.

And how much longer we could go on taking this kind of bombardment, without getting ourselves killed, was anyone's guess. Murph and Danny had picked up the fight on the left and were still firing, still hitting them pretty good. I was firing upward, trying to pick them off between the rocks, and Axe had jammed himself into a good spot in the rocks and was blazing away at the oncoming turbans.

Both Murph and I were hoping for a lull in the fire, which would signify we had killed a significant number. But that never came. What came were reinforcements. Taliban reinforcements. Groups of guys moving up, replacing their dead, joining the front line of this wide-ranging, large force on their home ground, armed to the teeth, and *still* unable to kill even one of us.

We tried to take the fight to them, concentrating on their strongest positions, pushing them to reinforce their line of battle. No three guys ever fought with higher courage than my buddies up there in those mountains. And damn near surrounded as we were, we still believed we would ultimately defeat our enemy. We still had plenty of ammunition.

But then Danny was shot again. Right through the neck, and he went down beside me. He dropped his rifle and slumped to the ground. I reached down to grab him and drag him closer to the rock face, but he managed to clamber to his feet, trying to tell me he was okay even though he'd been shot four times.

Danny couldn't speak now, but he wouldn't give in. He propped himself up against a rock for cover and opened fire again at the Taliban, signaling he might need a new magazine as his very lifeblood poured out of him. I just stood there for a moment, helplessly, fighting back my tears, witnessing a brand of valor I had never before been privileged to see. What a guy. What a friend.

Murph called out to me, "The only way's down, kid," as if I didn't know. I called back, "Roger that, sir."

I knew he meant the village, and it was true. That was our chance. If we could grab one of those houses and make a stand, we would be hard to dislodge. Four SEALs firing from solid cover will usually get the job done. All we needed to do was coax the Taliban down there. Although if things didn't get a whole lot better in the next few minutes, we might not make it ourselves.

8

The Final Battle for Murphy's Ridge

The ground shook. The very few trees swayed. The noise was worse than any blast all day...This was one gigantic Taliban effort to finish us. We hit the deck... to avoid the lethal flying debris, rock fragments and shrapnel.

Lieutenant Mike Murphy bellowed out the command, the third time he had done so in the battle. Same mountain. Same command. *"Fall back! Axe and Marcus first!"*

Again he really meant *Fall off!* And we were all getting real used to it. Axe and I sprinted for the edge, while Murph and Danny, tucked into the rocks, drew fire and covered our escape. I had no idea whether Danny could even move again, with all his wounds.

Lying right along the top of the cliff was a tree trunk with a kind of hollow underneath it, as if it had been washed out by the rains. Axe, who could think quicker on his feet than most people I've ever met, made straight for that hole because the tree trunk would give him cover as he plunged down to whatever the hell was over the goddamned cliff.

The slimly built Axe hit the ground like a javelin, skidded fast into the hollow, shot straight under the log, and out into space. I hit the ground like a Texas longhorn and came to a grinding halt, stuck fast under the log. Couldn't go forward, couldn't go back. Fuck me. Was this a bummer or what?

The Taliban had seen me by now. I was the only one they could see, and I heard a volley of bullets screaming around me. One shot smacked into the tree just to my right. The rest were hitting the dirt and sending up puffs of dust. I heaved at the log. I heaved with all my might, but I could not move that sucker. I was pinned down.

I was trying to look backward, wondering if Mikey had seen me and might try a rescue, when suddenly I saw the stark white smoke trail of an incoming RPG against the mountain. The RPG smashed into the tree trunk right next to me and exploded with a shattering blast as I tried frantically to turn away from it. I can't tell what happened next, but it blew the goddamned trunk clean in half and shot me straight over the cliff.

I guess it was about fifteen feet down to where Axe was moving into firing position, and I landed close. Considering I'd just been blown over the ledge like a freakin' human cannonball, I was pretty lucky to be still standing. And there right next to me on the ground was my rifle, placed there by the Hand of God Himself.

I reached down to pick it up and listened again for His voice. But this time there was no noise, just one brief second of silence in my mind, amid all the chaos and malevolence of this monstrous struggle for supremacy, apparently being conducted on behalf of His Holy Prophet Muhammad.

I was not sure whether either of them would have approved. I don't know that much about Muhammad, but, by all that's holy,

I don't think my own God wished me to die. If He had been indifferent to my plight, He surely would not have taken such good care of my gun, right? Because how on earth that was still with me, I will never know.

That rifle had so far fought three separate battles in three different places, been ripped out of my grasp twice, been blown over a cliff by a powerful grenade, fallen almost nine hundred feet down a mountain, and was *still* somehow right next to my outstretched hand. Fluke? Believe what you will. My own faith will remain forever unshaken.

Anyhow, I picked it up and moved back into the rocks where Axe was now picking up fire from the enemy. But he was well positioned and fighting back, blazing away on the left, the flank for which he'd fought so desperately for so long. Actually it had been about forty minutes, but it seemed like ten years, and we were both still going.

So, for that matter, were Mikey and Danny, and somehow they had both made the leap down here to the lower level, near the stream, where the Taliban assault was not quite so bad. Yet. We looked, by the way, shocking, especially Danny, who was covered head to toe in blood. Axe was okay but badly battered, and Mikey was soaked in blood from that stomach wound; not as bad as Danny, but not pretty.

When that grenade blew me over the cliff, it probably should have killed me, but the only new injury I had sustained was a broken nose, which I got when I hit the deck semiconscious. To be honest, it hurt like hell, along with my back, and I was bleeding all over my gear. However, I had not been seriously shot, as two of my team had.

Axe was holding the tribesmen off, leaning calmly on a rock, firing up the hill, the very picture of an elite warrior in combat.

No panic, rock steady, firing accurately, conserving his ammunition, missing nothing. I was close to him in a similar stance, and we were both hitting them pretty good. One guy suddenly jumped up from nowhere a little above us, and I shot him dead, about thirty yards range.

But we were trapped again. There were still around eighty of these maniacs coming down at us, and that's a heck of a lot of enemies. I'm not sure what their casualty rate was, because both Mikey and I estimated Sharmak had thrown 140 men minimum into this fight. Whatever, they were still there, and I was not sure how long Danny could keep going.

Mikey worked his way alongside me and said with vintage Murphy humor, "Man, this really sucks."

I turned to face him and told him, "We're gonna fucking die out here—if we're not careful."

"I know," he replied.

And the battle raged on. The massed, wild gunfire of a very determined enemy against our more accurate, better-trained response, superior concentration, and war-fighting know-how. Once more, hundreds of bullets were ricocheting around our rocky surroundings. And once more, the Taliban went to the grenades, blasting the terrain around us to pieces. Jammed between rocks, we kept firing, but Danny was in all kinds of trouble, and I was afraid he might lose consciousness.

That was when they shot him again, right at the base of the neck. I watched in horror as Danny went down, this beautiful guy, husband of Patsy, a friend of mine for four years, a guy who had always been last away while we retreated, a guy who had provided our covering fire until he couldn't stand anymore.

And now he lay on the ground, blood pouring from his five wounds. And I was supposed to be a fucking SEAL medic, and

I could not do a damn thing for him without getting us all killed. I dropped my rifle and climbed over the rock, running across open ground to get to him. All right. All right. No hero bullshit. I was crying like a baby.

Danny was saturated in blood, still conscious, still trying to fire his rifle at the enemy. But he was in a facedown position. I told him to take it easy while I turned him over. "C'mon, Dan, we're gonna be all right."

He nodded, and I knew he could not speak and would probably never speak again. What I really remember is, he would not let go of his rifle. I raised him by the shoulders and hauled him into an almost sitting position. Then, grasping him under the arms, I started to drag him backward, toward cover. And would you believe, that little iron man opened fire at the enemy once again, almost lying on his back, blasting away up the hill while I kept dragging.

We'd gone about eight yards when everything I dreaded came true. Here I was, just about defenseless, trying to walk backward, both hands full, when a Taliban fighter suddenly loomed up out of the rocks to our right. He was right on top of us, looking down, a smile on his face as he aimed that AK-47 straight at my head.

Neither of us saw him in time to return fire. I just said a quick prayer and stared back at him. Which was precisely when Axe banged two bullets right between his eyes, killed that tribesman stone dead instantly. I didn't have time to thank him, because the grenades were still coming in, and I just kept trying to drag Danny to safety. And, like Axe, Danny kept firing.

I got him to the rock face just a few yards from Mikey. And it was clear the enemy had nearly managed to surround us for the fourth time today. We could tell by the direction of the gunfire and occasionally the RPGs. Danny was still alive and willing to fight, and Mikey was now fighting shoulder to shoulder with Axe, and they were inflicting heavy damage.

I still thought we had a chance of getting out, but once more the only option was down, toward that village and onto the flat ground. Fighting uphill, as we had been doing since this battle started, did, in the words of our mission officer, really suck.

I yelled out loudly, *"Axe! Moving!"* He had time to shout back, *"Roger that!"* before they shot him in the chest. I watched his rifle fall from his grasp. He slumped forward and slipped down the rock he'd been leaning on, all the way to the ground.

I absolutely froze. This could not be happening. Matt Axelson, a family fixture, Morgan's best friend, a part of our lives. I started calling his name, irrationally, over and over. Privately I thought Danny was dying, and all I could see was a stain of blood gathering in the red dirt where Axe was slumped. For a brief moment I thought I might be losing it.

But then Axe reached for his rifle and got up. He leveled the weapon, got a hold of another magazine, shoved it into the breech, and opened fire again, blood pumping out of his chest. He held his same firing position, leaning against the rock. He showed the same attitude of solid Navy SEAL know-how, the same formidable steadiness, staring through his scope, those brilliant blue eyes of his scanning the terrain.

When Axe got up, it was the bravest thing I ever saw. Except for Danny. Except for Mikey, still commanding us after taking a bullet through his stomach so early in the battle.

And now Murph was masterminding a way down the escarpment. He had chosen the route and called up Axe to follow him down. And still the bullets were humming around us as the Taliban started their pursuit. Mikey and Axe were about seventy-five yards in front, and I was dragging Danny along while he did everything he could to help, trying to walk, trying to give us covering fire.

"It's okay, Danny," I kept saying. "We just need to catch up with the others. It's gonna be all right."

Right then a bullet caught him full in the upper part of his face. I heard it hit home, I turned to help him, and the blood from his head wound spilled over us both. I called out to him. But it was too late. He wasn't fighting the terrible pain anymore. And he couldn't hear me. Danny Dietz died right there in my arms. I don't know how quickly hearts break, but that nearly broke mine.

And still the gunfire never abated. I dragged Danny off the open ground maybe five feet, and then I said good-bye to him. I lowered him down, and I had to leave him or else die out here with him. But I knew one thing for certain. I still had my rifle and I was not alone, and neither was Danny, a devout Roman Catholic. I left him with God.

And now I had to get back to help my team. It was the hardest thing I've ever done in my life.

To this day I have nightmares about it, a chilling dream where Danny's still talking to me, and there's blood everywhere, and I have to walk away and I don't even know why. I always wake up in tears, and it will always haunt me, and it's never going to go away.

And now I could hear Murph yelling to me. I grabbed my rifle, ducked down, slipped and fell off a rock, then started to run toward him and Axe while they provided heavy covering fire nonstop aimed at the Taliban's rocky redoubt, maybe another forty yards back.

I reached the edge, ran almost blindly into a tree, bounced off, skidded down the slope, which was not very deep, and landed on my head right in the fucking stream. Like any good frogman, I was seriously pissed off because my boots got wet. I really hate that.

Finally I caught up with them. Axe was out of ammunition and I gave him a new magazine. Mikey wanted to know where Danny was, and I had to tell him that Danny had died. He was appalled, completely shocked, and so was Axe. Although Mikey would not say it, I knew he wanted to go back for the body. But we both knew there was no time and no reason. We had nowhere to take the remains of a fallen teammate, and we could not continue this firefight while carrying around a body.

Danny was dead. And strangely, I was the first to pull myself together. I said suddenly, "I'll tell you what. We have to get down this goddamned mountain or we'll all be dead."

And as if to make up our minds for us, the Taliban were again closing in, trying to make that 360-degree movement around us. And they were doing it. Gunfire was coming in from underneath us now. We could see the tribesmen still swarming, and I tried to count them as I had been trying to do for almost an hour.

I thought there were now only about fifty, maybe sixty, but the bullets were still flying. The grenades were still coming in, blasting close, sending up dust clouds of smoke and dirt with flying bits of rock. There had never been a lull in the amount of ordnance the enemy was piling down on us.

Right now, again tucked low behind rocks, the three of us could look down and see the village one and a half miles distant, and it remained our objective.

Again I told Mikey, "If we can just make it down there and get some cover, we'll take 'em all out on the flat ground."

I knew we were not in great shape. But we were still SEALs.

Nothing can ever take that away. We were still confident. And we were never going to surrender. If it came down to it, we would fight to the death with our knives against their guns.

"Fuck surrender," said Mikey. And he had no need to explain further, either to Axe or me. Surrender would have been a disgrace to our community, like ringing the bell at the edge of the grinder and putting your helmet in the line. No one who had made it through this far, to this no-man's-land in the Afghan mountains, would have dreamed of giving up.

Remember the philosophy of the U.S. Navy SEALs: "I will never quit...My Nation expects me to be physically harder and mentally stronger than my enemies. If knocked down, I will get back up, every time. I will draw on every remaining ounce of strength to protect my teammates...I am never out of the fight."

Those words have sustained many brave men down the years. They were engraved upon the soul of every SEAL. And they were in the minds of all of us.

Mikey suddenly said, above the rage of the battle, "Remember, bro, we're never out of it."

I nodded tersely. "It's only about another thousand yards to flat ground. If we can just get down there, we got a chance."

Trouble was, we couldn't get down there, at least not right then. Because once more we were pinned down. And we faced the same dilemma: the only escape was to go down, but our only defensive strategy was to go up. Once more, we had to get off this ground, away from the ricochets. Back up the left flank.

We were trying to fight the battle our way. But even though we were still going, we were battered half to death. I led the way back up the rocks, blasting away, shooting down anyone I could see. But they caught on to that real quick, and now they really unloaded on us, Russian-made rocket grenades. Coming straight down their right flank, our left.

The ground shook. The very few trees swayed. The noise was worse than any blast all day. Even the walls of this little canyon shook. The stream splashed over its banks. This was one gigantic Taliban effort to finish us. We hit the deck, jamming ourselves into our rocky crevasse, heads down to avoid the lethal flying debris, rock fragments and shrapnel. As before they did not kill anyone with this type of thunderous bombardment, and as before they waited till the dust had cleared and then opened fire again.

Above me I could see the tree line. It was not close, but it was nearer than the village. But the Taliban knew our objective, and as we tried to fight our way forward, they drove us back with sheer weight of fire.

We'd tried, against all the odds, and just could not make it. They'd knocked us back again. And we retreated down, making a long pathetic loop, back the way we'd come. But once more we landed up in a good spot, a sound defensive position, well protected by the rock face on either side. Again we tried to take the fight to them, picking our targets and driving them back, making some ground now toward the village.

They were up and screaming at us, yelling as the battle almost became close quarters. We yelled right back and kept firing. But there were still so many of them, and then they got into better position and shot Mikey Murphy through the chest.

He came toward me, asking if I could give him another magazine. And then I saw Axe stumbling toward me, his head pushed out, blood running down his face, bubbling out of the most shocking head wound.

"They shot me, bro," he said. "The bastards shot me. Can you help me, Marcus?" What could I say? What could I do? I couldn't help except by trying to fight off the enemy. And Axe was standing right in my line of fire.

I tried to help him get down behind a rock. And I turned to Mikey, who was obviously badly hurt now. "Can you move, buddy?" I asked him.

And he groped in his pocket for his mobile phone, the one we had dared not use because it would betray our position. And then Lieutenant Murphy walked out into the open ground. He walked until he was more or less in the center, gunfire all around him, and he sat on a small rock and began punching in the numbers to HQ.

I could hear him talking. "My men are taking heavy fire... we're getting picked apart. My guys are dying out here...we need help."

And right then Mikey took a bullet straight in the back. I saw the blood spurt from his chest. He slumped forward, dropping his phone and his rifle. But then he braced himself, grabbed them both, sat upright again, and once more put the phone to his ear.

I heard him speak again. "Roger that, sir. Thank you." Then he stood up and staggered out to our bad position, the one guarding our left, and Mikey just started fighting again, firing at the enemy.

He was hitting them too, having made that one last desperate call to base, the one that might yet save us if they could send help in time, before we were overwhelmed.

Only I knew what Mikey had done. He'd understood we had only one realistic chance, and that was to call in help. He also knew there was only one place from which he could possibly make that cell phone work: out in the open, away from the cliff walls.

Knowing the risk, understanding the danger, in the full knowledge the phone call could cost him his life, Lieutenant Michael Patrick Murphy, son of Maureen, fiancé of the beautiful Heather, walked out into the firestorm.

His objective was clear: to make one last valiant attempt to save his two teammates. He made the call, made the connection. He reported our approximate position, the strength of our enemy, and how serious the situation was. When they shot him, I thought mortally, he kept talking.

Roger that, sir. Thank you. Will those words ever dim in my memory, even if I live to be a hundred? Will I ever forget them? Would you? And was there ever a greater SEAL team commander, an officer who fought to the last and, as perhaps his dying move, risked everything to save his remaining men?

I doubt there was ever anyone better than Mikey, cool under fire, always thinking, fearless about issuing the one-option command even if it was nearly impossible. And then the final, utterly heroic act. Not a gesture. An act of supreme valor. Lieutenant Mikey was a wonderful person and a very, very great SEAL officer. If they build a memorial to him as high as the Empire State Building, it won't ever be high enough for me.

Mikey was still alive, and he carried on, holding the left. I stayed on the right, both of us firing carefully and accurately. I was still trying to reach slightly higher ground. But the depleted army of the Taliban was determined that I should not get it, and every time I tried to advance even a few yards, get even a few feet higher, they drove me back. Mikey too was still trying to climb higher, and he actually made it some of the way, into a rock strata above where I was standing. It was a good spot from which to attack, but defensively poor. And I knew this must surely be Mikey's last stand.

Just then, Axe walked right by me in a kind of a daze, making only a marginal attempt at staying in the cover of the rocks. Then I saw the wound, the right side of his head almost blown away. I shouted, *"Axe! Axe!* C'mon, old buddy. Get down there, right down there."

I was pointing at the one spot in the rocks we might find protection. And he tried to raise his hand, an act of confirmation that he'd heard me. But he couldn't. And he kept walking, slowly, hunched forward, no longer clutching his rifle. He was down to just his pistol, but I knew he could not hold that, aim, and fire. At least he was headed for cover, even though no one could survive a head wound like that. I knew Axe was dying.

Mikey was still firing, but suddenly I heard him scream my name, the most bone-chilling primeval scream: *"Help me, Marcus! Please help me!"* He was my best friend in all the world, but he was thirty yards up the mountain, and I could not climb to him. I could hardly walk, and if I'd moved two yards out of my protected position, they would have hit me with a hundred bullets.

Nonetheless, I edged out around the rocks to try to give him covering fire, to force these bastards back, give him a breather until I could find a way to get up there without getting mowed down.

And all the time, he was screaming, calling out my name, begging me to help him live. And there was nothing I could do except die with him. Even then, with only a couple of magazines left, I *still* believed I could nail these fuckers in the turbans and somehow save him and Axe. I just wanted Mikey to stop screaming, for his agony to end.

But every few seconds, he cried out for me again. And every time it happened, I felt like I'd been stabbed. There were tears welling uncontrollably out of my eyes, not for the first time on this day. I would have done anything for Mikey, I'd have laid down my own life for him. But my death right here in this outcrop of rocks was not going to save him. If I could save him, it would be by staying alive.

And then, as suddenly as it began, the screaming stopped. There was silence for a few seconds, as if even these Taliban warriors understood that Mikey had died. I moved slightly forward and looked up there, in time to see four of them come down and fire several rounds into his fallen body.

The screaming had stopped. For everyone except me. I still hear Mikey, every night. I still hear that scream above all other things, even above the death of Danny Dietz. For several weeks I thought I might be losing my mind, because I could never push it aside. There were one or two frightening occasions when I heard it in broad daylight and found myself pressed against a wall, my hands covering my ears.

I always thought these kinds of psychiatric problems were suffered by other people, ordinary people, not by Navy SEALs. I now know the reality of them. I also doubt whether I will ever sleep through the night again.

Danny was dead. Mikey was now dead. And Axe was dying. Right now there were two of us, but only just. I resolved to walk down to where Axe was hiding and to die there with him. There was, I knew, unlikely to be a way out. There were still maybe fifty of the enemy, perhaps by now hunting only me.

It took me nearly ten minutes, firing back behind me sporadically to try to pin them down...just in case. I was firing on the wild chance that there was a shot at survival, that somehow

Mikey's phone call might yet have the guys up here in time for a last-ditch rescue.

When I reached Axe, he was sitting in a hollow, and he'd fixed a temporary bandage on the side of his head. I stared at him, wondering where those cool blue eyes of his had gone. The eyes in which I could now see my own reflection were blood black, the sockets filled from the terrible wound in his skull.

I smiled at him because I knew we would not walk this way again, at least not together, not on this earth. Axe did not have long. If he'd been in the finest hospital in North America, Axe would still not have had long. The life was ebbing out of him, and I could see this powerful super-athlete growing weaker by the second.

"Hey, man," I said, "you're all fucked up!" And I tried, pitifully, to fix the bandage.

"Marcus, they got us good, man." He spoke with difficulty, as if trying to concentrate. And then he said, "You stay alive, Marcus. And tell Cindy I love her."

Those were his last words. I just sat there, and that was where I planned to stay, right there with Axe so he wouldn't be alone when the end came. I didn't give a flying fuck what happened to me anymore. Quietly, I made my peace with God, and I thanked Him for protecting me and saving my rifle. Which, somehow, I still had. I never took my eyes off Axe, who was semiconscious but still breathing.

Along with the other two, Axe will always be a hero to me. Throughout this brief but brutal conflict, he'd fought like a wounded tiger. Like Audie Murphy, like Sergeant York. They shot away his body, crippled his brain but not his spirit. They never got that.

Matthew Gene Axelson, husband of Cindy, fired at the

enemy until he could no longer hold his rifle. He was just past his twenty-ninth birthday. And in his dying moments, I never took my eyes off him. I don't think he could hear me any longer. But his eyes were open, and we were still together, and I refused to allow him to die alone.

Right then, they must have seen us. Because one of those superpowerful Russian grenades came in, landed close, and blew me sideways, right out of the hollow, across the rough ground, and over the edge of the goddamned ravine. I lost consciousness before I hit the bottom, and when I came to, I was in a different hollow, and my first thought was I'd been blinded by the explosion, because I couldn't see a thing.

However, after a few seconds, I gathered my wits and realized I was upside down in the freakin' hole. I still had my eyesight and a few other working parts, but my left leg seemed paralyzed and, to a lesser degree, so was my right. It took me God knows how long to wriggle out onto flat ground and claw my way into the cover of a rock.

My ears were zinging, I guess from the blast of the grenade. I looked up and saw I had fallen a pretty good way down, but I was too disoriented to put a number on it. The main difference between now and when I'd been sitting with Axe was that the gunfire had ceased.

If they'd reached Axe, who could not possibly have lived through the blast, they might not have bothered to go on shooting. They obviously had not found me, and I would have been real hard to locate, upside down in the hole. But whatever, no one seemed to be looking. For the first time in maybe an hour and a half, I was apparently not being actively hunted.

Aside from being unable to stand, I had two other very serious problems. The first was the total loss of my pants. They'd been blown right off me. The second was the condition of my left leg, which I could scarcely feel but which was a horrific sight, bleeding profusely and full of shrapnel.

I had no bandages, nothing medical. I had been able to do nothing for my teammates, and I could do nothing for myself, except try to stay hidden. It was not a promising situation. I was damn sure I'd broken my back and probably my shoulder; I'd broken my nose, and my face was a total mess. I couldn't stand up, never mind walk. At least one leg was wrecked, and maybe the other. I was paralyzed in both thighs, and the only way I could move was to belly crawl.

Unsurprisingly, I was dazed. And through this personal fog of war, there was yet one more miracle for me to recognize. Not two feet from where I was lying, half hidden by dirt and shale, well out of sight of my enemy, was my Mark 12 rifle, and I still had one and a half magazines left. I prayed before I grabbed it, because I thought it might be just a mirage and that when I tried to hold it... well, it might just disappear.

But it did not. And I felt the cold steel in the hot air as my fingers clasped it. I listened again for His voice. I prayed again, imploring Him for guidance. But there was no sound, and all I knew was that somehow I had to make it out to the right, where I'd be safe, at least for a while.

My God had not spoken again. But neither had He forsaken me. I knew that. For damned sure, I knew that.

I knew one other thing as well. For the first time, I was entirely alone. Here in these Taliban-controlled, hostile mountains, there was no earthly teammate for me, and my enemy was all around. Had they heeded the words of the goatherds? That there were four of us, and that right now they had only three bodies? Or did they assume I had been blown to pieces by the blast of the final Russian RPG?

I had no answer to those questions, only hope. With absolutely no one to turn to, no Mikey, no Axe, no Danny, I had to face the final battle by myself, maybe lonely, maybe desolate, maybe against formidable odds. But I was not giving up.

I had only one Teammate. And He moved, as ever, in mysterious ways. But I was a Christian, and He had somehow saved me from a thousand AK-47 bullets on this day. No one had shot me, which was well nigh beyond all comprehension.

And I still believed He did not wish me to die. And I would still try my best to uphold the honor of the United States Navy SEALs as I imagined they would have wished. No surrender. Fuck that.

When I judged I had fully gathered my senses and checked my watch, it was exactly 1342 local time. For a few minutes there was no gunfire, and I was beginning to assume they thought I was dead. Wrong, Marcus. The Taliban AKs opened up again, and suddenly there were bullets flying everywhere, all around, just like before.

My enemy was coming up on me from the lower levels and from both sides, firing rapidly but inaccurately. Their bullets were ripping into the earth and shale across a wide range, most of them, thank Christ, well away from me.

It was clear they thought I might be still alive but equally clear they had not yet located me. They were conducting a kind of recon by fire, trying to flush me out, blazing away right across the spectrum, hoping someone would finally hit me and finish me. Or better yet, that I would come out with my hands high so the murdering little bastards could cut my head off or indulge in one of their other attractive little idiosyncracies before telling that evil little television station al-Jazeera how they had conquered the infidels.

I think I've mentioned my view about surrender. I rammed another magazine into the breech of my miraculous rifle and somehow crawled over this little hill, through the hail of bullets, right into the side of the mountain. No one saw me. No one hit me. I wedged myself into a rocky crevasse with my legs sticking out into a clump of bushes.

There were huge rocks to both sides, protecting me. Overall I judged I was jammed into a fifteen-foot-wide ledge on the mountain. It was not a cave, not even a shallow cave, because it had a kind of open top way above me. Rocks and sand kept falling down on me as the Taliban warriors scrambled around above my position. But this crevasse provided sensational cover and camouflage. Even I realized I would be pretty hard to spot. They'd have to get real lucky, even with their latest policy of trying to flush me out with sheer volume of fire.

My line of vision was directly ahead. I realized I couldn't move or change position, at least in broad daylight I couldn't, and it was imperative I hide the blood which was leaking from my battered body. I took stock of my injuries. My left leg was still bleeding pretty bad, and I packed the wounds with mud. I had a big cut on my forehead, which I also packed with mud. Both legs were numb. I was not going anywhere. At least not for a while.

I had no medical kit, no maps, no compass. I had my bullets, and I had my gun, and I had a decent view off my mountain, straight ahead over the canyon to the next mountain. I had no pants, and no buddies, but no one could see me. I was wedged in tight, my back to the wall in every possible sense.

I eased myself into a relatively comfortable position, checked my rifle, and laid it down the length of my body, aiming outward. If enough of them discovered me, I guess I'd quickly be going to join Danny, Axe, and Mikey. But not before I'd killed a whole lot more of them. I was, I knew, in a perfect position for a stubborn, defensive military action, protected on all sides, vulnerable to a frontal assault only, and that would have to be by weight of numbers.

I could still hear gunfire, and it was growing closer. They were definitely coming this way. I just thought, *Don't move, don't breathe, do not make a sound.* I think it was about then I understood how utterly alone I was for the very first time. And the Taliban was hunting me. They were not hunting for a SEAL platoon. They were hunting me alone. Despite my injuries, I knew I had to reach deep. I was starting to lose track of time. But I stayed still. I actually did not move one inch for eight hours.

As the time passed, I could see the Taliban guys right across the canyon, running up and down, seemed like hundreds of them, plainly searching, scouring the mountain they knew so well, looking for me. I had some feeling back in my legs, but I was bleeding real bad, and I was in a lot of pain. I think the loss of blood may have started to make me feel light-headed.

Also, I was scared to death. It was the first time in my entire six-year career as a Navy SEAL I had been really scared. At one point, late in the afternoon, I thought they were all leaving. Across the canyon, the mountainside cleared, everyone running hard to the right, swarms of them, all headed for the same place. At least that's how it seemed to me across my narrow field of vision.

I now know where they were going. While I was lying there in my crevasse, I had no idea what the hell was going on. But now I shall recount, to the best of my gathered knowledge, what happened elsewhere on that saddest of afternoons, that most shocking massacre high in the Hindu Kush, the worst disaster ever to befall the SEALs in any conflict in our more than forty-year history.

The first thing to remember is that Mikey had succeeded in getting through to the quick reaction force (QRF) in Asadabad, a couple of mountain ranges over from where I was still holding out. That last call, the one on his cell phone that essentially cost him his life, was successful. From all accounts, his haunting words — *My guys are dying out here . . . we need help* — ripped around our base like a flash fire. *SEALs are dying!* That's a five-alarm emergency that stops only just on the north side of frenzy.

Lieutenant Commander Kristensen, our acting CO, sounded the alarm. It's always a decision for the QRF, to launch or not to launch. Eric took a billionth of a second to make it. I know the vision of us four — his buddies, his friends and teammates, Mikey, Axe, Danny, and me, fighting for our lives, hurt, possibly dead, surrounded by a huge fighting force of bloodthirsty Afghan tribesmen — flashed through his mind as he summoned the boys to action stations.

And the vision of terrible loss stood stark before him as he roared down the phone, ordering the men of 160th Special Operations Aviation Regiment (SOAR), the fabled Night Stalkers, to get the big army MH-47 helo ready, right there on the runway. It was the same one that had taken off just before us on the previous day, the one we tracked in to our ops area.

Guys I've already introduced charged into position, desperate to help, cramming as much ammunition as they could into their pouches, grabbing rifles and running for the Chinook, its rotors already screaming. My SDV Team 1 guys were instantly there. Petty Officers James Suh and Shane Patton reached the helo first. Then, scrambling aboard, came the massively built Senior Chief Dan Healy, the man who had masterminded Operation Redwing, who apparently looked as if he'd been shot as he left the barracks.

Then came the SEAL Team 10 guys, Lieutenant Mike McGreevy Jr. of New York, Chief Jacques Fontan of New Orleans, Petty Officers First Class Jeff Lucas from Oregon and Jeff Taylor from West Virginia. Finally, still shouting that his boys needed every gun they could get, came Lieutenant Commander Eric Kristensen, the man who knew perhaps better than anyone that the eight SEALs in that helo were about to risk a lethal daytime insertion in a high mountain pass, right into the jaws of an enemy that might outnumber them by dozens to one.

Kristensen knew he did not have to go. In fact, perhaps he should not have gone, stayed instead at his post, central to control and command. Right then, we had the skipper in the QRF, which was, at best, a bit unorthodox. But Eric Kristensen was a SEAL to his fingertips. And what he knew above all else was that he had just heard a desperate cry for help. From his brothers, from a man he knew well and trusted.

There was no way Eric was not going to answer that call. Nothing on God's earth could have persuaded him not to go. He must have known we were barely holding on, praying for help to arrive. There were, after all, only four of us. And to everyone's certain knowledge, there were a minimum of a hundred Taliban.

Eric understood the stupendous nature of the risk, and he never blinked. Just grabbed his rifle and ammunition and raced to board that aircraft, yelling at everyone else to hurry... *"Move it, guys! Let's really move it!"* That's what he always said under pressure. Sure, he was a commanding officer, and a hell of a good one. But more than that, he was a SEAL, a part of that brotherhood forged in blood. Even more important, he was a man. And right now he was answering an urgent, despairing cry from the very heart of his own brotherhood. There was only one way Eric Kristensen was headed, straight up the mountain, guns blazing, command or no command.

Inside the MH-47, the men of 160th SOAR waited quietly, as they had done so many times before on these hair-raising air-rescue ops, often at night. They were led by a terrific man, Major Steve Reich of Connecticut, with Chief Warrant Officers Chris Scherkenbach of Jacksonville, Florida, and Corey J. Goodnature of Clarks Grove, Minnesota.

Master Sergeant James W. Ponder was there, with Sergeants First Class Marcus Muralles of Shelbyville, Indiana, and Mike Russell of Stafford, Virginia. Their group was completed by Staff Sergeant Shamus Goare of Danville, Ohio, and Sergeant Kip Jacoby of Pompano Beach, Florida. By any standards, it was a crack army fighting force.

The MH-47 took off and headed over the two mountain ranges. I guess it seemed to take forever. Those kind of rescues always do. It came in to land at just about the same spot we had fast-roped in at the start of the mission, around five miles from where I was now positioned.

The plan was for the rescue team to rope it down just the same, and when the "Thirty seconds!" call came, I guess the lead guys edged toward the stern ramp. What no one knew was the Taliban had some kind of bunker back there, and as the MH-47 tilted back for the insert and the ropes fell away for the climb-down, the Taliban fired a rocket-propelled grenade straight through the open ramp.

It shot clean past the heads of the lead group and blew with a shattering blast against the fuel tanks, turning the helo into an inferno, stern and midships. Several of the guys were blown out and fell, some of them burning, to their deaths, from around thirty feet. They smashed into the mountainside and tumbled down. The impact was so violent, our search-and-rescue parties later found gun barrels snapped in half among the bodies.

The helicopter pilot fought for control, unaware of the carnage behind him but certainly aware of the raging fires around and above him. Of course, there was nothing he could do. The big MH-47 just fell out of the sky and crashed with thunderous impact onto the mountainside, swayed, and then rolled with brutal force over and over, smashing itself to pieces on a long two-hundred-yard downward trail to extinction.

There was nothing left except scattered debris when our guys finally got up there to investigate. And, of course, no survivors. My close SDV Team 1 buddies James, Chief Dan, and young Shane were all gone. It was as well I did not know this as I lay there in my crevasse. I'm not sure I could have coped with it. It was nothing less than a massacre. Weeks later I broke down when I saw the photographs, mostly because it was me they were all trying to rescue.

As I explained, at the time I knew nothing of this. I only knew something had happened that had caused a lot of Taliban to get very obviously excited. And soon I could see U.S. aircraft flying right along the canyon in front of me, A-10s and AH-64 Apache helicopters. Some of them were so close I could see the pilots.

I pulled my PRC-148 radio out of my pouch and tried to make contact. But I could not speak. My throat was full of dirt, my tongue was sticking to the roof of my mouth, and I had no water. I was totally unable to transmit. But I knew I was in contact because I could hear the aircrew talking. So I fired up my emergency distress beacon on the radio and transmitted that.

They picked it up. I know they did because I could hear them plainly. "Hey, you getting that beacon?" "Yeah, we got it...but no further information." Then they just flew off, over to my right, where I now know the MH-47 had gone down.

The trouble was, the Taliban steal those radios if they can, and they often used them to lure the U.S. helicopters down. I was unaware of this at the time, but now it's obvious to me, the American pilots were extremely jumpy about trying to put down in response to a U.S. beacon because they did not know who the hell was aiming that beacon, and they might get shot down.

Which would have been, anyway, little comfort to me, lying there on the mountainside only half alive, bleeding to death and unable to walk. And now it was growing dark, and I was plainly running out of options. I guessed my only chance was to attract the attention of one of the pilots who were still flying down my canyon at pretty regular intervals.

My radio headset had been ripped away during my fall down the mountain, but I still had the wires. And I somehow rigged up two of my chem lights, which glow when you break them in half, and fixed them to the defunct radio wires. And then I whirled this homemade slingshot around my head in a kind of luminous buzz saw the first moment I saw a helicopter in the area.

I also had an infrared strobe light that I could fire up, and I had the laser from my rifle, which I took off and aimed at the regular U.S. flyby. Jesus Christ! I was a living, breathing distress signal. *There's got to be someone watching these mountains. Someone's got to see me.* I was using this procedure only when I actually saw a helicopter. And soon my optimism turned to outright gloom. No one was paying attention. From where I was lying, it looked like I'd been abandoned for dead.

By now, with the sun declining behind the mountains, I had almost all of the feeling back in my legs. And this gave me hope that I might be able to walk, although I knew the pain might be a bit fierce. I was getting dangerously thirsty. I could not get the clogged dust and dirt out of my throat. It was all I could do to breathe, never mind speak. I had to find water, and I had to get the hell out of this death trap. But not until the veil of darkness fell over these mountains.

I knew I had to get myself out, first to water and then to safety, because it sure as hell didn't look like anyone was going to find me. I remember Axe's final words. They still rang clearly in my mind: "You stay alive, Marcus. And tell Cindy I love her." For Axe, and for Danny, and above all for Mikey, I knew I must stay alive.

I saw the last, long rays of the mountain sun cast their gigantic shadows through the canyon before me. And just as certainly, I saw the glint of the silver barrel of an AK-47 right across from me, dead ahead, on the far cliff face, maybe 150 yards. It caught the rays of the dying sun twice, which suggested the sonofabitch who was holding it was making a sweep across the wall of my mountain, right past the crevasse inside of which I was still lying motionless.

And now I could see the tribesman in question. He was just standing there, his shirtsleeves rolled up, wearing a blue and white checkered vest, holding his rifle in the familiar low-slung grip of the Afghans, a split second short of raising it to the firing position. The only conclusion was he was looking for me.

I did not know how many of his buddies were within shouting range. But I did know if he got a clear sight across that canyon and somehow spotted me, I was essentially history. He could hardly miss, and he kept staring across, but he did not raise his rifle. Yet.

I decided this was not a risk I was prepared to take. My own rifle was loaded and suppressed. There would be little noise to attract anyone else's attention. And very carefully, hardly daring to breathe, I raised the Mark 12 into the firing position and drew down on the little man on the far ridge. He was bang in the crosshairs of my telescopic sight.

I squeezed the trigger and hit him straight between the eyes. I just had time to see the blood bloom out into the center of his forehead, and then I watched him topple over the edge, down into the canyon. He must have fallen two hundred feet, screaming with his dying breath all the way. I was not in any way moved, except to thank God there was one less.

Almost immediately two of his colleagues ran into the precise spot where he had been standing, directly across from me. They were dressed more or less the same, except for the different colors of their vests. They stood there staring down into the canyon where the first man had fallen. They both carried AKs, held in the firing position but not fully raised.

I thought they might just take off, but they stood there, now looking hard across the void which separated my mountain from theirs. From where I was, they seemed to be looking right at me, scanning the cliff face for any sign of movement. I knew they had no idea if their pal had been shot, simply fallen, or perhaps committed suicide.

However, I think option one was their instinct. And right now they were trying to find out precisely who had shot him. I remained motionless, but those little black eyes were looking straight at me, and I realized if they both opened fire at once on my rocky redoubt, the chances of an AK-47 bullet, or bullets, hitting me were good to excellent. They had to go. Both of them.

Once more, I slowly raised my rifle and drew a bead on an armed Taliban tribesman. My first shot killed the one on the right instantly, and I watched him tumble over the edge. The second one, understanding now there was an enemy at large, raised his gun and scanned the cliff face where I was still flat on my back.

I hit him straight in the chest, then I fired a second time in case he was still breathing and able to cry out. He fell forward without a sound and went to join his two buddies on the canyon floor. Which left me all alone and thus far undiscovered.

Just a few hours previously, Mikey Murphy and I had made a military judgment which cost three lives, the lives of some of the best SEALs I ever met. Lying here on my ledge, surrounded on all sides by hostile Taliban warriors, I could not afford another mistake. I'd somehow, by the grace of God, been spared from the consequences of the first one, made way up there on that granite outcrop which ought to be named for Mikey, our superb leader. The Battle for Murphy's Ridge.

Every decision I made from now on would involve my own life or death. I needed to fight my way out, and I did not give a damn how many of the Taliban enemy I had to kill in order to achieve that. The key point was, I could not make another mistake. I could take no chances.

The far side of the canyon remained silent as the sun disappeared behind the high western peaks of the Hindu Kush. I figured the Taliban had probably split their search party in this particular area and that I'd gotten rid of one half. Out there, somewhere, in the deathly silence of the twilight, there would almost certainly be three more, looking for the one surviving American from that original four-man platoon that had inflicted such damage on their troops.

The friendly clatter of the U.S. Apaches had gone now. No one was looking for me. And by far my biggest problem was water. Aside from the fact I was still bleeding and couldn't stand up, the thirst was becoming desperate. My tongue was still clogged with dust and dirt, and I still could not speak. I'd lost my water bottle on the mountain during the first crashing fall with Mikey, and it had now been nine hours since I'd had a drink.

Also I was still soaking wet from when I fell in the river. I understood I was very light-headed from loss of blood, but I still tried to concentrate. And the one conclusion I reached was that I had to stand up. If a couple of those Taliban came around that corner to my left, the only way to approach me, and they had any form of light, I'd be like a jackrabbit caught in someone's headlights.

My redoubt had served me well, but I had to get out of it right now. When the bodies of those three guys were found at first light, this mountain would be swarming with Taliban. I dragged myself to my feet and stood there in my boxers in the freezing cold mountain air. I tested my right leg. Not too bad. Then I tested my left, and that hurt like the devil. I tried to brush some of the shale and dirt away from where I'd packed the wound, but the shards of the shrapnel were jutting out of my thigh, and every time I touched one, I nearly jumped through the ceiling. At least I would have, if there'd been one.

One of my main problems was I had no handle on the terrain. Of course I knew that the mountain reared up behind me and that I was trapped on the cliff face with no way to go except up. Which from where I stood, almost unable to hobble, was a seriously daunting task. I tested my left leg again, and at least it wasn't worse.

But my back hurt like hell. I never realized how much pain three cracked vertebrae could inflict on a guy. Of course, I never realized I had three cracked vertebrae either. I could move my right shoulder despite a torn rotator cuff, which I also didn't realize I had. And my broken nose throbbed a bit, which was kid's stuff compared with the rest. I knew one side of my face was shredded by the fall down the mountain, and the big cut on my forehead was pretty sore.

But my overriding thought was my thirst. I was only slightly comforted by the closeness of several mountain streams up here. I had to find one, fast, both to clean my wounds and to drink. That way I had a shot at yelling through the radio and locating an American helicopter or fighter aircraft in the morning.

I gathered up my gear, radio, strobes, and laser and repacked them into my pouch. I checked my rifle, which had about twenty rounds left in the magazine, with a full magazine remaining in the harness I still wore across my chest.

Then I stepped out of my redoubt, into the absolute pitch black and deathly silence of the Hindu Kush. There was no moon, and it was just starting to rain, which meant there wasn't going to be a moon in the foreseeable future.

I tested the leg again. It held my weight without giving way. I felt my direction around the huge rock which had been guarding my left flank all day. And then, with the smallest, most timid strides I had ever taken, I stepped out onto the mountain.

9

Blown-up, Shot, and Presumed Dead

Right behind me I heard the soft footsteps of the chasing gunmen . . . there were two of them, just above me in the rocks. Searching. I had only split seconds to work, because they were both on me, AKs raised . . . I went for my grenades.

Even in the pitch black of the night, I could feel the shadow of the mountain looming above me. I actually thought I could see it, a kind of dark force, darker than everything else, blacker than the rock walls upon which I was leaning.

I knew it was a hell of a long way to the top, and I would have to move sideways like a delta crab if I was going to make it. It was also going to take me all night, but somehow I had to get up there, all the way to the top.

I had two prime reasons for my strategy. First, it would be flat up there, so if it came down to another firefight, I would have a good chance. No guys firing down on me. Every SEAL likes his chances of winning a fight on flat ground.

The second issue was calling in help. No helicopter ever built could land safely on these steep Afghan cliffs. The only place within the mountain range where an MH-47 could put down was in the flat bowl of the fields below, where the villagers raised crops. Dope, that is.

And there was no way I was going to risk hanging out near a village. I was going up, to the upper flatlands, where a helo could get in and then get out. Also, my radio reception would be better up there. I could only hope the Americans were still scouring the mountains, looking for the missing Redwings.

Meanwhile, I thought I might be dying of thirst, and my parched throat was driving me onward to water and perhaps safety. So I took my first steps, guessing I was probably going to climb around five hundred feet straight up. But I'd travel a whole lot farther on the zigzag course I'd have to make up the mountain.

I began my climb, out there in the dark, by moving directly upward. I jammed my rifle into my belt so I had two hands to grip, but before I'd made the first twenty feet going slightly right, I slipped badly, which was a very scary experience. The gradient was almost sheer, straight down to the valley floor.

In my condition I probably would not have survived the fall, and I somehow saved myself from falling any more than about ten feet. Then I picked it up again, clawing my way up, facing the mountain and grabbing hold of anything I could with a grip like a mechanical digger. You'd have needed a chain saw to pry me off that cliff face. All I knew was, if I fell, I'd probably plummet several hundred feet to my death. Which was good for the concentration.

So I kept going, climbing mostly sideways, grabbing rocks, vines, or branches, anything for a grip. Every now and then I'd dislodge something or snap a branch that would not bear my weight. And I guess I must have made more noise than the Taliban army has ever made in mountain maneuvers.

I'd been going for a couple of hours when I sensed I heard something behind me. I say *sensed* because when you are operating in absolute darkness, with no sight at all, everything else is heightened, all of your senses, particularly sound and smell. Not to mention the sixth one, same one a goat or an antelope or a zebra has, the one that warns vulnerable grazing animals of the presence of a predator.

Now, I wasn't that vulnerable. And I sure as hell wasn't grazing. But right then I was in Predator Central. Those cutthroat tribal bastards were all over my case and, for all I knew, closing in on me.

I lay flat, stock-still on the mountain. And then I heard it again, the distinct snap of a twig or a branch. I estimated it was maybe two hundred yards behind me. Right then my hearing was at some kind of a peak in this ultraquiet high country. I could have picked up the soft fart of a billy goat a mile away.

Then I heard it once more. Not the billy goat, the twig. And I knew for absolute certain I was being followed. Fuck! There was still no moon, and I could still see nothing. But that would not be true of the Taliban. They'd been stealing equipment from the Russians, and then the Americans, for years. Everything they had was stolen, except for what bin Laden had purchased for them. And their supplies certainly included a few pairs of NVGs. The Russians were, after all, pioneers of that particular piece of battle gear, and we knew the mujahideen had stolen everything from them when the Soviet army finally pulled out.

The presence of an unseen Afghani tracker was very bad news for me, not least for the remnants of my morale. The thought that there was a group of killers out there, stalking me across this mountain, able to see me when I could not see them...well, that was a sonofabitch in any man's army.

I decided to press on and hope they did not decide to open fire. When I reached the top, I'd take them out. Just as soon as I could see the little bastards. First sign of light, I'd stake my position underneath some bushes where no one could see me, and then I'd deal with them as soon as they got within range. Meantime, I was so thirsty I thought I might die before that hour approached.

I was trying everything. I was breaking the thinnest tree branches off and sucking at them for liquid. I sucked at the grass when I found some, hoping for a few drops of mountain dew. I even tried to wring out my socks to find just a taste of water. There is nothing quite so terrible as dying of thirst. Believe me. I've been there.

As the night wore on, I began to hear the occasional U.S. military aircraft above the mountains, usually flying high. And when I heard one in time, I was out there whirling my buzz-saw lights, transmitting the beacon as well as I could, still a walking distress signal. But no one heard me. It occurred to me that no one believed I was alive. And that was a very grim thought. It would be pretty hard to find me up here, even if the entire Bagram base was searching for me in these endless mountains. But if no one believed I was still breathing, well, that was probably the end for me. I experienced an inevitable feeling of utter desolation. Worse yet, I was so weakened, and in such pain, I realized, once and for all, I was never going to make it to the top of the mountain. Actually, I might have made it, but my left leg, blasted by that RPG, was never going to stand the climb. I would just have to keep going sideways, struggling across the steep face of the mountain, sometimes down, sometimes up, and hope to get my chance.

I was still losing blood, and I still could not speak. But I could hear, and I could hear my pursuers, sometimes calling to each other. I remember thinking this was very strange because they normally moved around in total silence. Remember those goatherds? I never heard that first one coming until he was about four feet from me. That's just the way they are, treading softly, lean, light men with no encumbrances—not even water.

When those Afghans travel, they carry their guns and ammunition and nothing else. One guy carries the water for everyone; another hauls the extra ammunition. And this leaves the main force free to move very fast, very softly. They are born trackers, able to pick up a trail across the roughest ground, and they can walk right up on you.

Of course, that assumes they are only after one of their own. Trying to follow a great 230-pound hulk like myself, slipping and sliding, crashing and breaking branches, causing minor avalanches on the loose ground—I must have been an Afghan tracker's dream. Even I realized my chance of actually losing them was close to zero.

Maybe those calls I heard among them were not really commands. Maybe they were outbursts of suppressed laughter at my truly horrible rock-climbing abilities. Wait until it gets light, I thought. This playing field would even out real quick. That's if they didn't shoot me first, in the dark.

I kept skirting around the mountain. Way below I could see the lights from a couple of lanterns, and I thought I could see the flickering flame of a fire. That must have been the valley floor, and it gave me my first guidance as to the terrain, but not much. In fact, it gave me the impression the ground where I was standing was flat, which it really was not. I stopped for a minute to see if there was anything else down in that valley, any further sign of my enemy, but I could still see just about nothing except for the lanterns and the fire, all of them about a mile down.

I gathered myself and took a step forward. And in that split second I realized I had stepped into the void. I just fell clean off that mountain, straight down, falling through the air, not over the ground. I hit the side of the mountain with a terrific bang, knocked the breath right out of me. Then I rolled, crashing through a copse of trees, trying to grab something to slow me down.

But I was moving too fast, and gathering speed. I fell helplessly down a steep bit, which leveled out for a few yards and allowed me to slow down. Finally I stopped on the edge of yet another precipice, which I sensed rather than saw. And I just lay there gasping for breath for a good twenty minutes, scared to death I'd find myself paralyzed.

But I wasn't. I could stand. I still had my rifle, although my strobe light had gone. And somehow I had to get back up to my highest point. The lower I was positioned down this mountain, the less my chance of getting rescued. I must go upward, and so I set off again.

I climbed, slipped, and scrambled for two more hours, until I thought I was more or less back to the point where I'd fallen off the mountain. It was 0200 now, and I'd been going for a long time, maybe six or seven hours. The pain was becoming diabolical, but in a way I was relieved I still had feeling in that left leg.

The Taliban army was still following me. I heard them, louder as I climbed higher, as if they'd been waiting for me. They were certainly a bigger force now than they had been two hours ago. I could hear them all around, more and more people searching for me, dogs barking, maybe a half mile back.

By now I could hear the river, which I knew was the same one I'd fallen in the previous afternoon. The same river on whose banks my three buddies lay dead. Thirsty as I was, I could not bring myself to go in search of its ice-cold flowing waters gushing down the mountainside. That was the only water on this earth I could not drink, water from the river which flowed right by the bodies of Mikey, Danny, and Axe. I had to find a different one.

With no compass, only my watch, I had to revert to navigation by the stars, which mercifully were now out, the thick high banks of clouds having passed over. I found the Big Dipper and followed the long curve of its stars all the way to the right angle at the end, where the shape angles upward, pointing directly at the polestar. That's the North Star. We learned it in BUD/S.

If I turned directly toward it and held out my left arm at a right angle, that way was west, the way I was headed. I think at this point I may have been suffering from hallucinations, that very odd sensation when you cannot really tell reality from a dream.

Like most SEALs, I'd experienced it before, at the back end of Hell Week. But right now I was becoming very light-headed. I was a hunted animal all alone in wild country, and I tried to pretend my buddies were still alive. I invented some kind of a formation with Danny climbing out on my right flank, Axe up to the left, and Mikey calling the shots in the rear.

I pretended they were there, I just couldn't see them. I think I was reaching the end of my tether. But I kept reminding myself of Hell Week. I kept telling myself this was just Hell Week all over again; I'd sucked it up then, and I could suck it up now. Whatever these bastards threw at me, I could take it. I'd come through. I might have been losing my marbles, but I was still a SEAL.

I could not, however, deny the fact I was also becoming disheartened. For the moment my pursuers were quiet, and I suddenly came upon a huge tree with a couple of big logs resting directly underneath it. I crawled under one of them and rested for a while, just lying there, feeling damned sorry for myself.

In my head I played over and over again one of the verses of Toby Keith's country and western classic "American Soldier." I remember lying there quietly singing the words to myself, the part that said I might have to die…"I'll bear that cross with honor."

I sang those words all night. I can't tell you how much they meant to me. I can tell you, it's little things like that, the words of a song, which can give you the strength to go on. Nonetheless, the fact was I had no idea what to do.

It occurred to me I could just settle in right here and make it my last stand. But I quickly dismissed this as a strategy. In my mind I was still committed to Axe's last request: "You stay alive, Marcus. And tell Cindy I love her." Helluva lot of good it would do Cindy Axelson if I ended up shot to pieces on the slopes of this godforsaken mountain. And who then would ever know what my buddies had done? And how hard and bravely they had fought? No. It was all up to me. I had to get out and tell our story.

I was comfortable and very, very tired, but thirst drove me on. Screw this, I decided, and I dragged myself up again and kept walking, hobbling, that is, making the most of this apparent expanse of flatter ground. It was just beginning to get light, around 0600. I knew that six hours from now, the sun would be in the south, but it was such a high sun out here, almost directly overhead, and it made navigation that much more difficult. I remember wondering where the hell I would be next time I saw the friendly polestar.

Almost immediately I found myself on a trail which was going my way. I could tell by the tight feel of the ground it was pretty well used, which meant I would have to move with immense care. Trails frequently traveled invariably lead to people, and before long I saw a house up ahead, maybe even three or four. At this distance it was hard to tell.

My first thought was of a tap or a well. If I had to, I'd get into one of these primitive residences and get rid of the occupants somehow. Then I could clean up my wounds and drink. But as I grew closer I could see there were four houses, very close together. To get their water I'd probably have to kill twenty people, and that was too much for me. I elected to keep going, praying I'd stumble upon a river or a mountain stream before much longer.

Well, I didn't. The sun was up, and it was growing hotter. I kept going for another four or five hours, and the hallucinations were getting worse. I kept wanting to ask Mikey what we should do. My mouth and throat had just about seized up. I could barely move my parched tongue, which was now firmly stuck to the roof of my mouth. I was afraid if I tried to move it, it would tear the skin off. I cannot describe the feeling. I had to get water.

Every bone in my body was crying out for rest, but I knew if I stopped, and perhaps slept, I would die. I had to keep going. It was strange, but the thirst which was killing me was also the driving force keeping me on this long, desperate march.

I recall thinking there was no water this high up, and I resolved to go back down to slightly lower slopes where hopefully a stream might come cascading out of the rocks, the way it does up here. Right then the sun was burning down on me, really hot, and way above me, the high peaks were still snowcapped. Something had to be melting, for Christ's sake. And all that water had to be going somewhere. I just had to find it.

Down in these lower areas, I found myself in the most beautiful green forest, so beautiful I wondered whether it might be a mirage. There were soft ferns, deep green grasses, and tall shady evergreens, a scene of verdant, lush mountain growth. Jesus Christ, there had to be water down here somewhere.

I paused often, listening intently for the sound of a running stream. But there was only silence, that shattering, merciless silence of the high country where no roads carve into the landscape, where no machines disrupt and pollute the air. Where there are no automobiles or tractors; no television, radio, or even electricity. Nothing. Just nature, the way it's been for thousands of years up here in this land of truly terrible beauty and ravenous hatred.

Don't get me wrong. The gradients were still very steep, and I was working my way through the forest, through the gutters of the mountain. Much of the time I was just crawling, hands and knees, trying to ease the pain in my left leg. To be honest, I really thought I might be finished now. I was full of despair, wondering if I might black out, begging my God to help me.

Yea, though I walk through the valley of the shadow of death,
I will fear no evil: For Thou art with me; Thy rod and Thy
staff they comfort me...

That's the Twenty-third Psalm, of course. We think of it as the Psalm of the SEALs. It is repeated at all of our religious services, all funerals. Too many funerals. I know it by heart. And I clung to its message, that even in death I would not be abandoned.

Thou preparest a table before me in the presence of mine enemies:
Thou anointest my head with oil; my cup runneth over.
Surely goodness and mercy shall follow me all the days of my life:
and I will dwell in the house of the Lord for ever.

It was all I had, just a plaintive cry to a God Who was with me, but Whose ways were becoming unclear to me. I had been saved from more or less certain death, and I was still armed with my rifle. But I did not know what to do anymore, except keep trying.

I left the trail and once more went upward, heading for high ground again. I was listening, straining to hear the sound of the water I knew must be here somewhere. I was on a steep escarpment, hanging on to a tree with my right hand, leaning out away from the cliff face. Would I ever hear the tumbling sound of a mountain stream, or was I really destined to die of thirst up here where no American would ever find me?

I kept repeating the Twenty-third Psalm in my head, over and over, trying to stop myself from breaking down. I was scared, freezing cold, without shelter or proper clothes, and I just kept saying it...

The Lord is my shepherd; I shall not want.
He maketh me to lie down in green pastures: He leadeth me
beside the still waters.
He restoreth my soul: He leadeth me in the paths of righteousness
for His name's sake...

That's how far I was in the prayer when I heard the water for the first time. I could not believe it. There it was, unmistakable, way below me, a brook, maybe even a small waterfall. In this pure mountain air, amid this awesome silence, that was swiftly flowing water. I had to find a way down to it.

I guess I knew in that moment, I was not going to die of thirst, whatever else befell me. It was just one of those moments that make your life spin right out in front of you. I thought of home, and my mom and my dad, and my brothers and friends. Did any of them know about me? And what had happened? Maybe they thought I was dead. Maybe someone had told them I was dead. And in those fleeting seconds I was overwhelmed by the sadness, the heartbreaking, crushing sadness of what this would mean to my mom, the lady who always told me I was Mama's angel.

What I did not know at the time but learned later was that *everyone* thought I was dead. Back home it was now some time in the small hours of Wednesday morning, June 29, and several hours previously a television station had announced that a four-man SEAL reconnaissance team that was on a mission in the northeast mountains of Afghanistan had all been killed in action. My name was among the four.

The station, like the rest of the world's media, had also announced the loss of the MH-47 helicopter with everyone on board, eight SEALs and eight members of the 160th SOAR Night Stalkers. Which made twenty special forces dead, the worst special ops catastrophe ever. My mom collapsed.

By the middle part of that Tuesday evening, people had begun to arrive at the ranch, local people, our friends, people who wanted to be with my mom and dad, just in case there was anything they could do to help. They arrived in trucks, cars, SUVs, and on motorbikes, a steady stream of families who all said damn near the same thing: *We just want to be with you.*

Outside the door of the main house, the front yard was like a parking lot. By midnight there were seventy-five people in attendance, including Eric and Aaron Rooney, from the family that owns one of the big East Texas construction corporations; David and Michael Thornberry, local land, cattle, and oil people, with their father, Jonathon; Slim, Kevin, Kyle, and Wade Albright, my boyhood friends, a lot of them Aggies.

There was Joe Lord; Andy Magee; Cheeser; Big Roon; my brother Opie and our buddy Sean; Tray Baker; Larry Firmin; Richard Tanner; Benny Wiley; the strength coach at Texas Tech in Lubbock. Those big tough guys were all in grade school with me.

Another of our local construction moguls, Scott Whitehead, showed up. He never even knew us, but he wanted to be there. He turned out to be a tower of strength for my mom, still calls her every day. Master Sergeant Daniel, highly decorated U.S. Army, showed up in full uniform, knocked on the front door, and told my dad he wanted to help in any way he could. He still shows up nearly every day, just to make sure Mom's okay.

And of course there was my twin brother, Morgan, making all speed to the ranch, refusing point-blank to accept the broadcaster's "fact" that I was dead. My other brother Scottie got there first, but not being an identical twin brother to me, he could only know what he was told, not what the telepathic wavelengths told him. He was almost as devastated as Mom.

My dad hit the Internet to check if there was further news or any official announcement from the SEAL HQ in Hawaii, my home base. All he found was confirmation of the MH-47 crash and four other SEALs missing in action. However, one of the Hawaiian newspapers was reporting the death of all four of us. At which moment I guess he believed it was true.

Shortly after 2:00 a.m. in Texas, the SEALs began to arrive at the ranch from Coronado. Lieutenant John Jones (JJ) in company with Chief Chris Gothro flew in, with Bosun's Mate Teg Gill, one of the strongest men I know. Lieutenant David Duffield arrived from Coronado right afterward, with John Owens and Jeremy Franklin. Lieutenant Josh Wynn and Lieutenant Nathan Shoemaker came in from Virginia Beach. Gunner's Mate First Class Justin Pitman made the journey from Florida. I should stress that none of this was planned or orchestrated. They just came, strangers mingling with friends, united, I suppose, in grief for a lost brother.

And there to greet them all with my mom and dad was the mighty figure of Billy Shelton. No one had ever seen him in tears before. It's often that way with the toughest of men.

Chief Gothro immediately told my parents he did not give a damn what the media said. There was no confirmation that any of the original four-man SEAL team was dead, although it was highly likely they had not all survived. He knew about Mikey's last call: *My guys are dying out here.* But there was no certainty about any of it. He told Mom to have faith, told her no SEAL was dead until there was a body.

And then Morgan arrived and told them all straight-out I was alive, and that was an end to it. He said he'd been in contact with me, had felt my presence. He thought I may have been injured, but I was not dead. "Goddamn it, I know he's not dead," he said. "If he was, I'd know."

By now there were 150 people in the front yard, and the local sheriffs had somehow cordoned off the entire ranch. No one could enter the property without passing through these guardians. There were police cruisers parked along the wide dirt road which leads to the house. Some of the officers were inside the perimeter fences, praying, at short services conducted by two naval chaplains who had arrived from Coronado in the small hours. Just in case, I guess.

Some time before 0500 my mom answered the front door to see SEAL lieutenant Andy Haffele, with his wife, Kristina, standing there. "We wanted to help, any way we could," said Andy. "We just got here from Hawaii."

"Hawaii!" said Mom. "That's halfway around the world."

"Marcus once saved my life," said Andy. "I had to be here. I know there's still hope."

I can't explain what all this meant to Mom. She hovered somewhere between hope and total despair. But she's always said she'll never forget Andy and the long journey he and Kristina made to be with our family.

It began, I suppose, just as neighborly visits, interspersed with more professional arrivals from SPECWARCOM. But it would turn into a vigil. No one went home, they just stayed, day after day, night after night, all night, praying to God that I was still alive.

When I think about it, these many months later, I'm kind of overwhelmed: that much love, that much caring, that much kindness to my parents. And I think about it, all of it, every day, and I still have no idea how to express my gratitude, except to say I know the door of our home is open to each and every one of them, no matter the hour or the circumstance, for all the days of my life.

Meantime, back up the goddamned mountain, unaware of the mighty gathering still building at home, I was listening to the distant flow of water. Hanging on to the tree, leaning out, wondering how to get down there without killing myself in the process. That's when the Taliban sniper shot me.

I felt the sting of the bullet ripping into the flesh high up at the back of my left thigh. Christ, that hurt. Really hurt. And the impact of the AK bullet spun me around, knocked me into a complete backflip clean off the fucking mountain. When I hit, I hit hard, but facedown, which I guess didn't do my busted nose a lot of good and opened up the gash on my forehead.

Then I started rolling, sliding very fast down the steep gradient, unable to get a grip, which may have been just as well. Because these Taliban bastards really opened up on me. There were bullets flying everywhere, pinging and zinging into the ground all around me, ricocheting off the rocks, slamming into the tree trunks. Jesus Christ, this was Murphy's Ridge all over again.

But it's a lot harder to hit a moving target than you might think, especially one traveling as quick as I was, out of control, racing between rocks and trees. And they kept missing. Finally I came to a stop in a flatter area, and of course my pursuers had not made the downward journey nearly as fast as I had. I had had a decent start on them, and to my amazement I had come to little harm. I guess I missed all the obstacles, and the earth beneath me was softish and loose packed. Also, I still had my rifle, which to my mind was a bigger miracle than Our Lady of Lourdes.

I began to crawl, going for cover behind a tree and trying to assess the enemy positions. I could see one guy, the nearest of them, just standing and pointing at me, yelling at two others, who were out to the right. Before I could make any kind of a decision, they both opened fire on me again. I did not have much of a shot at them, because they were still maybe a hundred yards up the cliff face and the trees were shielding them.

Trouble was, I could not stand properly, and aiming the rifle was a problem, so I decided to make a break for it, on my hands and knees, and wait for a better spot to take them out. I crawled, not fast but steady, over terrible terrain, full of little hills and dipping gullies. It could hardly have been better country for a fugitive, which I now was, except I could not walk down the gullies, and I sure as hell couldn't get down those steep slopes on all fours, not having been born a freakin' snow leopard.

So every time I reached one of those small precipices, I just threw myself straight off and hoped for a reasonable landing. I did a lot of rolling, and it was a long, bumpy, and painful ride. But it beat the hell out of getting shot up the ass again.

I kept it up for about forty-five minutes, crawling, rolling, and falling, staying out in front of my pursuers, gaining ground on the downward falls, losing it again as they ran up on me. And nowhere on that snaking route down the hills did I find a decent spot to get rid of the gunmen who were hunting me down. The bullets kept flying, and I kept moving. But finally I hit some flatter ground and all around me were big rocks. I decided this would be Marcus's last stand. Or theirs. One way or another. Although I did not know exactly how many of them there were.

I remember thinking, *Now, how the hell would Morgan get out of this? What would he do?* And it gave me strength, the massive strength of my seven-minutes-older brother. I decided that in this position, he'd wait till he saw the whites of their eyes. No mistakes. So I crawled behind this big rock, checked my magazine, then flipped off the safety catch of my Mark 12. And waited.

I heard them coming but not until they were very, very close. They were not together, which was unnerving, because I could not account for them all. But I could see the spotter now, the guy who was literally tracking me down, not trying to shoot me; he didn't even carry a rifle. His job was to locate me and then call the others to bring fire down on me. Cheeky little prick.

But it's the Afghan way. This Sharmak was an excellent delegator. One guy carries the water, another the extra ammunition, and the marksmen don't have to spend their time searching the terrain. They have a specialist to do this.

This particular specialist was not having much trouble tracking me, probably because I was leaving tracks like a wounded grizzly, scuffing up the ground and bleeding like a stuck pig from both my forehead and my thigh all over the shale.

I moved carefully on my knees around the rock, now with my rifle raised, and there was the Taliban spotter standing right in front of me, not ten feet away—but he had not spotted me.

In that instant I fired, dropped him dead in his tracks. And the force of the bullet knocked him backward, with blood pumping out of his chest. I think I got him straight through the heart, and I heard him hit the deck. But simultaneously right behind me I heard the soft footsteps of the chasing gunmen. I turned around and there were two of them, just above me in the rocks. Searching. I had only split seconds to work, because they were both on me, AKs raised. Fuck! I could get one, but not both.

I went for one of my grenades, ripped out the pin, and threw it straight at them. I think they got a couple of shots away but not in time to get me before I plunged back behind the rock. This was up close and personal, not five feet between us. I was just imploring the Lord to let my grenade explode, and it did, blasting the two Afghans to smithereens, splitting rocks, sending up a sandstorm of earth and sand. Me? I just kept my head well down and hoped to Christ there were no more of them.

It was around this time I began to black out a little, not from the blast of the grenade, just a general blacking-out situation. Everything was catching up with me, and as I lay there waiting for the debris to stop falling out of the sky, I started to feel pretty rotten, dizzy, unsure of myself, shaky. I think I hung around down there behind the rock for a few minutes before I ventured out, still crawling, trying to see if the other Taliban guys were following. But there was nothing.

Obviously, I had to get away from here, because that explosion from the grenade must have attracted some attention somewhere. I sat there for a few more minutes, marveling at the silence, and pondered the world. And the conclusion I reached was I needed to learn to fight all over again, not like a Navy SEAL, but like a secretive Afghan mountain man. At least, if I planned to stay alive.

The last hour had taught me a few major lessons, the main one being I must gain the ability to fight alone, in direct contrast to everything I had ever been taught. SEALs, as you now know, fight in teams, only in teams, each man relying entirely on the others to do exactly the right thing. That's how we do it, fighting as one in a team of four or maybe ten or even twenty, but always as one unit, one mind, one strategy. We are, instinctively, always backing up, always covering, always moving to plug the gap or pave the way. That's what makes us great.

But up here, being hunted down, all alone—this was entirely another game. And first I had to learn to move like an Afghan mountain man, stealthily, staying out of sight, making no sound, causing no disturbance. Of course, we had learned all that back in California, but not on the heightened scale which was required up here, against a native enemy even more stealthy, quiet, and unseen than we are.

Crawling around on all fours was not going to help. I had to concentrate, work myself into the correct military position before I pounced on my prey. I had to conserve ammunition, make certain I was going to kill before I carried out the deed, and above all try to stay out of sight and not betray myself by lumbering around like the wounded grizzly I was.

I resolved that when I next had to strike out against my enemy, it would be with our customary deadly force, always ensuring I held the element of surprise. Those are the tactics that invariably win conflicts for the truly ruthless underdog like the mujahideen, al Qaeda, and, from now on, me.

I dragged myself back up onto my hands and knees. I listened carefully, like an eager hound dog, turning my head sideways to the wind. Nothing. Not a sound. Maybe they'd given up or perhaps they considered I was probably dead. Either way I was out of there.

With my rifle jammed in my belt I began moving west, toward the water. It was still way below me, and since I was trying to avoid falling down this freakin' mountain again, I would zigzag my way down the steep slopes until I found it.

I've long lost count of the distance, but it felt like three or four miles, crawling along, resting, praying, hoping, trying my best, just like Hell Week. I think I did black out two or three times. But finally I heard the waterfall. I heard it hissing in the afternoon sun, tumbling off a high rock and into a deep pool before running down to the lower levels of the stream.

Somehow I arrived right on the top of that waterfall, maybe twenty feet above the flow. It really was beautiful, the sun glinting on the surface and all around it the trees on the mountain, high above the valley, on the edge of which was an Afghan village, way, way below me, maybe a mile.

For the first time for as long as I could remember, no one was trying to hunt me down. I could hear nothing, I could see no one, everything seemed tranquil. I'd plainly taken out the scouting party, because if there'd been anyone sneaking along behind me, I'd have heard it, believe me. I might not yet move like a tribesman, but I had developed the hearing of one.

I'd been without water for so long, I figured another half a minute would not make much difference, and so I pulled out my rifle scope to take a look down at the village from this excellent vantage point. I forced myself up, hanging on to a rock with my left hand, right above the water.

The view from there was outstanding, and I could see the village, its upper houses clinging to the mountain, built right into the rock face by guys who were obviously craftsmen. It was like something out of a child's picture book, like the home of the wicked witch or something, gingerbread houses on a big rock-candy mountain.

I put the scope away, and, not daring to look at the state of my left leg, I took a step forward, trying to find a spot where I could begin to slide down on my backside to the waiting ice-cold pool below me. That's when that left leg finally gave way. Perhaps it was the newly shot part, or maybe the blown-up parts, or just the tendons which could take no more strain. But that leg buckled and flung me forward, really badly.

I twisted and fell headlong downward, sliding over loose, smooth ground, shale and sand, gaining speed rapidly, tumbling over, feet in the air, sometimes digging the toes of my boots in, fighting for a foothold, any hold would be fine. I rocketed straight past that lower pool and kept right on going. I can't even imagine the speed I was going, but I could see it was a hell of a long way to the bottom, and I could not stop.

Up ahead of me was a sapling, and I lunged at it as I shot headlong past, trying to get a hold of anything to slow me down. My fingers closed on its thin, whippy trunk and I tried to pull myself up, but I was just going too fast, and it flipped me right over and landed me on my back. For a fleeting moment, I thought I was dead.

Didn't make much difference whether I was dead or alive, my battered body just kept going for almost a thousand feet, then the mountain kind of swerved and I went with it, tumbling and sliding for another five hundred feet to what was more or less the bottom of that escarpment. I landed in a heap, feeling like I'd broken every bone in my body. I was out of breath, blood was trickling down my face from the cut on my forehead, and I generally felt just about as sorry for myself as it's possible to be.

You're probably not going to believe this, but my rifle was again right beside me, and once more it was the thirst that saved me. Instead of just lying there, a bloodstained heap in the hot afternoon sun, I thought of that water, now right above me. At least it had been when I'd flashed past it a few moments ago.

I knew I had to climb back up there or die. So I grabbed my rifle and began the long crawl to the drink that should restore my life. I scrambled and slipped over the loose ground, and I am certain by now you have comprehended what a truly horrible mountaineer I am. I can only plead the gradient. It was unbelievably steep, not quite sheer but almost. A great rock climber would probably have taken full gear in order to scale it.

Personally I'm not sure which I was worse at, going up or falling down. But it was two hundred feet to that water. It took me two more hours. I blacked out twice, and when I reached it, I plunged my head in, just to free up my tongue and throat. Then I washed my burning face, cleaned the gash just below my hairline, and tried to get the blood to wash off the back of my leg. I couldn't tell whether the sniper's bullet was still lodged in there or not.

All I knew was I needed to drink a lot of water and then try to attract attention and get to a hospital. Otherwise I did not think I would survive. I decided to move up a few yards to where the water was lapping off a rock and splashing into a small pool. I lowered my head and drank. It was the sweetest water I had ever tasted.

And I was just getting into this real luxury when I noticed there were three guys standing right above me, two of them with AKs. For a moment I thought I was hallucinating. I stopped drinking. And I remember I was talking to myself, just mumbling really, flicking between reality and dream.

Then I realized one of them was yelling at me, shouting something I was supposed to understand, but in my befuddled state I just couldn't get it. I was like a badly wounded animal, ready to fight to the end. I understood nothing, not the hand of friendship, not the possibility of human decency. The only sensation I could react to was threat. And everything was a threat. Cornered. Scared. Suddenly afraid of dying. Ready to lash out at anything. That was me.

The only thought I had was *I'll kill these guys...just give me my chance.* I rolled away from the pool and held my rifle in my get-ready position. Then I began to crawl away over the rocks, braced all the time for a volley of AK bullets to rip into me and finally finish me off.

But I "reasoned" I had no choice. I would have to risk getting killed by these guys before I could hit back. Dimly I recall that first character was still yelling his head off, literally screaming at me. Whatever the hell he was saying seemed irrelevant. But he sounded like the outraged father of one of the many Afghani tribesmen who'd been removed from the battlefield by the men seconded to SEAL Team 10. Probably by me.

As I made my way, slowly, painfully, almost blindly to the bigger rocks up ahead, it did cross my mind that if these guys really wanted to shoot me they could have done it by now. In fact, they could have done it any time they wanted. But the Taliban had been hunting me down for too long. All I wanted was cover and a fair position from which to strike back.

I flicked off the safety catch on my rifle and kept crawling, straight into a dead end surrounded by huge boulders on all sides. This was it. Marcus's last stand. And, slowly, I half rolled, half turned around to face my enemy once again. The problem was, right here my enemy had kind of fanned out. The three guys somehow had gotten above me and yet surrounded me, one to the left, one to the right, and one dead ahead. Christ, I thought. I've only one hand grenade left. This is trouble. Big trouble.

Then I noticed there was even bigger trouble out in the clearing. There were three more guys moving up on me, all armed with AKs slung over their backs. And they too fanned out and somehow climbed higher, but they positioned themselves behind me. No one fired. I raised my rifle and drew down on the one who was doing the screaming. I tried to draw a bead on him, but he just moved swiftly behind a huge tree, which meant I was aiming at nothing.

I swung around and tried to locate the others, but the blood from my forehead was still trickling down my face, obscuring my vision. My leg was turning the shale beneath me to a dark red. I no longer knew what the hell was happening except that I was in some kind of a fight, which I was very obviously about to lose. The second three guys were moving down the rocks in rear of me, quickly, easily, right on top of me.

The guy behind the tree was now back out in the open and still yelling at me, standing there with his rifle lowered, I guessed demanding my surrender. But I couldn't even do that. I just knew that I desperately needed help or I was going to bleed to death. Then I did what I never thought I would do in the whole of my career. I lowered my rifle. Defeated. My whole world was spinning out of control in more ways than one. I was fighting to avoid blacking out again.

I just lay there in the dirt, blood seeping out, still clutching my rifle, still, in a sense, defiant, but unable to fight. I had no more strength, I was on the edge of consciousness, and I was struggling to understand what the screaming tribesman was trying to communicate.

"American! Okay! Okay!"

Finally I got it. These guys meant me no harm. They'd just stumbled on to me. They weren't chasing me and had no intention of killing me. It was a situation I was relatively unused to this past couple of days. But the vision of yesterday's goatherds was still stark in my mind.

"Taliban?" I asked. "You Taliban?"

"No Taliban!" shouted the man who I assumed was the leader. And he ran the edge of his hand across his throat, saying once more, *"No Taliban!"*

From where I was lying, this looked like a signal that meant "Death to the Taliban." Certainly he was not indicating that he was one of them or even liked them. I tried to remember whether the goatherds had said, "No Taliban." And I was nearly certain they had not. This was plainly different.

But I was still confused and dizzy, uncertain, and I kept on asking, "Taliban? Taliban?"

"No! No! No Taliban!"

I guess if I'd been at my peak, I'd have accepted this several minutes ago, before Marcus's Last Stand and all that. But I was losing it now. I saw the leader walk up to me. He smiled and said his name was Sarawa. He was the village doctor, he somehow communicated in rough English. He was thirtyish, bearded, tall for an Afghan, with an intellectual's high forehead. I recall thinking he didn't look much like a doctor to me, not wandering around on the edge of this mountain like a native tracker.

But there was something about him. He didn't look like a member of al Qaeda either. By now I'd seen a whole lot of Taliban warriors, and he looked nothing like any of them. There was no arrogance, no hatred in his eyes. If he hadn't been dressed like a leading man from *Murder up the Khyber Pass,* he could have been an American college professor on his way to a peace rally.

He lifted up his loose white shirt to show me he had no concealed gun or knife. Then he spread his arms wide in front of him, I guess the international sign for "I am here in friendship."

I had no choice but to trust him. "I need help," I said, uttering a phrase which must have shed an especially glaring light on the obvious. "Hospital—water."

"Hah?" said Sarawa.

"Water," I repeated. "I must have water."

"Hah?" said Sarawa.

"Water," I yelled, pointing back toward the pool.

"Ah!" he exclaimed. *"Hydrate!"*

I could not help laughing, weakly. Hydrate! Who the hell was this crazy-assed tribesman who knew only long words?

He called over a kid who had a bottle. I think he went and filled it with fresh water from the stream. He brought it back to me and I kept chugging away, glugging down the water, two good-sized bottles of it.

"Hydrate," said Sarawa.

"You got that right, pal," I confirmed.

At which point we began to converse in that no-man's-land of language, the one where no one knows hardly a word of the other's native tongue.

"I've been shot," I told him and showed him my wound, which had never really stopped bleeding.

He examined it and nodded sternly, as if he understood the clear truth that I badly needed medical attention. Heaven knows how severely my left leg would be infected. All the dirt, mud, and shale I'd inflicted on it couldn't have done it much good.

I told him I was a doctor too, thinking it might help somehow. I knew there would likely be savage retribution for a non-Taliban village sheltering an American fugitive, and I was praying they would not just leave me here.

I wished to hell I still had some of my medical gear with me, but that was lost a lifetime ago on the mountain with Mikey, Axe, and Danny. Anyway, Sarawa seemed to believe I was a doctor, although he seemed equally certain he knew where I'd come from. With a succession of signals and a very few words, he conveyed to me he knew all about the firefight on the mountain. And he kept pointing directly at me, as if to confirm he absolutely knew I had been one of the combatants.

The tribal bush telegraph up here must be fantastic. They have no means of fast communications, no phones, cars, nothing. Just one another, goatherds wandering the mountainside, passing on the necessary information. And here was this Sarawa, who had presumably been miles away from the action, informing me about the battle which I had helped fight the previous day.

He patted me reassuringly on the shoulder and then retreated into a kind of conference with his fellow villagers while I talked to the kid.

He had only one question, and he had a lot of trouble asking it, trying to make an American understand. In the end I got his drift: *Were you really the lunatic who fell down the mountain? Very far. Very fast. Very funny. All my village saw you do it. Very big joke. Ha! Ha! Ha!*

Jesus Christ! I mean, Muhammad! Or Allah! Whoever's in charge around here. This kid really was from a gingerbread village.

Sarawa returned. They gave me some more water. And again he checked over my wound. Didn't look one bit happy. But there were more important things to discuss than the state of my backside.

I did not, of course, realize this. But the decision Sarawa and his friends were making carried huge responsibilities and, possibly, momentous consequences: They had to decide whether to take me in. Whether to help me, shelter me, and feed me. Most important, whether to defend me.

These people were Pashtuns. And the majority of the warriors who fought under the banner of the former rulers of Afghanistan, plus a vast number of bin Laden's al Qaeda fighters, were members of this strict and ancient tribe, almost thirteen million of whom live right here in Afghanistan.

That steel core of the Taliban sect, that iron resolve and deadly hatred of the infidel, is unwaveringly Pashtun. The backbone of that vicious little tribal army is Pashtun. The Taliban moves around these mountains only by the unspoken approval and tacit permission of the Pashtuns, who grant them food and shelter. The two communities, the warriors and the general mountain populace, are irrevocably bound together. The mujahideen fighting the Russians were principally Pashtun.

Never mind "No Taliban." I knew the background. These guys might be peace-loving villagers on the surface, but the tribal blood ties were wrought in iron. Faced with an angry Taliban army demanding the head of an armed American serviceman, you would essentially not give a secondhand billy goat for the American's chances.

And yet there was something I did not know. We're talking *lokhay warkawal*—an unbending section of historic *Pashtunwalai* tribal law as laid out in the hospitality section. The literal translation of *lokhay warkawal* is "giving of a pot."

I did mention this briefly when I outlined the Pashtun tribal background much earlier. But this is the part where it really counts. This is where the ole *lokhay warkawal* gets shoved into context. Right here, while I'm lying on the ground bleeding to death, and the tribesmen are discussing my fate.

To an American, especially one in such terrible shape as I was, the concept of helping out a wounded, possibly dying man is pretty routine. You do what you can. For these guys, the concept carried many onerous responsibilities. *Lokhay* means not only providing care and shelter, it means an unbreakable commitment to defend that wounded man to the death. And not just the death of the principal tribesman or family who made the original commitment for the giving of a pot. It means the whole damned village.

Lokhay means the population of that village will fight to the last man, honor-bound to protect the individual they have invited in to share their hospitality. And this is not something to have a chitchat about when things get rough. It's not a point of renegotiation. This is strictly nonnegotiable.

So while I was lying there thinking these cruel heartless bastards were just going to leave me out here and let me die, they were in fact discussing a much bigger, life-or-death issue. And the lives they were concerned with had nothing to do with mine. This was *Lokhay*, boy, spelled with a big *L*. No bullshit.

For all I knew, they were deciding whether to put a bullet through my head and save everyone a lot of trouble. But by now I was drifting off, half asleep, half alert, and the distinction was minimal. Sarawa was still talking. Of course it occurred to me that these men might be just like the goatherds, loyal spies for the Taliban. They could easily take me in and then send their fastest messengers to inform the local commanders they had me, and I could be picked up and executed anytime they wanted.

I wished fervently this was not the case. And though I thought I understood Sarawa was a nice guy, I couldn't know the truth about him; no one could, not under those circumstances. Anyway, there was nothing much I could do about it, except maybe shoot them all, and a fat chance I would have had of getting away. I could hardly move.

So I just waited for the verdict. I kept thinking, *What would Morgan do? Is there any way out of this? What's the correct military decision? Do I have any options?* Not so you'd notice. My best chance of living was to try and befriend Sarawa, try somehow to ingratiate myself with his friends.

Disjointed thoughts were blundering through my mind. What about all the death there had been in these mountains? What if these guys had lost sons, brothers, fathers, or cousins in the battle against the SEALs? How would they feel about me, an armed, uniformed member of the U.S. military, staging various gun battles, blowing Afghanis up on their very own tribal lands?

I obviously didn't have any answers, nor could I know what they were thinking. But it couldn't be good. I knew that.

Sarawa came back. He sharply ordered two men to raise me up, one of them under each of my arms to give me support, and lift me off the ground. He ordered another to lift my legs.

As they approached me, I took out my last grenade and carefully pulled the pin, which placed that little bastard right in firing mode. I held it in one hand, clasped across my chest. The tribesmen did not seem to notice. All I knew was, if they tried to execute me or tie me up or invite their murderous Taliban colleagues in, I would drop that thing right on the floor and take the whole fucking lot of them with me.

They lifted me up. And slowly we began to head down to the village. I did not understand, not then, but this was the biggest break I'd had since the Battle for Murphy's Ridge first started. These friendly Pashtun tribesmen had decided to grant me *lokhay*. They were committed to defend me against the Taliban until there was no one left alive.

10

An American Fugitive Cornered by the Taliban

Then I found a piece of flinty rock on the floor of the cave, and, lying painfully on my left side, I spent two hours carving the words of the Count of Monte Cristo onto the wall of my prison: *God will give me justice.*

Sarawa and his friends did not attempt to take away my rifle. Yet. I carried it with me in one hand while they slowly lifted me down the steep track to the village of Sabray, a distance of around two hundred yards and home to perhaps three hundred households. In my other hand I clutched my last grenade, no pin, ready to take us all to eternity. It was a little after 1600, and the sun was still high.

We passed a couple of local groups, and both of them reacted with obvious astonishment at the sight of an armed, wounded American holding his rifle but being given help. They stopped and they stared, and both times I locked eyes with one of them. Each time he stared back, that hard glare of pure hatred with which I was so familiar. It was always the same, a gaze of undisguised loathing for the infidel.

They were, of course, confused. Which was not altogether surprising. Hell, I was confused. Why was Sarawa helping me? The worrying part was Sarawa seemed to be swimming against the tide. This was a village full of Islamic fanatics who wanted only to see dead Americans. Up here in these lawless mountains, the plan to smash New York's Twin Towers had been born.

At least, those were my thoughts. But I underestimated the essential human decency of the senior members of this Pashtun tribe. Sarawa and many others were good guys who wished me no harm, and neither would they permit anyone else to do me harm. Nor would they kowtow to the bloodlust of some of their fellow mountain men. They wanted only to help me. I would grow to understand that.

The hostile, wary looks of the goatherds on the trail were typical, but they did not reflect the views of the majority. We continued on down to the top house in Sabray. I say *top house* because the houses were set one above the other right into the almost sheer face of the mountain. I mean, you could step off the trail and walk straight onto the flat roof of a house.

You had to descend farther to reach the front door. Once inside, you were more or less underground in a kind of man-made cave of mud and rocks with a plain dirt floor, obviously built by craftsmen. There were rock stairs going down to another level, where there was another room. This, however, was an area best avoided, since the villagers were likely to keep goats in there. And where there are goats, there is goat dung. All over the place. The smell is fiendish, and it pervades the entire dwelling.

We arrived outside this house, and I tried to let them know I was still dying of thirst. I remember Sarawa handed me a garden hose with a great flourish, as if it had been a crystal goblet, and turned on a tap somewhere. I replaced the pin in my hand grenade, a process deeply frowned upon by the U.S. military, and stuck it safely in the battle harness I still wore.

Now I had two free hands again, and the water was very cold and tasted fabulous. Then they produced a cot from the house and set it up for me, four of them raising me up and lowering me carefully onto it under the supervision of Sarawa.

Above me I could see U.S. warplanes screaming through the high mountain sky. Everyone except me was pointing up at them. I just stared kind of wistfully, wondering when the hell they would come for me.

By now the entire population of Sabray was surrounding my cot, watching as Sarawa went to work. He carefully cleaned the wounds to my leg, confirming what I had suspected, that there was no bullet lodged in my left thigh. Indeed, he located the bullet's exit hole. Christ! I'd been bleeding from both places. No wonder I didn't have much blood left.

Then he took out a small surgical instrument and began pulling the metal shrapnel out of my leg. He spent a long time getting rid of every shard from that RPG he could find. That, by the way, hurt like hell. But he kept going. And then he cleaned it all again, thoroughly, applied antiseptic cream, and bound me up.

I just lay there, totally exhausted. Pretty soon, I guess around six o'clock, they came back and moved me inside, four of them carrying the cot. They gave me clean clothes, which was the best thing since my first drink of water. They were soft Afghan garments, a loose shirt and those baggy pants, unbelievably comfortable. I felt damn near human. Actually, they gave me two sets of clothes, identical, white for daytime, black for night.

The only hitch came as I changed from my battered U.S.

battle dress, really only my cammy top, into the tribal garments. My shoulder still ached like the devil, and they had to give me a hand. And when they saw the somewhat extravagant tattoo I have on my back—a half of a SEAL Trident (Morgan has the other half)—they damn near fainted.

They thought it was some kind of warlike tribal emblem, which I suppose it was. And then they thought I might be the devil incarnate, and I had to keep telling them I was a doctor, anything to stop them believing I was a special warrior from the U.S. Armed Forces, a man who sported a symbol of a powerful voodoo on his back, which was surely evil and would definitely, one day, wipe them all out. Happily, I managed to win that argument, but they were real pleased that I now had my shirt on, and they pulled down my sleeve to cover my upper arm, where a part of the design was visible.

By the time they began to leave, they were smiling, and I had become, for the rest of my stay in the village and I suppose far beyond, Dr. Marcus.

My final request was to be taken out to the communal head for a pee, and they took me but made me adopt the traditional Afghan body position for this operation. I remember falling over backward, which made them all laugh helplessly.

However, they carried me back safely to my cot, still giggling, and I suddenly realized with horror they had removed my rifle. I demanded to know where it was, and the tribesmen tried hard to explain they needed to take it away, *lokhay* or no *lokhay,* because if the Taliban ever did get into this room, they would not believe I was a wounded doctor, not with a sniper rifle like that. *Lokhay* or no *lokhay.*

At that stage I did not understand them, and anyhow there was little I could do about it. So I just cast it from my mind. And

I lay there in the fading light when they finally left me entirely alone.

I had had water and I'd eaten some of that flat bread they bake in the East. They had offered me a dish full of warm goat's milk into which I was supposed to dip it. But the combination was without doubt the worst-tasting sensation I'd ever had. I damn near threw up, and I asked them to take the milk away, telling them it was against my religion! I thus tackled that hard, awful bread bone dry. But I was grateful, and I tried to make that clear. Hell, I could have been dead up the mountain. But for them, I would have been.

And now once again I was alone. I stared around me, looking for the first time at my surroundings. A thick, loose-woven Afghan carpet covered the floor, and colored cushions were placed against the wall. There were carved hanging ornaments but no pictures. There was glass in the windows, and below this house I could see others had thatched roofs. They were definitely skilled builders up here, but I was uncertain where the raw materials came from, the rocks, glass, and straw.

Inside my room there was one very large, locked wooden box. In there, I learned, were the most valued possessions of every member of the household. And there was not much. Trust me on that. But what they had they seemed prepared to share with me.

I'd been given a couple of blankets, and as the night drew in, I discovered why. The temperature plummeted from the searing heat of the day straight into the thirties.

I noticed there was also an old iron woodstove in one corner of the room, where I later learned they baked bread every day. The system up here is for the two main houses, like this one, to do the baking for everyone, and the bread is then distributed. I lay there wondering where all the smoke went when they lit the stove, since there was no chimney. But that was a discovery yet to come. Answer: nowhere. That wood smoke stayed right in my bedroom.

I drifted into a half sleep, my wounds still throbbing but thankfully not becoming infected. *Hooyah*, Sarawa! Right?

The door to my new residence was quite thick but ill fitting. It would keep out the wind and the rain, but the guys had to give it a mighty shove to open it. I'd already noticed that, and I knew no one could enter the room without waking me, so I had no need to sleep on high alert.

What happened next, however, took me by surprise. The door gave way to a kick that shattered the silence. I opened my eyes in time to see eight armed Taliban fighters come barging into the room. The first one came straight over to my cot and slapped me across the face with all his force. That really pissed me off, and he was a very lucky boy that I could not move and was effectively a prisoner. If he'd even thought about putting his hands on me when I was fit, I'd have ripped his fucking head off. Little prick.

I knew they were Taliban because of their appearance, very clean cut, manicured beards, clean teeth, hands, and clothes. They were well fed and could speak broken English. None of them was very big, maybe around five feet eight on average, and they all wore those old Soviet leather belts, the ones with the red star in the middle of the buckle. They wore Afghan clothes, but each one had a different-colored vest. Every man carried a knife and a Russian pistol jammed into his belt. Everything made in Moscow. Everything stolen.

There was nothing I could get my hands on to defend myself. I had no rifle, no grenade, just my own personal badge of courage, the Lone Star of Texas on my arm and chest. I needed some of that courage because these bastards laid into me, kicking my left leg and punching my face and upper body, beating me to hell.

I didn't give that much of a shit. I can suck this kind of crap up, like I've been trained. Anyway, they didn't have a decent punch among them. Essentially they were all very lucky boys, because in normal circumstances, I could have thrown any one of them straight through the freakin' window. My main worry was they might decide to shoot me or tie me up and march me off somewhere, maybe over the border to Pakistan, to film me and then cut off my head on camera.

If I'd thought for one moment that was their intention, it would have been bad news for all of us. I was hurt, but not so bad as I was making out, and I was formulating a fallback plan. Up above me in the rafters, I could see a four-foot-long iron bar, just resting there. Could I get it if I stood up? Yes.

In a life-or-death situation, I'd grab that bar, carefully select the most violent of them, and smash it right through him. He'd never get up again. Then I'd lay into the front two, taking them entirely by surprise. At the same time, using the bar, I'd ram the whole group into a corner, crushing them together, as per standard SEAL combat strategy, making it impossible for anyone to draw down on me, pull a knife, or get out.

I'd probably have to obliterate the skulls of another couple of them before using one of those Russian pistols to finish anyone still alive. Could I have done it? I think so. My buddies back in SEAL Team 10 would have been mighty disappointed in me if I'd failed.

My absolute fallback position would have been to kill them all, grab their weapons and ammunition, then barricade myself in the house until the Americans came to get me.

The problem was, where would all this get me in the short

term? What was the point of being a bad-ass SEAL, the way some guys would be? The house was surrounded by more Taliban, all of them with AKs. I saw those guards come in and then go out again. Some of the little creeps were right outside the window. Anyway, the entire sprawl of the village of Sabray was surrounded by the Taliban. Sarawa had told me so, and it beat me why I'd been left alone...unless they knew...unless they were indoctrinated...unless I really was in the hands of off-duty Taliban warriors.

But the guys at my bedside were not off duty. They were right on my case, demanding to know why I was there, what the American planes were doing, whether the United States was planning an attack on them, who was coming to rescue me (good question, right?). I knew that right now discretion was, by a long way, the better part of valor, because my objective was simply to try and stay alive, not to get into a brawl with knife-wielding tribesmen or, worse, get myself shot.

I kept telling them I was just a doctor, out here to help with our wounded. I also told them a huge lie, that I had diabetes. I was not a member of the special forces, and I needed water, which they ignored. The main trouble was, strangely, my beard, because they knew the U.S. Army did not permit beards. Only the U.S. Special Forces allows that.

I managed to persuade them I needed to go outside, and they gave me this one single opportunity, one last desperate try to slip away. But I could not move fast enough, and they just dragged me back inside, threw me on the ground, and beat me even more seriously than they had before. Broke the bones in my wrist. That hurt, and I've since needed two operations to correct it.

By now they had lit their lanterns, maybe three of them, and the room was quite light. And their inquisition went on for maybe six hours. Yelling and beating, yelling and kicking. They told me my buddies were all dead, told me they'd already cut everyone's head off and that I was next. They said they had shot down an American helicopter, killed everyone. They were just full of bravado, shouting, boasting they would in the end kill every American in their country and then some... *We will kill you all! Death to the Satan! Death to the infidel!*

They pointed out with huge glee that I was their main infidel and I had mere moments to live. I took a sidelong glance at that iron bar, perhaps my last hope. But I told them nothing, stuck to my guns, kept on telling them I was only a doctor.

At one stage, one of the village kids came in, about seventeen years old. I was pretty certain he had been in one of the groups I'd passed on the way down here. And he had what I now call the Look. That sneering hatred of me and my country.

The Taliban guys let him come in and watch them knocking me around. He really liked it, and I could tell they regarded him as "one of us." He was allowed to sit on the bed while they kicked at the bandage on my left thigh. He just loved it. Kept running the edge of his hand over his throat and laughing, "Taliban, heh?... Taliban!" I'll never forget his face, his grin, his triumphant stare. And I kept looking right up at that iron bar. The kid, too, was a very lucky boy.

Then my interrogators found my rifle laser sight and my camera and wanted to take pictures of one another. I showed them how to use the laser to achieve their pictures, but I showed them the wrong way around and told them to stare into the beam with their naked eye. I guess the last favor I did them was to blind the whole fucking lot of 'em! Because that beam would have burned their retinas right out. Sorry, guys. That's show business.

Right after that, must have been around midnight, a new

figure entered the room, accompanied by two attendants. I knew this was the village elder, a small man with a beard, a man who commanded colossal respect. The Taliban immediately stood up and stepped aside as the old man walked to the spot where I was lying. He kneeled down and offered me water in a little silver cup, gave me bread, and then stood up and turned on the Taliban.

I was not certain what he was saying, but I found out later he was forbidding them to take me away. I think they knew that before they came, otherwise I'd probably have been gone by then. But there was no mistaking the authority in his voice. It was a small, quiet voice, calm, firm, and no one spoke while he spoke. No one interrupted either.

They hardly said a word while this powerful little figure laid down the law. Tribal law, I guess. When he left, he walked out into the night very upright, the kind of posture adopted by men who are unused to defiance. You could spot him a mile off, kind of like an Afghan Instructor Reno. Christ! What if he could see me now?

Upon the departure of the village elder, six hours after they had arrived, at around 0100, the Taliban suddenly decided to leave. Painful eyes, I hoped.

Their leader, the chief talker, was a thin character almost a head taller than all the rest. He led them outside, and I heard them walk off, moving softly up to the trail which led out of Sabray and into the mountains. Once more I was left, bleeding badly and very bruised, eternally grateful to the village elder, drifting off into a form of half-awake sleep, scared, really scared those bastards would somehow come back for me.

Bang! Suddenly, there went that door again. I nearly jumped out of my new Afghan nightshirt with fright. Were they back?

With their execution gear? Could I get up and fight again for my life?

But this time it was Sarawa. And I had to ask myself, Who was he really? Had he tipped someone off? Was he in the clutches of the Taliban? Or had they just come for me and broken in when no one was looking?

I *still* had not been informed of the concept of *lokhay*. Possibly because they had no way to inform me, and anyway I had no choice but to trust them. It was my only shot at survival.

Sarawa was carrying a small lantern, accompanied by a few of his friends. I sensed them but could not really see in the pitch dark, not in my condition in this flickering light.

Three of the villagers lifted me off the floor and carried me toward the door. I remember seeing their silhouettes on the mud walls, sinister, shadowy figures wearing turbans. Honestly, it was like something out of *Arabian Nights*. Big Marcus being hauled away by Ali Baba and his forty thieves to meet the fucking genie. I could not, of course, know they were acting on the direct orders of the village elder, who had told them to get me out of there in case the Taliban decided to ignore the ancient rules and take me by force.

Once outside, they doused the light and set up their formation. Two guys to walk in front with AK-47s and one guy in the rear also carrying an AK. The same three guys as before carried me, Sarawa included, and began to walk out of the village, downward along a trail. We traveled for a long way, the guys walking for more than an hour, maybe even two. And they walked tirelessly, like Bushmen or Bedouins.

In the end we headed down a new trail all the way to a river—I guess the same one where I'd met them—by the waterfall, on a higher reach. I must have been a complete dead weight, and not for the first time I was amazed by their strength.

When we reached the river, they stopped and adjusted their grip on me. Then they walked straight into it and in near total silence carried me across, in the darkness of this moonless night. I could hear the water rippling past but nothing more as they waded softly through it. On the other side, they never broke stride and now began to make their way up a steep gradient through the trees.

It was lush and beautiful in the daylight. I'd seen it, and even in this cold night, I could feel its soft, dark green isolation, heavy with ferns and bushes. Finally we reached what I took to be a cave set deep into the mountainside. They lowered me to the ground, and I tried to talk to them, but they could not see my signals or understand my words, so I drew a blank. But I did manage to make Sarawa understand I suffered from diabetes and required water at all times. I guess the dread of dying of thirst remained uppermost in my mind, and right then I knew I could not get down to that river, not by myself.

They carried me to the back of the cave and set me down. I think it was around 0400 when we got there. It was Thursday, June 30. They left me with no food, but they did come up with a water container, an aged Pepsi bottle actually, the most evil-smelling piece of glass on this planet. I thought it must have been used for goat shit in a previous life. But it was all I had, a bottle from a sewer, but filled with water.

I was afraid to put it to my lips, in case I contracted typhoid. Somehow I held it above my face and poured its contents into my mouth like one of those Spanish guys tending their bulls, or whatever they do.

I had no food or weapon, and Sarawa and his guys were on their way out. I was terrified they'd never come back and had just made a decision to dump me. Sarawa told me he'd be back in five minutes, but I was not sure I could believe him. I just lay there on the rocky floor, in the dark, all alone, shivering in the cold, uncertain of what would befall me next.

In the remains of that night, I fell to pieces, finally lost my mind and sobbed hopelessly out of pure fear, offering no further resistance to anything. I thought I could not take it any longer. Reno would have kicked my ass, for sure and certain. Hopefully on the right side, not the left.

I kept on thinking of Morgan, crazily trying to communicate with him, trying to get my thought waves tuned in with his, begging God to let him hear me. And soon it began to get light. Sarawa had been gone for over two hours. Jesus Christ! They'd dumped me out here to die; Morgan didn't know where I was or whether I was dead or alive; and my SEAL buddies had given me up for dead.

My brain would have been racing but for the fact that I had suddenly been attacked by a tribe of big black Afghan ants, and that really got my attention. I might have given up, but I was fucked if I was going to be eaten alive by these little sonsabitches. I got myself raised up and laid into 'em with my Pepsi bottle.

Most of them probably died from the smell, but I killed enough to beat them off for a while. And the hours ticked by. Nothing. No Pashtun tribesmen. No Sarawa. No Taliban. I was getting desperate. The ants were trickling back. And I no longer had the strength to mount a full assault on them. I went into selective-killing mode, going for the leaders with my Pepsi bottle.

Then I found a piece of flinty rock on the floor of the cave, and, lying painfully on my left side, I spent two hours carving the words of the Count of Monte Cristo onto the wall of my prison: *God will give me justice.*

I wasn't sure I quite believed it anymore. He'd been out of touch for some time now. But I was still alive. Just. And maybe there was help on the way. He works in awful mysterious ways. Still, even my rifle was gone now, like most of my hope.

I was just beginning to drift off again, maybe a little before 0800, when the place seemed to come alive. I could hear the little bells around the necks of the goddamned goats, and they seemed to be above me. When sand and rocks started raining down on me, I realized there was no roof to my cave. I was open to the sky, I could hear those goat hooves pounding away up there somewhere, and the sand kept pouring down on me.

The good news was it buried the ants, but I was trying to stop it getting in my eyes, and so I turned facedown, shielding my eyes with my hands, my right wrist aching like hell from that Taliban gun butt. Suddenly, to my complete horror, I saw the barrel of an AK-47 easing round the corner of the rock which guarded my left side. I couldn't hide, I couldn't even take cover, and I sure as hell couldn't fight back.

The barrel kept coming, then the rest of the rifle, the hands, and the face—the face of one of my buddies from Sabray, grinning cheerfully. I was in such shock I could not even bring myself to call him a crazy prick, which he plainly was. But he brought me bread and that appalling goat's milk and filled my water bottle. The one from the sewer.

Half an hour later Sarawa came, five hours after he said he would. He looked at my bullet wound and gave me more water. Then he posted a guard at the entrance to my roofless cave. The guard was thirtyish and, like the rest of them, whip-thin and bearded. He sat on a rock a little way above my entrance, his AK-47 slung over his shoulder.

I kept drifting off, lying there on the floor, and every time I came awake I leaned out to see if the guard was still there. His name was Norzamund, and he always smiled real friendly and gave me a wave. But we could not speak, no common words. He came down once to fill my water bottle and I tried to get him to share his with me. No dice.

So I lifted the evil Pepsi bottle and splashed the water directly into my mouth. Then I chucked it to the back of the cave. Next time Norzamund brought water, he went back and found the goddamned thing and filled it yet again.

I was alone in the late afternoon, and I saw the goatherds come by a couple of times. They never waved or made contact, but neither did they betray my position. If they had I do not believe I would be here. Even now I'm not sure whether *lokhay* works for a guy who's left the village.

Norzamund had left me some fresh bread, for which I was grateful. He went home shortly after dark, and for several hours I saw no one. I tried to stay calm and rational because it seemed Sarawa and his men were intent on saving me. Even the village elder was plainly on my side. That's nothing to do with my charm, by the way. That's strictly *lokhay*.

I sat there by myself all through that long evening and into the night. June 30 became July 1; I checked my watch around midnight so I knew when that happened. I tried not to think of home and my mom and dad, tried not to give in to self-pity, but I knew it was around 3:00 p.m. back home in Texas, and I wondered if anyone had the slightest clue about how much trouble I was in and whether they realized how badly I needed help.

* * *

What I definitely did not know was that there were now well over two hundred people gathered at the ranch. No one went home. It was as if they were willing a hopeless situation to become hopeful, as if their prayers for me could somehow be answered, as if their presence could somehow protect me from death, as if they believed that if they just stayed in place, no one would announce I had been killed in action.

Mom says she was witnessing a miracle. She and Dad were serving three meals a day to every person on that ranch, and she never knew where the food came from. But it kept coming, big trucks from a couple of food distributors were arriving with steaks and chicken for everyone, maybe two hundred meals at a time. No charge. Local restaurants were trucking stuff in, seafood, pasta, hamburgers. There was Chinese food for fifty, then for sixty. Eggs came, sausage, ham, and bacon. Dad says the barbecues never went out.

Everyone was there to help, including the Herzogg family, big local cattle ranchers, churchgoers, patriots, ready to step up for a friend in need. Mrs. Herzogg showed up with her daughters and without asking just went to work cleaning the place up. And they did it every day.

The navy chaplains made everyone recite the Twenty-third Psalm, just like I was doing. During the open-air services, everyone would stand up and solemnly sing the navy hymn:

Eternal Father, strong to save,
Whose arm hath bound the restless wave,
Who bid'st the mighty ocean deep
Its own appointed limits keep...

And of course they always ended with the special verse exclusively for the Navy SEALs, the everlasting anthem for SPEC-WARCOM:

Eternal Father, faithful friend,
Be quick to answer those we send,
In brotherhood and urgent trust,
  On hidden missions dangerous,
O hear us when we cry to Thee,
For SEALs in air, on land, and sea.

People just slept whenever and wherever they could. We have a large wood guesthouse at the entrance to the property, and people just went in there. The SEALs came into the house and slept where they could, on beds, on sofas, in chairs, wherever. And every three hours, there was a telephone call, patched in directly from the battlefield in Afghanistan. It was always the same: "No news." No one ever left Mom alone, but she was beside herself with worry.

As June turned into July, many were beginning to lose faith and believe I was dead. Except for Morgan, who would not believe it and kept saying he'd been in communication, mentally. I was hurt but alive. Of that he was certain.

The SEALs also would not even consider the possibility that I was dead. He's missing in action, MIA. That was their belief. And until someone told them different, that's all they would accept. Unlike the stupid television station, right? They thought they could say any damn thing they felt like, true or not, and cause my family emotional trauma on a scale only a community as close as we are could possibly understand.

*   *   *

Meanwhile back in the cave, Norzamund came back with two other guys, again frightening the life out of me. It was about 0400 on Friday, July 1, and they had no lantern. They communicated with whispers and hissing signals for silence. Once more they lifted me up and carried me down the hill to the river. I tried to throw the foul-smelling water bottle away, but they found it and brought it right back. Guess there was a heavy shortage of water bottles in the Hindu Kush. Anyway, they looked after that bottle like it was a rare diamond.

We crossed the river and turned up the escarpment, back to the village. It seemed to take a real long time, and at one point I flicked on the light on my watch, and they almost went wild with fury: *No! No! No! Dr. Marcus. Taliban! Taliban!*

Of course I didn't know what they were talking about. The light was tiny, but they kept pointing at it. I soon realized that light was an acute danger to all of us, that the village of Sabray was surrounded by the Taliban, waiting for their chance to capture or kill me. My armed bearers had the same Pashtun upbringing and knew the slightest flicker of a light, no matter how small, was unusual out here on the mountain and could easily attract the attention of an alert watchman.

I switched that sucker off, real quick. And one of my guys, walking out in front with his AK, had some English. He came back to me and whispered: "Taliban see light, they shoot you, Dr. Marcus."

Finally we reached high ground, and I picked up the word *helicopter*. And right here I thought someone might be coming to rescue me. But it was just a false alarm. Nothing came. I stretched out on the concrete, and some time before dawn, Sarawa showed up with his medical bag and attended to my leg. He removed the blood-soaked dressings, washed out the wounds, and applied antiseptic cream and fresh bandages. Then, to my astonishment, he produced some insulin for the diabetes I didn't have.

Guess I was a better liar than I thought. And I obviously had to take it. The stuff I do for my country. Unbelievable, right?

They moved me into a house up there near the top of the village, and soon after I arrived I met my first real friend, Mohammad Gulab, the thirty-three-year-old son of the village elder, and the resident police chief. Everyone called him Gulab (pronounced *Goo-larb*), and his position in the community was very strong. He made it clear the Taliban were not going to take me while he had anything to do with it.

He was an extremely nice guy, and we became good friends, or as close to good friends as it's possible to be when the language barrier is almost insurmountable. Mostly we tried to communicate about families, and I understood he had a wife and six children and God knows how many cousins and uncles. Conveying news about my identical twin brother was a tough one, so we just settled for brother, mainly because Gulab unfailingly thought Morgan was me. Like a lot of other folk have done down the years.

Gulab had a friend with him who was also a solid man, plainly an appointed relief guard. Between them they never left me alone. By this time I knew why. The village was entirely embarrassed when the Taliban had crept in here armed to the teeth and conducted an interrogation regardless of the wishes of the people. Those warriors had been on the verge of causing the ultimate retribution under the laws of *lokhay*, which would have obliged the village to go to war to the last man on my behalf.

I did not yet comprehend the full implications of *lokhay* but I knew it was important and that I would not be surrendered. And now I had a full-time guard detail in my room. This did not prevent other visitors from coming in, and my first on that morning in my new house was a little boy, maybe eight or nine years old.

He sat on the edge of my cot and tried to teach me a Muslim prayer: *La La e La La — Muhammad del la su La La.* I pretty soon got the hang of it and repeated it with him. He was thrilled, clapped his hands and laughed, and charged out through the door to round up a posse of other kids. Gulab tried to inform me that the repetition of that prayer meant that I was now a Muslim. And almost immediately the first little boy came racing back into the room with all his buddies, about twenty of them, all eager to pray with the new Texan convert.

I tried to explain I was a doctor, and they understood this pretty quickly, started saying over and over, "Hello, Dr. Marcus," laughing like hell and falling about like kids do. I could tell they really liked me, and I borrowed a marker pen one of them had and wrote each of their names in English on their arms. Then I let them write their names on mine.

We exchanged words for ears, nose, and mouth. Then for water *(uba)* and for walk *(ducari),* both of which I found useful. In the end they left, but other local tribesmen came in to speak to Gulab, and I began, with his encouragement, to converse with the guys who walked the goats, the men who would understand distance. Slowly, during the course of the day, we established there was a small American base two miles away.

They pointed out the window directly at a mountain which looked like a spare part from the Rockies. It towered above us, a great wall of granite that would have caused a mountain goat to back off. "Over there, Dr. Marcus, far side," one of them managed to say. And since I probably could not have reached the window, never mind the mountain, I put that plan on the back burner for the moment.

They had been referring to the village of Monagee, in the district of Manrogai, where I knew the U.S. military had some kind of an outpost. But it was out of the question right now. I couldn't get there or anywhere else until my leg improved. Nonetheless, the goatherds had some good information about the terrain and the distances to various villages and U.S. bases. These guys walk around the mountains for a living. Local knowledge. That's key to every serving SEAL, especially one who was planning a kind of soft jailbreak, like me.

With the goatherds, I was able to work out that from the scene of the original battlefield where the others died, on that terrible night of June 28 I had traveled around seven miles, four walking, three crawling. Seven miles! *Wow!* I couldn't believe that. But these herders knew their land. And they, like everyone else, knew all about the Battle for Murphy's Ridge, where it had been fought and the very bad losses sustained by the Taliban... "You shoot, Dr. Marcus? You shoot?"

Me? Shoot? Never. I'm just a wandering doctor trying to look after my patients. But I was real proud of traveling seven miles over the mountain in my beat-up condition after the battle.

I took my ballpoint pen and marked distances, drew maps, made diagrams of the mountains on my right thigh. When that got a little crowded, I had to use my left. (Shit! That hurt. That really hurt!)

At noon the kids came back for prayers, bringing with them several adults, clearly eager to meet the new American convert, no longer an infidel. We prayed together to Allah, kneeling—painfully, in my case—on the floor. After which we all shook hands, and I think they welcomed me to their prayers. Never told 'em, of course, I slipped in a quick one to my own God while I was at it, respectfully wondering, if it was all right with Him, whether I could get my rifle back anytime soon.

They all came back for afternoon prayers at 1700, and again at sunset. The little kids, my first friends, had to leave for bed right after that, but I remember they all came and hugged me before they left, and, not having mastered "Good-bye" or "Good night" yet, they repeated their first American phrase again and again as they left the room: "Hello, Dr. Marcus."

The older kids, the young teenagers, were allowed to stay and talk with me for a while. Gulab helped them to communicate and we parted as friends. The trouble was, I was getting sick now, and I was beginning to feel pretty ropy, not just the pain of my wounds but kind of like flu, only a bit worse.

When the kids had finally left, I received a visit from the village elder himself. He brought me bread, gave me fresh water, then sat down for maybe three hours while we discussed, as best we could, how I could get to an American base. It was clear I was a major problem to the village. Threats were already being received from the Taliban, informing the villagers how urgent it was for their cause that I be surrendered to them immediately.

The old man imparted this to me but took the view I was in no shape to travel and that it would simplify matters for a member of his Pashtun tribe to make the journey, on foot, to the big U.S. base at Asadabad and inform them of my whereabouts. I had no clue at the time he was preparing to make the journey himself, some thirty to forty miles alone in the mountains.

He asked me to write out a letter for him to take to Asadabad. I wrote, *This man gave me shelter and food, and must be helped at all costs*. At the time I was under the distinct impression that he and I were going to make the journey together, possibly with an escort and a few guys to help carry me. Departure time was set for 1930, right after evening prayers.

But I had misunderstood. The old man had no intention of traveling with me, correctly reasoning I'd be a far greater nuisance on such a trek over the mountains than I would be lying here. Also, if the Taliban found out we'd gone, we would be highly susceptible to ambush. I never saw him again, to thank him for his kindness.

I waited all afternoon and half the night for him to come and have me collected. But of course he never did. I remember being hugely disappointed, not for the first time, that more definite plans were not being formulated for my evacuation.

At one point during the evening, the tribal leaders came and had a meeting in my room. They just sat on the floor and talked, but they brought me back the little silver cup I'd had in the first house. And they poured me several cups of that chai tea they drink and, I think, grow on a small scale up here. The ceremony included sweet candy, which you eat while you drink your tea. And that tasted great after my enforced diet of very, very dry baked flat bread.

Gulab stayed with me and was cheerful as ever, but he either could not or would not answer questions about his father and his immediate plans. I think the tribal leaders felt it was better for me not to know—classified, Pashtun-style, FYO and all that. The work of the elder was information provided on a need-to-know basis only. I was getting used to operating outside the loop, everyone's freakin' loop, that is.

Gulab spent much of the evening trying to explain to me the complex threads that hold together the Pashtun tribes and al Qaeda, still working in conjunction with the Taliban army. The United States had been busy trying to clear all of them the hell out of Afghanistan for four years but with only limited success.

The jihadists seem to have some kind of hammerlock on tribal loyalties, using a whole spectrum of Mafia-style tactics, sometimes with gifts, sometimes with money, sometimes promising protection, sometimes with outright threats. The truth is, however, neither al Qaeda nor the Taliban could function without the cooperation of the Pashtun villages.

And often, deep within the communities, there are old family ties and young men who sympathize with the warlike mentality of the Taliban and al Qaeda chiefs. Kids barely out of grade school—joke, they don't have grade schools up here—are drawn toward the romantic cutthroats who have declared they'll fight the American army until there is no one left.

I guess there's something very alluring about that to some kids. You can see these potential Taliban recruits in any of the villages. I've seen dozens of them, too young to have that much hate and murder in their eyes and hearts. Christ, one of the little bastards had sat on my bed urging eight armed men to torture me. Nice. He couldn't have been more than seventeen.

But there is another side to this. Sabray was obviously governed wisely by Gulab's father. And there was a sense of law and order and discipline in an essentially lawless land. Al Qaeda effectively owns great swaths of land in Kunar Province, which had now been my home for the better part of three months. And this is mostly because of the terrain.

I mean, how the hell do you impose national government on a place like this? With no roads, no electricity, no mail, little communication, where the principal industry is goats' milk and opium, the main water company is a mountain stream, and all freight is moved by mule cart, including the opium. You're whistling Dixie. It's never going to happen.

Al Qaeda are running around in broad daylight, mostly doing what the heck they want, until we show up and chase the little pricks back over the border to Pakistan. Where they stay. For about ten minutes, before launching their next foray into these tribal mountains, which their ancestors have ruled for centuries.

These days there are less gifts and a lot more fear. The Taliban is a ruthless outfit, with instincts about killing their enemies which have barely changed in two thousand years. They should somehow by now have frightened the bejesus out of my buddy Gulab and his father, but they had not succeeded, so far as I could see. There's just something unbreakable about them all, a grim determination to follow the ancient laws of the Pashtuns—laws which may yet prove too strong even for the Taliban and al Qaeda.

But from where I was sitting, in the smoky main room of one of Sabray's high houses, talking to the village cop, that's not the way the tide was running. And until the United States decides to wield a very large stick up here in support of the elected government of the people, in Kabul, I'm not looking for any serious change real soon. The enemy is prepared to go to any lengths to achieve victory, terrorizing its own people, if necessary, and resorting to barbaric practices against its enemy, including decapitating people or butchering them.

We are not allowed to fight them on those terms. And neither would we wish to. However, we could fight in a much more ruthless manner, stop worrying if everyone still loved us. If we did that, we'd probably win in both Afghanistan and Iraq in about a week.

But we're not allowed to do that. And I guess we'd better start getting used to the consequences and permit the American liberals to squeak and squeal us to ultimate defeat. I believe that's what it's called when you pack up and go home, when a war fought under your own "civilized" terms is unwinnable.

We're tougher, better trained, better organized, better armed, with access to weapons which cannot be resisted. The U.S. Armed Forces represent the greatest fighting force this world has ever seen, and we keep getting our butts kicked by a bunch of illegal thugs who ought to be eliminated.

Look at me, right now in my story. Helpless, tortured, shot, blown up, my best buddies all dead, and all because we were afraid of the liberals back home, afraid to do what was necessary to save our own lives. Afraid of American civilian lawyers. I have only one piece of advice for what it's worth: if you don't want to get into a war where things go wrong, where the wrong people sometimes get killed, where innocent people sometimes have to die, then stay the hell out of it in the first place.

Because that's what happens. In all wars, down all the years of history. Terrible injustices, the killing of people who did not deserve to die. That's what war is. And if you can't cope with it, don't do it.

Meantime, I was stuck in the house waiting for the old man to show up, when he was already miles away, walking through the mountains, the thirty or so miles to Asadabad. Once I wandered outside when no one was looking, and I tried to find him. But he seemed to have gone missing. Even then I never dreamed that little old guy was walking to Asadabad by himself.

I couldn't really tell, but I sensed something was making my guys jumpy. And about ten or eleven o'clock that night, we moved. They had just brought me fresh water and bread, which I consumed gratefully, and then I was instructed to pack up and leave. By this time my leg was a little better, even though it hurt, and with some assistance I was able to walk.

We made our way in the dark down to a different house and stepped off the trail directly onto the roof. We had some kind of a sheet, and the three of us laid down close together for warmth. It was very, very cold, but I guess they felt there was some danger if I'd remained in my old spot. Maybe they had suspicion of someone in the village, worry that someone had tipped off the Taliban as to my precise whereabouts. But whatever, these guys were taking no chances. If Taliban gunmen burst into my old house, they would not find me.

I was up here on the freakin' roof, huddled with Gulab and his buddy, freezing to death but safe. And once more I was amazed by the silence, that mountain silence. There was not one single sound in the entire village of Sabray, and for a Westerner that's really hard to imagine.

Gulab and his pal made no sound. I could scarcely hear them breathing. Whenever we did anything, they were always telling me *shhhhh*, when I had thought I was being silent as the grave. It's another world up here, so quiet it defies the logic of Western ears. Maybe that's why no one has ever conquered these high lands of the Afghan tribesmen.

I slept on and off through the night, up there on the roof. Once I dared to change position, and you'd have thought I'd set off a fire alarm from the reaction of my new friends. *"Shhhhh, Dr. Marcus... Quiet."* It just showed how jumpy they were, how nervous of the hushed killers of the Taliban army.

At dawn we packed up and returned to the house. I wanted to sleep some more, but there was a big tree right outside the window that had a view down the mountain, and in that tree lived the world's loudest rooster. That sucker could have awakened a graveyard. And he did not give a damn about dawn, first light and all that. He let it fly right after midnight and never let up. There were several times when, if it had come to a straight coin toss between taking out Sharmak or the rooster, I could easily have spared Sharmak.

The tribal chiefs came back again around 0700 to conduct their early morning prayers in my room. Of course I joined them in reciting the bits I had learned, and then, when the adults left, the door flew open and a whole bunch of kids came charging through the door, shouting, *"Hello, Dr. Marcus."*

They never knocked, just came tumbling in, grabbing me and hugging me. And it went on intermittently throughout the day. Sarawa had left his medical bag in my room, and I fixed up their cuts and scrapes, and they taught me bits of their language. Those kids were great. I'll never forget them.

By that Saturday morning, July 2, I was still in a lot of pain; my shoulder, back, and leg were often killing me. Gulab knew this, and he sent an old man from the village to see me. He came with a plastic pouch containing tobacco opium, which looks like green bread dough. He gave me the pouch, and I took a pinch of the stuff, put it in my lip, and waited.

I'm here to tell you, that was a miracle. The pain slowly vanished, completely. It was the first time I'd ever done drugs, and I loved it! That opium restored me, set me free. I felt better than I had since we all fell down the mountain. What with the Muslim prayers and now my becoming a devotee of the local dope, I was drifting into the life of an Afghan peasant. *Hooyah,* Gulab, right?

The old man left the bag with me, and it helped me get through the next hours more than I can say. When you've lived through a lot of pain for a few days, the relief is terrific. For the first time

I understood the power of that drug, which is, of course, the one the Taliban and al Qaeda feed to suicide bombers before they obliterate themselves and everyone else within range.

There's nothing heroic about suicide bombers. They're mostly just dumb, brainwashed kids, stoned out of their minds.

Outside the house, I could see the U.S. helicopters flying overhead, Black Hawk 60s and MH-47s, obviously looking for something. Hopefully me. I knew from what the Taliban had said that one of our helos was down, but not, of course, who had been on board, that eight more of my buddies from Alfa Platoon were dead, including Shane Patton, James Suh, and Chief Healy.

I also did not know that neither Mikey's, Danny's, nor Axe's body had been found and that the helos were circling the area trying to pick up any trace of the original four who had set off on the ill-fated Operation Redwing. The aircrew did not know whether any of us were alive or dead. And back home, the media were vacillating between dead and missing, whichever made the best story on the day, I guess. Didn't help any in East Texas, I can say that.

Anyway, when I saw those helos, I charged outside. I took off my shirt and waved it over my head, yelling, *"Here I am, guys! I'm right here. It's me, Marcus! Right here, guys!"*

But they just flew off, leaving me a somewhat forlorn figure standing outside the house, trying to put on my shirt, and wondering again whether anyone would ever come and rescue me.

In the fullness of time I understood the quandary for the American military. Four SEALs, fighting for their lives, had made one final communication that we were dying up here. Since then, there had been neither sight nor sound of the four of us.

Militarily, there were several possibilities, the first being we were all now dead. The second was we were all still alive. The third was there were survivors, or at least a survivor, and they were somewhere on the loose, possibly wounded, in steep country where there is almost no possibility of making a safe landing in any aircraft.

I guess the last possibility was that we had been taken prisoners and that in time there would be either a ransom note demanding an enormous cash payment or a television film showing us first as prisoners and then being executed.

The last option was unlikely when the missing were Navy SEALs. We don't habitually get captured. Either we kill our enemy or our enemy kills us. SEALs don't put their hands up or wave white flags. Period. The command post knew that back in Asadabad, or Bagram.

They would not have been expecting a communiqué from the Taliban saying SEALs had been captured. There's an old SEAL motto: Never assume a frogman's dead unless you find his body. Everyone knows that.

The most likely scenario, aside from all dead, was that one or more of the Redwings was hurt, out of communication, and unable to make contact. The problem was location. Where were we? How could we be found?

Plainly, the Taliban were not saying a thing; therefore, they had no prisoners. Equally, the missing SEALs weren't saying anything. Dead? Probably. Wounded in action and still holding out in the mountains, out of contact? As the days went by, this must have seemed increasingly less likely.

By now Gulab had told me that his father had departed to walk to Asadabad alone. All my hopes rested in the soft tread of this powerful yet tiny old man.

11

Reports of My Death Greatly Exaggerated

He literally dragged me into a standing position, and then... He was running and trying to make me keep up with him, and he kept shouting, signaling, again and again: Taliban! Taliban are here! In the village! Run, Dr. Marcus, for God's sake, run!

Gulab had now become the principal figure in my life. He called the security shots, made sure I had food and water, and was, in my mind, the link between us and his father as the old man toiled through the mountains to Asadabad.

The Afghani policeman betrayed no sign of stress, but he did reveal to me that a letter had been received earlier from the commander of the Taliban forces. It was a written demand that the villagers of Sabray hand over the American immediately.

The demand came from the rising officer of the Taliban army in the northeast, the firebrand "Commodore Abdul," right-hand man to Sharmak and a character who plainly saw himself as some kind of Eastern Che Guevara. His reputation was apparently growing as an ambush leader and as an officer who was expert at bringing in new recruits through the passes.

I never knew, but it would not have surprised me to learn he had been in the front line of the army that confronted the team on the ridge, though I have no doubt the strategy was planned by the senior man, Sharmak, who had done so much damage already.

They did not, however, faze Gulab. He and his father had replied that it made no difference how bad the Taliban wanted the American, they were not going to get him. When Gulab told me, he made a very distinct, brave, dismissive gesture. And he spent some time trying to convey his personal position: *They can't frighten me. My village is well armed, and we have our own laws and rights. The Taliban need our support a lot more than we need theirs.*

He was a gallant and confident man, at least on the surface. But I noticed he took no chances when there was any kind of suggestion the Taliban were coming in. I guess that's why we ended up sleeping on the roof.

Also, he had not the slightest interest in a reward. I offered to give him my watch in return for his unending decency to me. I implored him to take my watch, because it was all I had to offer. But he always refused to accept it. As for money, what use could that have been to him? There was nothing to spend it on. No shops, the nearest town miles and miles away, a journey that had to be made on foot.

A couple of the sneering kids did ask for money, teenagers, maybe sixteen- or seventeen-year-olds. But they were planning to join the Taliban and leave Sabray, to fight for "freedom." Gulab told me he had no intention of leaving here. And I understood that. He was part of the fabric of the village. One day he would be the village elder. His family would grow up here. It was all he had ever known, all he had ever wanted. This very beautiful corner of the Hindu Kush was where he belonged. What use was money to Mohammad Gulab of Sabray?

The last of the kids had left my room, and I was lying there contemplating the world, when there was a kick on the door that nearly took it off its hinges. No one kicks a door in quite like that except a Taliban raiding party. That was all I could imagine. But around here, where doors don't fit, a good bang with your sandal is about the only way to get the sonofabitch open, short of a full-blooded shoulder charge.

But the sudden shock of a door being kicked in about five feet from your head is a nerve-racking experience. And I'm neurotic about it to this day. Because the sound of the crash on the door is the sound I heard before I was tortured. It sometimes dominates my dreams. I wake up sweating, a tremendous crash echoing in my mind. And no matter where I am, I need to check the door lock before I can sleep again. It's pretty goddamned inconvenient at times.

Anyway, this was not the Taliban. It was just my own guys opening the door, which must have been shut firmly by the kids. I restarted my heart, and my room stayed kind of quiet until midmorning, when the door catapulted open with a violent *bang!* that shook the goddamned mountain, never mind the room. And once more I almost jumped out of my Afghan jumpsuit. And this time they were shouting at me. I could not understand what, but something had broken out, things were on the move. Jesus Christ! I had to steady this group down. There were adults and kids, all mixed up, and they were all yelling the same thing— *"Parachute! Parachute! Parachute! Dr. Marcus, come quick!"*

I made my way outside, aching to high heaven all the way. I resolved to have another shot of that opium soon as I returned, but for now it was all eyes upward, straight at the clear blue, cloudless skies. What could we see? Nothing. Whatever had landed was down, and I stood there trying to make them understand I needed to know if there had been a man on the end of that parachute, and if so, how many parachutes there had been. Was this a drop zone for my buddies to come right in and get me?

The upshot of this was also nothing. The tribesmen simply could not understand me. The kids, who I detected were the ones who had actually spotted the parachute, or parachutes, were just as mystified. All the hours of study we had done together had come to nothing.

There was a sudden conference, and most of the adults upped and left. I went back in. They returned maybe fifteen minutes later and brought with them all my gear, which they had hidden away from the eyes of the Taliban. They gave me back my rifle and ammunition, my H-gear (that's my harness), and in its pocket, my PRC-148 intersquad radio, the one for which I'd lost the little microphone earpiece. It still had its weakish battery and its still-operational emergency beacon.

I was aware that if I grabbed the bull by the horns and went right outside and let rip with this communications gear, I would once more be a living, breathing distress signal, which the Americans might catch from a cruising helo. On the other hand, the Taliban, hidden all around in the hills, could scarcely miss me. I found this a bit of a dilemma.

But the rearmament guys of Sabray also brought me my laser and the disposable camera. I grabbed my rifle and held it like you might caress a returning lover. This was the weapon God had granted me. And, so far as I could tell, still wanted me to have. We'd traveled a long way together, and I probably deserved some kind of an award for mountain climbing, maybe the Grand Prix

Hindu Kush presented to Sherpa Marcus. Sorry, forget all that, I meant mountain *falling*, the Grand Prix Hindu Crash, awarded unanimously to Sherpa Marcus the Unsteady.

Outside, I put on my harnesss, locked and loaded the rifle, and prepared for whatever the hell might await us. But with my harness back, I was not yet done with the kids. That harness contained my notebook, and we had access to the village ball-point pen.

I marched them back into the house and carefully drew two parachutes on the page. I drew a man swinging down from the first one. On the second one, I drew a box. I showed both pictures to the kids and asked them, Which one? And about twenty little fingers shot forward, all aimed directly at the parachute with the box.

Beautiful. I had intel. There had been some kind of a supply drop. And since the local tribesmen do not use either aircraft or parachutes, those supplies had to be American. They also had to be aimed at the remnants of my team. Everyone else was dead. I was that remnant.

I asked the kids exactly where the chutes had dropped, and they just pointed to the mountain. Then they got into gear and raced out there, I guess to try and show me. I stood outside and watched them go, still a bit baffled. Had my buddies somehow found me? Had the old man reached Asadabad? Either way, it was one hell of a coincidence the Americans had made a supply drop a few hundred yards from where I was taking cover. The mountains were endless, and I could have been anywhere.

I went back into the house to rest my leg and talk for a while with Gulab. He had not seen the parachute drop, and he had no idea how far along the road his father had journeyed. In my mind, I knew what every active combat soldier knows, that Napoleon's army advanced on Moscow at one mile every fifteen minutes, with full packs and muskets. That's four miles an hour, right? That way, the village elder should have made it in maybe eleven hours.

Except for two mitigating factors: (1) he was about two hundred years old, and (2) from where I stood, the mountain he was crossing had a gradient slightly steeper than the Washington Monument. If the VE made it by Ramadan 2008, I'd be kinda lucky.

One hour later, there it goes again. *Bang!* That goddamned door went off like a bomb. Even Gulab jumped. But not as high as I did. In came the kids, accompanied by a group of adults. They carried with them a white document, which must have looked like a snowball in a coal mine up here where the word *litter* simply does not exist.

I took it from them and realized it was an instruction pamphlet for a cell phone. *"Where the hell did you get this?"* I asked them.

"Right out there, Dr. Marcus. Right out there." Everyone was pointing at the mountainside, and I had no trouble with the translation.

"Parachute?" I said.

"Yes, Dr. Marcus. Yes. Parachute."

I sent them right out there again, trying to make it clear that I needed the mountainside searched for anything like this, anything that might have come in on the parachutes.

My guys don't drop cell phone pamphlets, but they might have been trying to drop me a cell phone and the pamphlet just came with it. Either way, I could not find out for myself, so I had to get the guys to do it for me. Gulab stayed, but the others went with the kids, like a golf crowd fanned out to look for Tiger's ball in deep rough.

Gulab and I settled down. We had a cup of tea and some of those delicious little candies, then lounged back on our big cushions. Suddenly, *bang!* The door nearly cannoned off its hinges. I shot tea all over the rug, and in came everyone again.

This time they had found a 55-90 radio battery and an MRE (meal ready to eat). The guys must have thought I was starving. Correct. But the battery did not fit my PRC-148 radio, which sucked, because if it had, I could have fired up a permanent distress signal straight into the sky above the village. As things were, I had no idea if my present weak radio beacon would reach much higher than the rooftops.

I had no need to interrogate the kids further. If there had been anything else out there on the mountain, they'd have found it. There obviously wasn't. Whatever the drop had contained, the Taliban had beaten the kids to it. The one bit of reverse good news was they clearly had the cell phone or phones, and they would probably try to use them. And the entire U.S. electronic surveillance system in the province of Kunar would be listening, ready to locate the caller.

But then I noticed something which made my blood boil. Almost every one of the kids had been battered. They had bruises on their faces, cut lips, and bloody noses. Those little pricks out there had beaten up my kids, punched them in their faces, to stop them getting the stuff from the drop. There is no end to the lengths these people will go to to win this war.

And I'll never forget what they did to the kids of Sabray. I spent the rest of the day patching them up, all those brave little guys trying not to cry. I nearly wiped out the entire contents of Sarawa's medical bag. Whenever I hear the word *Taliban,* I think of that day first.

More strategically, it did seem the American military believed there was at least one SEAL still alive down here. The question was, What now? No one wanted to risk sending in another MH-47 helicopter, since the Taliban seemed to have become very adroit at knocking them down. Mind you, they have had a lot of practice, right back from when they were using those old Stinger missiles to knock the Russians out of the sky.

And we all knew the danger point was landing, when the ramp was down, ready for an insert. That's when the mountain men aimed the RPGs straight in the back, to explode right in the fuel-tank area. And I guess the U.S. flight crews could never be sure of any Afghan village, who might be in it, what weapons they had, and how skilled they might be at using them.

I knew they'd need a pretty good aerial group to soften the place up before they could come in and get me. And I was desperate to give them some kind of a guide. I rigged up my radio emergency beacon to transmit through the open window. I had no idea how much battery I had left, so I just turned it on, aimed it high, and left it there on the window ledge, hopefully pinpointing my whereabouts to any overhead flights by the air force or the Night Stalkers.

To my surprise, U.S. reaction happened a whole lot quicker than I thought it would. That afternoon. The U.S. Air Force came thundering in, dropping twelve-hundred-pound bombs on the mountainside beyond the village, right where the Taliban had picked up the stuff from the parachute drop.

The blasts were incredible. In my house, well, I thought the whole building was coming down. Rocks and dust cascaded into the room. One of the walls sustained a major structural fault as blast after blast shook the mountain from top to bottom. Outside, people were screaming as the bombs hit and exploded; thatched roofs were blown off; there was a dust storm outside. Mothers and kids were rushing for cover, the tribesmen were at a complete loss. Everyone had heard of American airpower, but they had not seen it firsthand, like this.

In fact none of the bombs, I guess by design, hit Sabray. But they came close. Damned close. All around the perimeter. There must have been a big lesson right here, and a very simple one. If you allow the Taliban and al Qaeda to make camp in and around your village, no good can possibly come of it.

However, that wasn't much comfort to my villagers as they tried to clean up the mess, rebuild walls and roofs, and calm down frightened kids, most of whom had had a very bad day. And all because of me. I looked out at the havoc around me and felt the most terrible sadness. And Gulab understood what I was feeling. He came over and put his arm around me and said, "Ah, Dr. Marcus, Taliban very bad. We know. We fight."

Jesus. Just what I need. A brand-new battle. We both retreated into the house and sat down for a while, trying to plot a course for me which would cause the least possible trouble to the farmers of Sabray.

It seemed apparent that my presence here was causing a more and more threatening attitude from the Taliban, and the last thing I wanted was to cause pain and unhappiness among these people who had sheltered me. But my options were narrow, despite the Americans being, it seemed, hot on my trail. One of the main problems was that Gulab's father had not made contact with us, because there was no way he could. And we had no way of knowing whether he had made it to a military base.

The Taliban were probably not overwhelmingly thrilled at being bombed by the U.S. Air Force and had probably sustained many casualties out there on the mountain. It occurred to both Gulab and me that the word *revenge* might not be far from the curled lips of these hate-filled Muslim fanatics and that I might be the most convenient target.

That meant a major problem and probably loss of life for the people of Sabray. Gulab himself was under pressure since he'd received that threat from the Taliban. He had a wife, children, and many relatives to think about. In the end, the decision made itself. Clearly, I had to leave, just to keep the village from becoming a battleground. *Lokhay* had worked well, but we both wondered if its mystical tribal folklore could hold out indefinitely in the face of the wounded and somewhat embarrassed Taliban and al Qaeda fighters.

The U.S. bombardment of the mountainside had for a while raised my hopes and expectations. After all, here were my own guys, swooping over these tribesmen from the Middle Ages, hitting them hard with high-tech modern ordnance. That's got to be good, right?

But not everything's good. Retribution, against me and my protectors, was now uppermost in my mind. I think it was the tight-fisted old oil baron John Paul Getty who once observed that for every plus that takes place in this world, there is, somewhere, somehow, a minus. He got that right.

The question was, Where should I go? And here, my options were very limited. I could never make the long walk to the base at Asadabad, and anyhow that would seem inane since the village elder was either in there or very nearly. And the only place of refuge close by was the U.S. outpost at Monagee, two miles away over a steep mountain.

I did not relish the plan, and neither would the guys who would need to assist me on the journey. But so far as Gulab and

I could tell, there was nothing else we could do except hunker down and prepare for a Taliban attack, and I really did not want to put anyone through that. Especially the kids.

We thus resolved that I should walk with him and two others over the mountain to the village of Monagee, which sounds Irish but is strictly Pashtun and is cooperative with the U.S. military. The plan was to wait until long after dark and then slip out into the high pastures around eleven o'clock, stealthily passing right under the noses of the probably sleeping Taliban watchmen.

I could only hope my left leg would stand up to the journey. I'd lost a ton of weight, but I was still a very big guy to be half carried by a couple of slender Afghan tribesmen, most of whom were five foot eight and 110 pounds soaked to the skin. But Gulab did not seem too worried, and we settled down to wait out the long dark hours before eleven, when we would make our break.

Night fell, quite abruptly, as it does up here in the peaks when the sun finally slips behind them. We lit no lanterns, offering no clue to the Taliban. We just sat there in the dark, sipping tea and waiting for the right moment to leave.

Suddenly, from right out of the blue, there was the most colossal thunderstorm. The rain came swiftly, lashing rain, driving sideways over the mountain. It was rain like you rarely see, the kind of stuff usually identified with those hurricanes they keep replaying on the Weather Channel.

It belted down on the village of Sabray. All windows and doors were slammed tight shut, because this was monsoon rain, driving in, right across the country from the southwest. No one would have set foot outside home because that wind and rain would have swept anyone away, straight off the mountain.

Outside, great gushes of water cascaded down the steep main trail through the village. It sounded like we were in the middle of a river, the water racing past the front door. An area like this cannot, of course, flood, not up here, because the gradient is far too steep to hold water. But it can sure as hell get wet.

We had a rock-and-mud roof that was sound, but I did wonder how some of the households down below us were getting along. Everything here is communal, including the cooking, so I guess everyone was just crowded in together in the undamaged houses, out of the rain.

Up above us, the mountaintops were lit up by great bolts of forked lightning, ice blue in color, jagged, electric neon in the sky. Thunder rolled across the Hindu Kush. Gulab and I got down close to the thick rock wall at the back of the room because our own house was by no means watertight. But the rain was not driving through the gaps in the rocks and mud. Our spot was dry, but we were still deafened and dazzled by this atrocity of nature raging outside.

That level of storm can be unnerving, but when it goes on for as long as this one, you become accustomed to its fury. Every time I looked out the window, the lightning flashed and crackled above the highest peaks. But occasionally it illuminated the sky beyond our immediate range of hills, and that was just about the creepiest sight you've ever seen, like the wicked witch of the Kush was about to come hurtling through the sky on a broomstick.

Lightning out in front, naked and violent, is one thing. But similar bolts hidden from view, turning the heavens into a weird, electric blue, made a landscape like this look unearthly, enormous black summits, stark against the universe. It was a forbidding sight for a wounded warrior more used to the great flat plains of Texas.

But slowly I became used to it and finally fell into a deep sleep flat out on the floor. Our departure time of 2300 came and went and still the rain lashed down. Midnight came, and with it, a new calendar date, Sunday, July 3, which this year would be the midpoint of the Fourth of July weekend, a time for celebration all over the U.S.A., at least in most parts, except for those in profound mourning for the lost special forces.

While I was sitting out the storm, the mood back home on the ranch, according to Mom, was very depressed. I had been missing in action for five days. The throng gathered in our front yard now numbered almost three hundred. They had never left, but the crowd was growing very solemn.

There was still a police cordon around the property. The local sheriffs had been joined by the judges, and the state police were busy providing personal escorts in the form of cruisers to accompany the SEALs on their twice-daily training runs, front and rear.

Attending the daily prayers were local firemen, construction men, ranchers, bookstore owners, engineers, mechanics, teachers, two charter-boat fishing captains. There were salesmen, mortgage brokers, lawyers from Houston, and local attorneys. All of them fighting off my demise in the best way they knew how.

Mom says the whole place was lit up all night by the lights from the automobiles. Someone had brought in portacabins, and there seemed little point in people going anywhere. Not until they knew whether I was still alive. According to Mom, they separated into groups, one offering prayers every hour, others singing hymns, others drinking beers. Local ladies who had known Morgan and me all our lives were unable to hold back their tears. All of them were in attendance for only one reason, to comfort my parents if the worst should be announced.

I don't know that much about other states, because my experience in California has been strictly sheltered in the SPECWARCOM compound. But in my opinion, that nearly weeklong vigil carried out in an entirely impromptu manner by the people of Texas says a huge amount about them, their compassion, their generosity, and their love for their stricken neighbors.

Mom and Dad did not know all of them by any means, but no one will ever forget the single-minded purpose of their visits. They just wanted to help in any way they could, just wanted to be there, because one of their own was lost on the battlefield far, far away.

And as the weekend wore on, no Stars and Stripes were flying. I guess they were not sure whether to raise them to halfmast or not. My dad says it was obvious people were becoming disheartened—the sheer regularity of the signal by phone from Coronado: "No news." The grimness of the media announcing stuff like: "Hope is fading for the missing Navy SEALs...seems like those early reports of the death of all four will be proved accurate...Texas family mourns their loss...Navy still refusing to confirm SEALs deaths..."

It beats the hell out of me. In the military, if we don't know something, we say we don't know and proceed to shut up until we do. Some highly paid charlatans in the media think it's absolutely fine to take a wild guess at the truth and then tell a couple of million people it's cast-iron fact, just in case they might be right.

Well, I hope they're proud of themselves, because they nearly broke my mom's heart, and if it had not been for the stern authority of Senior Chief Petty Officer Chris Gothro, I think she might have had a nervous breakdown.

That morning he found her in the house, privately crying, and right then Senior Chief Gothro stepped in. He stood her up, turned her around, and ordered her to look him straight in the eye. "Listen, Holly," he said, "Marcus is missing in action. That's MIA in our language. That's all. Missing means what it says. It means we cannot at present locate him. It does not mean he's dead. And he's not dead until I tell you he's dead, understand?

"We do not have a body. But we do have movement on the ground. We cannot tell right now who it is, or how many there are. But no one, repeat, no one in SPECWARCOM believes he is dead. I want you to understand that, clearly."

The austere words of a professional must have hit home. Mom rallied after that, aided and comforted by Morgan, who still claimed he was in contact with me and that whatever else was happening, I was not dead.

There were now thirty-five SEALs on the property, including Commander Jeff Bender, Admiral Maguire's public relations officer and a fantastic encouragement to everyone. Navy SEAL chaplain Trey Vaughn from Coronado was a spiritual pillar of strength. Everyone wanted to talk to him, and he dealt with it all with optimism and hope. When the mood was becoming morbid and there were too many people in tears, he would urge them to be positive. "Stop that crying right now...we need you...we need your prayers...and Marcus needs your prayers. But most of all we need your energy. No giving up, hear me?" No one will ever forget Trey Vaughn.

There were also two naval chaplains from the local command who just showed up out of nowhere. Chief Bruce Misex, the navy recruiter boss from Houston, who'd known me a long time, turned up and never left. As the days had worn on, shipments of seafood started to arrive from the gulf ports to the south: fresh shrimp, catfish, and other white fish. One lady brought an enormous consignment of sushi every day. And families who had spent generations in the South stuck hard by that old southern tradition of bringing covered dishes containing pots of chicken and dumplings to a funeral.

Dad thought that was a bit premature, but there were a lot of people to feed, and he assumed a loose command of the cooking. Everyone was grateful for everything. He says it was strange but there was never any question of anyone going home. They were just going to stay there, for better or for worse.

Meanwhile, back in the freakin' thunderstorm, more than thirty pounds lighter than when I first set off on this mission, I was sleeping like a child. Gulab said at 0300 it had been raining for nearly six hours without ever slowing up. I was out to the world, the first time I had slept soundly for a week, oblivious to the weather, oblivious to the Taliban.

I slept right through the night and woke up in broad daylight after the rain. I checked my watch and rounded on Gulab. I was supposed to be in Monagee, for chrissakes, why the hell hadn't he made sure I was? What kind of a guide was he, allowing me to oversleep?

Gulab was sanguine. And since we were growing very efficient at communicating, he was able to tell me he knew it was the first time I had been able to sleep for a long time, and he thought it would be better to leave me. Anyway, he said, we could not possibly have gone out in that weather because it was too dangerous. The overnight walk to Monagee had been out of the question.

One way and another, I took all this pretty badly. I actually stormed out of the house, racked by yet another disappointment; after the helicopters that never came, Sarawa's sudden vanishing while I was in the cave, the village elder taking off without me. And now the trip to Monagee in ruins. Christ. Could I ever believe a goddamned word these people said?

I'd been asleep for so long, I decided to indulge myself in a luxurious and prolonged pee. I walked outside wearing my harness and a very sour expression, temporarily forgetting entirely that I owed my life to the people of this village. I left my rifle behind and walked slowly down the steep hill, which was now as slippery as all hell because of the rain.

At the conclusion of this operation, I took myself up the hill a little way and sat down on the drying grass, mainly because I did not wish to be any ruder to Gulab than I already had been, but also because I just wanted to sit alone for a while and nurse my thoughts.

I still considered my best bet would be to find a way to get to the nearest American military base. And that was still Monagee. I stared up at the towering mountain I would have to cross, the rain and dew now glinting off it in the early morning sun, and I think I visibly flinched.

It really would be one heck of a climb, and my leg was aching already, not at the thought of it but because I'd walked a hundred yards; bullet wounds tend to take a while to heal up. Also, despite Sarawa's bold efforts, that leg was, I knew, still full of shrapnel, which would not be much of a help toward a pain-free stroll over the peak.

Anyway, I just sat there on the side of the mountain and tried to clear my mind, to decide whether there was anything else I could do except sit around and wait for a new night when Gulab and the guys could assist me to Monagee. And all the time, I was weighing the possibility of the Taliban coming in on some vengeful attack in retribution for yesterday's bombardment.

The fact was, I was a living, breathing target as well as a distress signal. There sat the mighty Sharmak, with his second in command, "Commodore Abdul," and a large, trained army, all of them with essentially nothing else to do except kill me. And if they managed to make it into the village and hit the house I was staying in, I'd be lucky to fend them off and avoid a short trip to Pakistan for publicity and execution.

Christ, those guys would have loved nothing more in all the world than to grab me and announce to the Arab television stations they had defeated one of the top U.S. Navy SEAL teams. Not just defeated, wiped them out in battle, smashed the rescue squad, blown up the helicopter, executed all survivors, and here they had the last one.

The more I thought about it, the more untenable my position seemed to be. Could the goatherds of Sabray band together and fight shoulder to shoulder to save me? Or would the brutal killers of al Qaeda and the Taliban in the end get their way? It was odd, but I still did not realize the full power of that *lokhay*. No one had fully explained it to me. I knew there was something, but that ancient tribal law was still a mystery to me.

I stared around the hills, but I could see no one outside of the village. Gulab and his guys always behaved as if the very mountainside was alive with hidden danger, and while he did not in my mind make much of an alarm clock, he had to be an expert on the bandit country which surrounds his own Sabray.

It was thus with rising concern that I saw Gulab racing down the hill toward me. He literally dragged me into a standing position and then pulled me down the trail leading to the lower reaches of the village. He was running and trying to make me keep up with him, and he kept shouting, signaling, again and again: *Taliban! Taliban are here! In the village! Run, Dr. Marcus, for God's sake, run!*

He pushed his right shoulder up under my left arm to bear some of my fast-dwindling weight, and I half hobbled, half ran, half fell down the hill. Of course by my own recent standards this was like a stroll on the beach.

I suddenly realized we might have to fight and I'd left my rifle back in the house. I had my ammunition in the harness, but nothing to fire it with. And now it was my turn to yell, *"Gulab! Gulab! Stop! Stop! I don't have my gun."*

He replied something I took to be Afghan for "What a complete fucking idiot you've turned out to be."

But whatever had put the fear of God into him was still right there, and he had no intention of stopping until he had located a refuge for us. We ducked and dived through the lower village trails until he found the house he was looking for. Gulab kicked the door open, rammed it shut behind him, and helped me down onto the floor. And there I sat, unarmed, largely useless, and highly apprehensive about what might happen in the next hour.

Gulab, without a word, opened the front door and took off at high speed. He went past the window like a rocket, running hard up the gradient, possibly going for the Hindu Kush allcomers 100-meters record. God knows where he was going, but he'd gone.

Three minutes later he kicked open the door and came charging back into the house. He was carrying my rifle as well as his own AK-47. I had seventy-five rounds left. I think he had more in his own ammunition belt. Gravely he handed me the Mark 12 sniper rifle and said simply, "Taliban, Dr. Marcus. We fight."

He looked more serious than I'd ever seen him. Not afraid, just full of determination. Up on that mountain, when he had first seen me, Sarawa had made the decision with his buddies that I, a wounded American, should be granted *lokhay*. The doctor knew perfectly well from the first moment by that gushing mountain river that the situation might ultimately come to this. Even if I didn't.

It was a decision that, right from the start, had affected everyone in the village. I think most people had accepted it, and it had obviously been endorsed by the village elder. I'd seen a few angry faces full of hatred, but they were not in the majority. And now the village chief of law and order, Mohammad Gulab, was prepared to stand by that unspoken vow his people had given to me.

He was doing it not for personal gain but out of a sense of honor that reached back down the generations, two thousand years of *Pashtunwalai* tradition: You will defend your guest to the death. I watched Gulab carefully as he rammed a new magazine into his AK. This was a man preparing to step right up to the plate. And I saw that light of goodness in his dark eyes, the way you always do when someone is making a brave and selfless action.

I thanked Gulab and banged a new magazine into my rifle. I stared out the window and assessed the battlefield. We were low down on almost flat terrain, but the Taliban's attack would be launched from the higher ground, the way they always preferred it. I wondered how many other rock-and-mud houses in Sabray were also shielding men who were about to fight.

The situation was serious but not dire. We had excellent cover, and I didn't think the enemy knew precisely where I was. So far as I could see, the Battle for Murphy's Ridge represented a two-edged sword. First of all, the tribesmen could be seething with fury about the number of their guys killed in action by Mikey, Axe, Danny, and me. This might even mean a suicide bomber or an attack so reckless they'd risk any number of warriors just to get me. I wasn't crazy about either option.

On the other hand, they might be slightly scared at the prospect of facing even one of that tiny American team that had wiped out possibly 50 percent of a Taliban assault force.

Sure, they knew I was wounded, but they also knew I would be well armed by the villagers, even if I had lost my own rifle. I guessed they would either throw everything at me, the hell with the expense, or take it real steady, fighting their way through the village house by house until they had Gulab and me cornered.

But an impending attack requires quick, expert planning. I needed to operate fast and make Gulab understand our tactics. He immediately gave way to my experience, which made me think he had never quite accepted my story about being a doctor. He knew I'd fought on the ridge, and right now he was ready to do my bidding.

We had two areas to cover, the door and the window. It wouldn't have been much good if I'd been blasting away through the window at Taliban down the street when a couple of those sneaky little bastards crept through the front door and shot me in the back.

I explained it was up to Gulab to cover the entrance, to make sure I had the split second I would need to swing around and cut 'em down before they could open fire. Ideally I would have preferred him to issue an early warning that the enemy was coming. That way I might have been able to get into the shadows in the corners and take 'em out maybe six at a time instead of just gunning down the leader.

Ideally I would have liked a heavy piece of furniture to ram in front of the door, just to buy me a little extra time. But there was no furniture, just those big cushions, which were obviously not sufficiently heavy.

Anyway, Gulab understood the strategy and nodded fiercely, the way he always did when he was sure of something. "Okay, Marcus," he said. And it did not escape me, he'd dropped the *Dr.* part.

When battle began, Gulab would man the end of the window that gave him the best dual view of the door. I would concentrate on whatever frontal assault might be taking place. I'd need to shoot steadily and straight, wasting nothing, just like Axe and Danny did on the mountain while Mikey called the shots.

I tried to tell Gulab to stay calm and shoot straight, nothing hysterical. That way we'd win or, at worst, cause a disorderly Taliban retreat.

He looked a bit vacant. I could tell he was not understanding. So I hit him with an old phrase we always use before a conflict: "Okay, guys, let's rock 'n' roll."

Matter of fact, that was worse. Gulab thought I was about to give him dancing lessons. It might have been funny if the situation had not been so serious. And then we both heard the opening bursts of gunfire, high up in the village.

There was a lot of it. Too much. The sheer volume of fire was ridiculous, unless the Taliban were planning to wipe out the entire population of Sabray. And I knew they would not consider that because such a slaughter would surely end all support from these tribal villages up here in the mountains.

No, they would not do that. They wanted me, but they would never kill another hundred Afghan people, including women and children, in order to get me. The Taliban and their al Qaeda cohorts were mercilessly cruel, but this Ben Sharmak was not stupid.

Besides, I detected no battlefield rhythm to the gunfire. It was not being conducted with the short, sharp bursts of trained men going for a target. It came in prolonged volleys, and I listened carefully. There was no obvious return of fire, and right then I knew what was happening.

These lunatics had come rolling out of the trees into the village, firing randomly into the air and aiming at nothing, the way they often do, all jumping up and down and shouting, *"Death to the infidel."* Stupid pricks.

Their loose objective is always to frighten the life out of people, and right now they seemed to be succeeding. I could hear women screaming, children crying, but no return of fire from the tribesmen of Sabray. I knew precisely what that would sound like, and I was not hearing it.

I looked at Gulab. He was braced for action, leaning in the window with me, one eye on the front door. We both clicked our safety catches open.

Up above we could still hear the screaming, but the gunfire subsided. Little sonsabitches were probably beating up the kids. Which might have inspired me to get right back up there and take on the whole jihadist army single-handed, but I held back, held my fire, and waited.

We waited for maybe forty-five minutes and then it was quiet. As if they had never been here. That unseen village calm had returned, there was no sense of panic or sign of injured people. I left it to Gulab to call this one. "Taliban gone," he said simply.

"What happens now?" I asked him. "Bagram?"

Gulab shook his head. "Bagram," he said. Then he signaled for the umpteenth time, "Helicopter will come."

I rolled my eyes heavenward. I'd heard this helicopter crap before. And I had news for Gulab. "Helicopter no come," I told him.

"Helicopter come," he replied.

As ever, I could not really know what Gulab knew or how he had discovered what was happening. But right now he believed the Taliban had gone into the house where I had been staying and found I was missing. No one had betrayed me, and they had not dared to conduct a house-to-house search for fear of further alienating the people and, in particular, the village elder.

This armed gang of tribesmen, who were hell-bent on driving out the Americans and the government, could not function up here in these protective mountains entirely alone. Without local support their primitive supply line would perish, and they would rapidly begin to lose recruits. Armies need food, cover, and co-operation, and the Taliban could only indulge in so much bullying before these powerful village leaders decided they preferred the company of the Americans.

That's why they had just evacuated Sabray. They would still surround the village, awaiting their chance to grab me, but they would not risk causing major disruption to the day-to-day lives of the people. I'd been here for five nights now, including the night in the cave, and the Taliban had crossed the boundaries of Sabray only twice, once for a few hours of violence late in the evening, and once just now for maybe an hour.

Gulab was certain they had gone, but he was equally certain we could not dare go back to the house. It was almost ten in the morning by now, and Gulab was preparing to leave and take me with him, once more out into the mountains.

*   *   *

It had passed midnight back in Texas and the vigil at our ranch continued. The media was still voicing its opinion that the SEAL team was dead, and the latest call from Coronado had been received. There was still no news of me. They all knew there would be another call at 0400, and everyone waited out there in the hot July night, their hopes diminishing, according to Mom, as the hours ticked by.

People were starting to speculate how I could possibly have survived if no one at the American base knew where I was. But news was really scarce, except for the part some members of the media invented. And people were beginning to lose heart.

Except, apparently, for Morgan and the other SEALs, none of whom would even consider I was dead. At least that's what they always told everyone. "MIA," they kept repeating. "MIA. He's not dead till we say he's dead."

Morgan continued to tell everyone that he was thinking about me and I was thinking about him. He was in contact, even if no one else was. And Senior Chief Gothro kept a careful eye on my mom in case she disintegrated.

But she remembers that night to this day, and how there were people growing sadder by the minute. And how the SEALs held it all together, the chaplains, the officers, the noncoms, some ordering, some imploring, but asking everyone to keep the faith.

"Marcus needs you!" Chaplain Trey Vaughn told this large and disparate gathering. "And God is protecting him, and now repeat after me the words of the Twenty-third Psalm. 'Yea, though I walk through the valley of the shadow of death, I will fear no evil: for Thou art with me; Thy rod and Thy staff they comfort me.'"

Solemnly, some of the toughest men in the U.S. Armed Forces stood shoulder to shoulder with the SEAL chaplain, each of them thinking of me as an old and, I hope, trusted friend and teammate. Each of them, at those moments, alone with his God. As I was with mine, half a world away.

At 0400 the call came through to the ranch from Coronado. Still no news. And the SEALs started the process all over again, encouraging, sharing their optimism, explaining that I had been especially trained to withstand such an ordeal. "If anyone can get out of this, it's Marcus," Chaplain Vaughn said. "And he'll feel the energy in your prayers — and you will give him strength — and I *forbid you to give up on him — God will bring him home.*"

Out there in the dry summer pastures, surrounded by thousands of head of cattle, the words of the United States Navy Hymn echoed into the night. There were no neighbors to wake. Everyone for miles around was in our front yard. Mom says everyone was out there that night, again nearly three hundred. And the policemen and the judges and the sheriffs and all the others joined Mom and Dad and the iron men from SPECWARCOM, just standing there, singing at the top of their lungs, "'O hear us when we cry to Thee, for SEALs in air, on land and sea...'"

Back in Sabray, Gulab and I were making a break for it. Clutching our rifles, we left our little mud-and-rock redoubt in the lower street and headed farther down the mountain. Painfully, I made the two hundred yards to a flat field which had been cultivated and recently harvested. It was strictly dirt now, but raked dirt, as if ready for a new crop.

I had seen this field before, from the window of house two, which I could just see maybe 350 yards back up the mountain.

I guess the field was about the size of two American football fields; it had a dry rock border all around. It was an ideal landing spot for a helicopter, I thought, certainly the only suitable area I had ever seen up there. It was a place where a pilot could bring in an MH-47 without risking a collision with trees or rolling off a precipice or landing in the middle of a Taliban trap.

For a few moments, I considered writing a large *SOS* in the dirt, but Gulab was anxious, and he half carried, half manhandled me out of the field and back onto the lush mountain slopes, and there he found me a resting place at the side of the trail where I could take cover under a bush. And this carried a bonus, because the bush contained a full crop of blackberries. And I lay down there in the shade luxuriously eating the berries, which were not quite ripe but tasted damned good to me.

It was very quiet again now, and my trained sniper's ear, honed perhaps better than ever before, detected no unusual sound in the undergrowth. Not a snapped twig, not an unusual rustling in the grass. No unusual shadow behind a tree. Nothing.

We waited there for a short while before Gulab stood up and walked a little way, then turned and whispered, "We go now." I got hold of my rifle and twisted onto my right side, ready to heave myself upward, a movement that this week had taken a lot of concentration and effort.

I don't know why it happened. But something told me to look up, and I cast my eyes to the slope behind us. And right there sitting very quietly, his gaze steady upon me and betraying nothing, was Sharmak, the Taliban leader, the man I had come to capture or kill.

I'd seen only a grainy, not very good photograph of him, but it was enough for me. I was certain it was him. And I think he knew I knew. He was a lean character, like all of them, forty-ish, with a long, black, red-flecked beard. He wore black Afghan garb, a reddish vest, and a black turban.

I seem to recall he had green eyes, and they were filled with a hatred which would have melted a U.S. Army tank. He stared right through me and spoke not one word. I noticed he was unarmed, and I tightened my grip on the Mark 12 and very slowly turned it on him until the barrel was aimed right between his eyes.

He was not afraid. He never flinched, never moved, and I had a powerful instinct to shoot that bastard dead, right here on the mountain. After all, it was what I had come for; that or capture him, and that last part wasn't going to happen.

Sharmak was surrounded by his army. If I'd shot him, I would not have lasted twenty seconds. His guys would have gunned down both me and Gulab and then, minus their beloved commander in chief, probably would have massacred the entire village, including the kids. I considered that and rejected shooting him.

I also considered that Sharmak was clearly not about to shoot me. The presence of Gulab made it a complete standoff, and Sharmak was not about to call in his guys to shoot the oldest son of Sabray's village elder. Equally, I did not feel especially inclined to commit suicide. Everyone held their fire.

Sharmak just sat there, and then Gulab nodded to the Taliban boss, who I noticed made an infinitesimal incline of his head, like a pitcher acknowledging a catcher's signal. And then Gulab walked slowly across to talk to him, and Sharmak stood up, and they turned their backs on me and moved farther up the mountainside, out of my sight.

There was only one subject they could possibly be discussing. Would the people of Sabray now agree to give me up? And I could not know how far Gulab and his father would still go to defend me.

I just slumped back under the blackberry bush, uncertain of my fate, uncertain what these two mountain tribesmen would decide. Because each of them, in his way, had so far proved to be unbending in his principles. The relentless killer, a man who saw himself as the warrior-savior of Afghanistan, now in conference with the village cop, a man who seemed prepared to risk everything just to defend me.

12

"Two-two-eight!
It's Two-two-eight!"

In her mind, there could be only one possible reason for
the call... They'd found my body on the mountain...
A voice came down the line and demanded, "Is the
family assembled?"

They were gone for five minutes, and they came back together.
Ben Sharmak stood for a few moments staring at me, and then
he climbed away, back to his army. Gulab walked down the hill
to me and tried to explain Sharmak had handed him a note that
said, *Either you hand over the American—or every member of your
family will be killed.*

Gulab made his familiar dismissive gesture, and we both
turned and watched the Taliban leader walking away through
the trees. And the village cop offered me his hand, helped me to
my feet, and once more led me through the forest, half lifting me
down the gradients, always considerate of my shattered left leg,
until we reached a dried-up riverbed.

And there we rested. We watched for Taliban sharpshooters,
but no one came. All around us in the trees, their AKs ready,
were familiar faces from Sabray ready to defend us.

We waited for at least forty-five minutes. And then, amid the unholy silence of the mountain, two more guys from my village arrived. It was obvious they were signaling for us to leave, right now.

Each of them gave me support under my arms and led me up through the trees on the side of this steep escarpment. I have to admit I no longer knew what was going on, where we were going, or what I was supposed to be doing. I realized we could not go back to the village, and I really did not like the tone of that note Gulab had shoved in his pocket.

And here I was, alone with these tribesmen, with no coherent plan. My leg was killing me, I could hardly put it to the ground, and the two guys carrying me were bearing the whole of my weight. We came to a little flight of rough rock steps cut into the gradient. They got behind pushing me up with their shoulders.

I made the top step first, and as I did so, I came face to face with an armed Afghani fighter I had not seen before. He carried an AK-47, held in the ready-to-fire position, and when he saw me, he raised it. I looked at his hat, and there was a badge containing the words which almost stopped my heart — BUSH FOR PRESIDENT!

He was Afghan special forces, and I was seized by panic because I was dressed in the clothes of an Afghan tribesman, identical to those of the Taliban. But right behind him, bursting through the undergrowth, came two U.S. Army Rangers in combat uniform, rifles raised, the leader a big black guy. Behind me, with unbelievable presence of mind, Gulab was roaring out my BUD/S class numbers he'd seen on my Trident voodoo tattoo: *"Two-two-eight! It's Two-two-eight!"*

The Ranger's face suddenly lit up with a gigantic smile. He took one look at my six-foot-five-inch frame and snapped,

"American?" I just had time to nod before he let out a yell that ripped across the mountainside— *"It's Marcus, guys! We got him— we got him!"*

And the Ranger came running toward me and grabbed me in his arms, and I could smell his sweat and his combat gear and his rifle, the smells of home, the smells I live with. American smells. I tried to keep steady, not break down, mostly because SEALs would *never* show weakness in front of a Ranger.

"Hey, bro," I said. "It's good to see you."

By this time there was chaos on the mountain. Army guys were coming out of the forest from all over the place. I could see they were really beat up, wearing battered combat gear, all of them with several days' growth of beard. They were covered in mud, unkempt, and all grinning broadly. I guessed, correctly as it happened, they'd been out here searching for my team since early last Wednesday morning. Hell, they'd been out all night in that thunderstorm. No wonder they looked a bit disheveled.

It was Sunday now. And Jesus, was it great to hear the English language again, just the everyday words, the diverse American accents, the familiarity. I'm telling you, when you've been in a hostile, foreign environment for a while with no one to whom you can explain anything, being rescued by your own kind—tough, confident, organized guys, professional, hard-trained, armed to the teeth, ready for anything, bursting with friendship—well, it's a feeling of the highest possible elation. But I wouldn't recommend the preparation for such a moment.

They moved into action immediately. An army captain ordered a team to get me up out of the forest, onto higher ground. They carried me up the hill and sat me down next to a goat pen. U.S. Corpsman Travis instantly set about fixing up my wounds. He removed the old dressings which Sarawa had given me and applied new antiseptic cream and fresh bandages. He gave me clean water and antibiotics. By the time he'd finished I felt damn near human.

The atmosphere was unavoidably cheerful, because all the guys felt their mission was accomplished. All Americans in combat understand that feeling of celebration, reflecting, as we all do, that so much could have gone wrong, so much we had evaded by our own battlefield know-how, so many times it could have gone either way.

These Rangers and Green Berets were no different. Somehow, in hundreds of square miles of mountainous terrain, they'd found me alive. But I knew they did not really understand the extreme danger we were all in. I explained to them the number of Taliban warriors there were out here, how many there had been against us on Murphy's Ridge, the presence of Sharmak and his entire army, so close, maybe watching us...no, forget that. Most certainly watching us. We were all together, and we would make a formidable fighting force if attacked, but we would be badly outnumbered, and we were now all inside a Taliban encirclement. Not just me.

I debriefed them as thoroughly as I could, first of all explaining that my guys were all dead, Mikey, Axe, and Danny. I found that especially difficult, because I had not told anyone before. There had been no one for me to report to, definitely no one who would understand what those guys meant to me and the gaping hollow they would leave in my life for the rest of my days.

I consulted my thighs, where I still had my clear notes of routes, distances, and terrain. I showed them the areas where I knew the Taliban were encamped, helped them mark up their maps. *Here, here, and here, guys, that's where they are.* The fact was, the bastards were everywhere, all around us, waiting for their chance. I did have a feeling that Sharmak might have grown wary of facing heavy American firepower head-on. He'd had half his army wiped out on the ridge by just four of us. There were a lot more of us now, gathered around the goat pens while Travis did his number.

I asked the Ranger captain how many guys he had. And he replied, "We're good. Twenty."

In my view that was probably a bit light, since Sharmak could easily be back to his full strength of maybe 150 to 200 warriors, reinforced by al Qaeda.

"We got gunships, Apache Sixty-fours, standing by," he said. "Whatever we need. We're good."

I stressed once more that we were undoubtedly surrounded, and he replied, "Roger that, Marcus. We'll act accordingly."

Before we left, I asked them how the hell they'd found me. And it turned out to be my emergency beacon in the window of the little rock house in the mountain. The flight crews had picked it up when they were flying over and then tracked it back to the village. They were pretty certain the owner of that PRC-148 radio was one of the original SEAL team but had to consider the fact it might have been stolen by the Taliban.

They did not, however, think it had been operated by Afghan tribesmen in this instance, and they thought it unlikely the beacon had been switched on and aimed skyward by guys who had not the slightest idea what it was for.

They thus reasoned that one of the SEALs was right down there in that village, or in any event pretty damned close. So the guys just closed in on me, somehow moving their own dragnet right past the Taliban dragnet. And suddenly there I was, dressed up like Osama bin Laden's second in command, arms wrapped around a couple of tribesmen like we were three drunks falling up the hill, the village policeman right behind yelling, *"Two-two-eight!"*

Led by Gulab, we set off for the village and moved back into my second house, the one where we'd sat out the storm. The army threw a security perimeter all the way around Sabray, and they carried me up past that big tree and into the main room. I noticed that rooster was right there in the tree; he was quiet for a change, but the memory of him still made me want to blow his freakin' head off.

The guys rustled up some tea and we settled down for a detailed debriefing. It was noon in Sabray, and in attendance was a very serious group of army personnel, from captains on down, mostly Rangers and Green Berets. Before we started, I was compelled to tell 'em I had hoped to be rescued by the SEALs—because now I'd definitely have to put up with a lot of bullshit from them, telling me, "See that, the SEALs get in trouble, and they gotta send for the army to get 'em out, like always."

That got a loud cheer, but it did not disguise my eternal gratitude to them and what they had risked to save me. They were really good guys and took total control in the most professional way. First they radioed into base that I had been found, that I was stable and unlikely to die, but regretfully, the other three team members had died in action. I heard them confirm they had me safe but that we were still in a potentially hostile Afghan village and that we were surrounded by Taliban and al Qaeda troops. They were requesting evacuation as soon as night fell.

The debriefing went on for a long time as I tried to explain details of my actions on and off the battlefield. And all the time, the kids kept rushing in to see me. They were all over the place, hanging on to my arm, their own arms around my neck, talking, shouting, laughing. The adults from the village also came in, and I had to insist they could stay, especially Sarawa, who had reappeared, and Gulab, who had never left. I owed my life to each of them.

So far, no one had found the bodies of Mikey, Danny, and Axe. And we spent a long time going over satellite photographs for me to pinpoint the precise places they had died. The army guys had some data on the battle, but I was able to fill in a lot of stuff for them. Especially to explain how we had fallen back under Mikey's command, and then kept falling back, how we never had any option but to establish our defense farther down the mountain, always farther down.

I recounted how Axe had held our left flank with such overwhelming gallantry, and how Danny, shot so many times, kept firing, trying to hold our right flank until his dying breath. And how, in the end, there were just too many of them, with too much firepower, too many of those big Russian-made grenades, the ones that finally blew Axe and me clean out of the battle.

Taliban casualties had been, of course, high. It seemed everyone knew that. I think all of us in that little room, including Gulab, thought the Taliban would not risk another frontal assault on the Americans. And so we waited until the sun began to slip behind the mountains, and I said good-bye to all the kids, several of whom were crying. Sarawa just slipped quietly away. I never saw him again.

Gulab led us down to the flat field at the base of the village, and with the comms up and running, we waited it out. The Ranger security guard was in formation around the perimeter, in case the Taliban decided to give it one last shot. I knew they were out there, and I never took my eyes off that mountain slope as we all sat there, around twenty army personnel and maybe ten villagers, the guys who had stuck by me from the beginning.

We all sat in the dark, backs to the stone wall, looking at the field, just waiting. Way over the high horizon, shortly before 2200, we could hear the unmistakable distant beat of a big U.S. military helicopter, clattering in over the mountains.

We saw it circling, far away from the slopes where I believed the main Taliban and al Qaeda forces were camped. And then suddenly Gulab grabbed my arm, hissing, *"Marcus! Marcus! Taliban!"*

I stared up at the escarpment and there in the darkness I could see white lights, moving quickly, across the face of the mountain. *"Taliban, Marcus! Taliban!"* I could tell Gulab was really uneasy, and I called over the army captain and pointed out the danger.

We all reacted instantly. Gulab, who was unarmed, grabbed my rifle, and he and two of his buddies helped me climb the wall and jump down the much deeper drop on the other side. Several of the villagers ran like hell up the hill to their rocky homes. Not Gulab. He took up position behind that wall, aiming my sniper rifle straight at the enemy on the hillside.

The army comms guys moved into action, calling in the United States air armada we knew was out there—fighter bombers and helicopters, ready to attack that mountain if there was even a suggestion the Taliban might try to hit the incoming rescue helo.

I considered it was obvious that they were planning one last offensive, one last-ditch attempt to kill me. I grabbed a pair of NVGs and took up my position as spotter behind the wall, trying to locate the mountain men, trying to nail them once and for all.

We could still see the rescue helo way out in the distance when the U.S. Armed Forces, who'd plainly had it up to their eyeballs with this fucking Ben Sharmak, finally let it rip. They came howling across those pitch-black crevasses and blasted the living hell out of those slopes: bombs, rockets, everything they had. It was a storm of murderous explosive. No one could have lived out there.

The lights went out for the Taliban that night. All those little white beams, their fires and lanterns—everything went out. And I just crouched there, calling out the information to the comms guy next to me, identifying Taliban locations, the stuff I'm trained to do. I was standing up now with a smile on my face, watching my guys pulverize those little bastards who beat up my kids and killed my teammates. Fuck 'em, right?

It was a grim smile, I admit, but these guys had chased me, tortured me, pursued me, tried to kill me about four hundred times, blown me up, nearly kidnapped me, threatened to execute me. And now my guys were sticking it right to 'em. Beautiful. I saw a report confirming thirty-two Taliban and al Qaeda died out there that night. Not enough.

The shattering din high in the Hindu Kush died away. The U.S. air offensive was done. The landing zone was cleared and made safe, and the rescue helo came rocketing in from the south.

The Green Berets were still in communication, and they talked the pilot down, into the newly harvested village opium field. I remember the rotors of the helo made a green bioluminescent static in the night air.

And I could hear it dropping down toward us, an apparition of howling U.S. airpower in the night. It was an all-encompassing, shattering, deafening din, thundering rather than echoing, between the high peaks of the Hindu Kush. No helicopter ever smashed the local sound barriers with more brutality. The eerie silence of those mountains retreated before the second decibel onslaught of the night. The ground shuddered. The dust whipped up into a sandstorm. The rotors screamed into the pure mountain air. It was the most beautiful sound I ever heard.

The helo came in slowly and put down a few yards from us. The loadmaster leaped to the ground and opened the main door. The guys helped me into the cabin, and Gulab joined me. Instantly we took off, and neither of us looked out at the blackness of the unlit village of Sabray. Me, because I knew we could not see a thing; Gulab, because he was uncertain when he would pass this way again. The Taliban threats to both himself and his family were very much more serious than he had ever admitted.

He was afraid of the helicopter and clung to my arm throughout the short journey to Asadabad. And there we both disembarked. I was going on to Bagram, but for the moment Gulab was to stay on this base, out there in his own country, and assist the U.S. military in any way he could. I hugged him good-bye, this rather inscrutable tribesman who had risked his life for me. He seemed to expect nothing in return, and I had one more shot at giving him my watch. But he refused, as he had done four times in the past.

Our good-bye was painful for me, because I had no words in his language to express my thanks. I'll never know, but perhaps he too would have said something to me, if he'd only had the words. It might even have been warm or affectionate, like... well... "Noisy bastard, footsteps like an elephant, ungrateful son of a gun." Or "What's the matter with our best goat's milk, asshole?"

But there was nothing that could be said. I was going home. And he may never be able to go home. Our paths, which had crossed so suddenly and so powerfully in a life-changing encounter for both of us, were about to diverge.

I boarded the big C-130 for Bagram, back to my base. We touched down on the main runway at 2300, exactly six days and four hours since Mikey, Axe, Danny, and I had occupied this very same spot, lying here on this ground, staring up at the distant snowcapped peaks, laughing, joking, always optimistic, unaware of the trial by fire which awaited us high in those mountains. Less than a week. It might have been a thousand years.

I was greeted by four doctors and all the help I could possibly need. There was also a small group of nurses, at least one of whom knew me from my volunteer work in the hospital. The others were stunned at the sight of me, but this one nurse took one look at me standing at the top of the ramp and burst into tears.

That's how terrible I looked. I'd lost thirty-seven pounds, my face was scoured from the crash down mountain one, my broken nose needed proper setting, I was racked with pain from my leg, my smashed wrist hurt like hell and so did my back, as it will when you've cracked three vertebrae. I'd lost God knows how many pints of blood. I was white as a ghost, and I could hardly walk.

The nurse just cried out, "Oh, Marcus!" and turned away, sobbing. I declined a stretcher and leaned on the doctor, ignoring the pain. But he knew. "Come on, buddy," he said. "Let's get you on the stretcher."

But again I shook my head. I'd had a shot of morphine, and I tried to stand unassisted. I turned to the doc and looked him in the eye, and I told him, "I walked on here, and I'm walking off, by myself. I'm hurt, but I'm still a SEAL, and they haven't finished me. I'm walking."

The doctor just shook his head. He'd met a lot of guys like me before, and he knew it wouldn't do a damn bit of good arguing.

I guess he understood the only thought I had in my mind was *What kind of a SEAL would it make me if they had to help me off the plane? No sir. I won't agree to that.*

And so I entered my home base once more, moving very slowly down the ramp under my own steam until I touched the ground. By this time, I noticed two other nurses were in tears. And I remember thinking, *Thank Christ Mom can't see me yet.*

Right about then I think I caved in. The doctors and nurses ran forward to help me and get me stretchered into a van and directly to a hospital bed. The time for personal heroics had passed. I'd sucked up every goddamned thing this fucking country could throw at me, I'd been through another Hell Week to the tenth power, and now I was saved.

Actually, I felt particularly rough. The morphine was not as good as the opium I'd been given. And every goddamned thing hurt. I was met formally by the SEAL skipper, Commander Kent Pero, who was accompanied by my doctor, Colonel Carl Dickens.

He came with me in the van, Commander Pero, a very high-ranking SEAL officer who had always remembered my first name, ever since the day we first met. He sat beside me, gripping my arm, asking me how I was. I recall telling him, "Yes, sir, I'm fine."

But then I heard him say, "Marcus." And he shook his head. And I noticed this immensely tough character, my boss's boss, had tears streaming down his face, tears of relief, I think, that I was alive. It's funny, but it was the first time in so long that I was with someone who really cared about me, the first time since Mikey and Axe and Danny had died.

And I found it overwhelming, and I broke down right there in the van, and when I pulled myself together, Commander Pero was asking me if there was anything I needed, because no matter what it was, he would get it.

"Yes, sir," I replied, drying my eyes on the sheet. "Do you think I could get a cheeseburger?"

The moment I was secured in Bagram, they made news of my rescue available. I had been in the hands of the U.S. military for some hours, but I know the navy did not want anyone to start celebrating until I was well and truly safe.

The call went around the world like a guided missile: Bagram — Bahrain — SATCOM to SPECWARCOM, Coronado — direct phone link to the ranch.

The regular call had come in on time at around one that afternoon, and they were expecting another "no news" update at four. But now the phone rang at three. Early. And according to my dad, when Chief Gothro came outside and walked through the crowd to collect my mom, telling her there was a call from Coronado, she almost fainted. In her mind, there could be only one possible reason for the call, and that was the death of her little angel (that's me).

Chief Gothro half carried her into the house, and when they arrived at the bedroom where the phone was installed, the first thing she saw was Morgan and my other brother, Scottie, with their arms around each other, sobbing uncontrollably. Everyone thought they knew the military. There could be only one reason for the early call. They'd found my body on the mountain.

Chief Gothro walked my mom to the phone and informed her that whatever it was, she had to face it. A voice came down the line and demanded, "Chief, is the family assembled?"

"Yessir."

"Mr. and Mrs. Luttrell?"

"Yes," whispered Mom.

"We got him, ma'am. We got Marcus. And he's stable."

Mom started to collapse right there on the bedroom floor. Scottie moved swiftly to save her from hitting it. Lieutenant JJ Jones bolted for the door, stood on the porch, and called for quiet. Then he shouted, *"They got him, guys! Marcus has been rescued."*

They tell me the roar which erupted over those lonely pastures way down there in the back country of East Texas could have been heard in Houston, fifty-five miles away. Morgan says it wasn't just your average roar. It was spontaneous. Deafening. Everyone together, top of their lungs, a pure outpouring of relief and joy for Mom and Dad and my family.

It signaled the conclusion of a five-day vigil in which a zillion prayers had been offered by God-fearing folk; they understood in that split second after the announcement that those prayers had been asked and answered. For them, it was a confirmation of faith, of the unbreakable hope and belief, of the SEAL chaplain Trey Vaughn and all the others.

Immediately, they raised the flag, and the Stars and Stripes fluttered in the hot breeze. And then the SEALs linked arms with my family and my friends and my neighbors, people who they might never see again but to whom they were now irrevocably joined for all the days of their lives. Because no one, according to Mom, could ever forget that one brief moment they shared, that long-awaited moment of release, when fears and dreads were laid to rest.

I was alive. I guess that's all it took. And all these amazing guys, with hearts as wide as the Texas prairies, burst suddenly into song: "God bless America, land that I love..."

That's Mrs. Herzogg and her daughters; Billy Shelton; Chief Gothro; Mom and Dad; Morgan and Scottie; Lieutenant Andy Haffele and his wife, Kristina; Eric Rooney; Commander Jeff

Bender; Daniel, the master sergeant; Lieutenant JJ Jones; and all the others I already mentioned. Five days and five nights, they'd waited for this. And here I was, safe in a hospital bed eight thousand miles away, thinking of them, as they were thinking of me.

Matter of fact, at the time I was just thinking of a smart-ass remark to make to Morgan, because they'd told me I was about to be patched through to my family, on the phone. I guessed Morgan would be there, and if I could come up with something sufficiently slick and nonchalant, he'd know for sure I was good. Of course, it wasn't as important to talk to him as it was to speak to Mom. Morgan and I had been in touch all along, the way identical twins usually are.

Right around this time, I was assigned a minder, Petty Officer First Class Jeff Delapenta (SEAL Team 10), who would never leave my side. And remember, damn near everyone on the base wanted to come and have a chat. At least that's how it seemed to me. But Jeff was having none of it. He stood guard over my room like a German shepherd, taking the view that I was very sick and needed peace and rest, and he, PO1 Jeff, was going to make good and sure I got it.

Doctors and nurses, fine. High-ranking SEAL commanders, well... okay, but only just. Anyone else, forget it. Jeff Delapenta turned away generals! Told 'em I was resting, could not be disturbed under any circumstances whatsoever. "Strict orders from his doctors... Sir, it would be more than my career's worth to allow you to enter that room."

I spoke privately to my family on the phone and refrained from mentioning to Mom that I had now contracted some kind of Afghan mountain bacteria that attacked my stomach like Montezuma's revenge gets you in Mexico. I swear to God, it came from that fucking Pepsi bottle. That sucker could have poisoned the population of the Hindu Kush.

Didn't stop me loving that first cheeseburger, though. And as soon as I was rested, the real intensive debriefing began. It was right here that I learned, for the first time, of the full ramifications of *lokhay*, that the people of Sabray were indeed prepared to fight for me until no one was left alive. One of the intel guys told me those details, which I had suspected but never knew for sure.

These debriefing meetings revealed sufficient data to pinpoint precisely where the bodies of my guys were lying. And I found it really difficult. Just staring down at the photographs, reliving, as no one could ever understand, the place where my best buddy fell, torturing myself, wondering again if I could have saved him. Could I have done more? That night, for the first time, I heard Mikey scream.

On my third day in the hospital, the bodies of Mikey and Danny were brought down from the mountains. They were unable to find Axe. I was told this, and later that day I dressed, just in shirt and jeans, so Dr. Dickens could drive me out for the Ramp Ceremony, one of the most sacred SEAL traditions, in which we say a formal good-bye to a lost brother.

It was the first time anyone had seen me outside of my immediate entourage, and they probably received a major shock. I was scrubbed and neat, but not much like the Marcus they knew. And I was ill from my brutal encounter with that goddamned Pepsi bottle.

The C-130 was parked on the runway, ramp down. There were around two hundred military personnel in attendance when the Humvees arrived bearing the two coffins, each draped with the American flag. And all of them snapped to attention, instantly, no commands, as the SEALs stepped forward to claim their brothers.

Very slowly, with immense dignity, they lifted the coffins high, and then carried the bodies of Mikey and Danny the fifty yards to the ramp of the aircraft.

I positioned myself right at the back and watched as the guys carefully bore my buddies on their first steps back to the United States. A thousand memories stood before me, as I guess they would have done to anyone who'd been at Murphy's Ridge.

Danny, crashing down the mountain, his right thumb blown off, still firing, shot again and again and again, rising up as I dragged him away, rising up to aim his rifle at the enemy once more, still firing, still defiant, a warrior to his last breath. And here he comes in that polished wood coffin.

Out in front was the coffin that carried Mikey Murphy, our officer, who had walked out into the firestorm to make that last call on his cell phone, the one that placed him in mortal danger, the one chance, he believed, to save us.

Gunned down by the Taliban, right through the back, blood pouring out of his chest, his phone in the dust, and he still picked it up. "Roger that, sir. Thank you." Was anyone ever braver than that? I remember being awestruck at the way he somehow stood up and walked toward me, tall and erect, and carried right on firing until they finally blew half his head away. "Marcus, this really sucks."

He was right then. And he was still right at this moment. It did suck. As they carried Mikey to the plane, I tried to think of an epitaph for my greatest buddy, and I could only come up with some poem written by the Australian Banjo Paterson, I guess for one of his heroes, as Mikey was mine:

He was hard and tough and wiry—just the sort that won't
   say die—
   There was courage in his quick, impatient tread;
And he bore the badge of gameness in his bright and fiery eye,
And the proud and lofty carriage of his head.

That was Lieutenant Michael Patrick Murphy precisely. You can trust me on that. I lived with him, trained with him, fought with him, laughed with him, and damn near died with him. Every word of that poem was inscribed for him.

And now they were carrying him past the crowd, past me, and suddenly my senior commanders came over and told me it would be fitting for me to stand right by the ramp. So I moved forward and stood as rigidly to attention as my back would allow.

The chaplain moved up the ramp, and as the coffins moved forward, he began his homily. I know it was not a funeral, not the one their families would attend back home in the States. This was our funeral, the moment when we, his other family, all serving overseas together, would say our final good-byes to two very great men. The voice of the priest, out there on the edge of the aircraft hold, was soft. He stood there speaking in praise of their lives and asking one last favor from God—"To let perpetual light shine upon them…"

I watched as around seventy people, SEALs, Rangers, and Green Berets, filed forward and walked slowly into the aircraft, paused, saluted with the greatest solemnity, and then disembarked. I stayed on the ground until last of all. And then I too walked slowly forward up the ramp, to the place where the coffins rested.

Inside, beyond the SEAL escort to the coffins, I saw a very hard combat veteran, Petty Officer Ben Saunders, one of Danny's closest friends, weeping uncontrollably. Ben was a tough mountain boy from West Virginia, expert tracker and climber, kind of spiritual about the wild lands. And now he was pressed against the bulkhead, too upset to leave, too broken up to go down the steps. (He was SDV Team 2, same as Danny.)

I knelt down by the coffins and said my good-bye to Danny. Then I turned to the one that contained Mikey, and I put my arms around it, and I think I said, "I'm sorry. I'm just so sorry." I don't really remember it very clearly. But I remember how I felt. I remember not knowing what to do. I remember thinking how Mikey's remains would soon be taken away, and how some people would forget him, and others would remember him slightly, and a few would remember him well and, I know, with affection.

But the death of Mikey would affect no one as it would affect me. No one would miss him in the way that I would. And feel his pain, and hear his scream. No one would encounter Mikey in the small hours, in their worst nightmares, as I would. And still care about him, and still wonder if they had done enough for him. As I do.

I stepped out of the aircraft and walked unaided to the bottom of the steps. Dr. Dickens met me and drove me back to the hospital. I stood there and listened for the C-130 to take off, to hear it roar off the runway and carry Mikey and Danny westward into the setting sun, a few miles closer to heaven.

And the words from a thousand memorial services flickered through my mind: "Age shall not weary them, nor the years condemn. / At the going down of the sun and in the morning / We will remember them." Right here in bed in Bagram, Afghanistan, I was conducting my own military service for my two fallen buddies.

My new worry was Axe. Where was he? Surely he could not have lived? But the guys could not find him, and that was bad. I'd pinpointed that hollow where we both had rested and waited for death while the unseen Taliban rained fire down on us from behind the rocks and finally blew us both across the open ground to oblivion.

I'd survived, but I had not been shot five times like Axe. And I knew to the inch where he was last time I saw him. I talked to the guys again, and the SEAL command was not about to leave him up there. They were going in again, this time with more intel if possible, more searchers, and more local guidance.

I suggested they find the village elder from Sabray, if he was still in residence. Because he of all people could surely lead them to the dead SEAL. I learned right then from the intel guys that the gentleman I referred to was the headman of all the three villages we had observed. He was a man hugely revered in the Hindu Kush, because this is a culture that does not worship youth and cheap television celebrity. Those tribesmen treasure, above all things, knowledge, experience, and wisdom.

We did contact him immediately, and a few days later, the same old man, Gulab's father, my protector, walked through the mountains again for maybe four or five miles. This time he was at the head of an American SEAL team, the Alfa Platoon, which contained many of my buddies, Mario, Corey, Garrett, Steve, Sean, Jim, and James. (No last names. Active special ops guys, right?)

There was also a group from Echo Platoon. All day they tramped over the steep mountainside, and they took extra water and food with them, in case it took longer. But this time they were not coming back without Axe. No sir. We never leave anyone alone.

The elder hardly spoke one word to them. But he walked directly to the exact place where the body of Matthew Gene Axelson was lying. His face had been blasted by close-range gunfire, in that quaint, old-fashioned way the Taliban have when they find a mortally wounded American. By the way, if anyone should dare to utter the words *Geneva Convention* while I'm writing this, I might more or less lose control.

Anyway, they found Axe, with the bullets the Taliban rifles had emptied into his face as he lay dying, just as they had done to Mikey. But Axe was in a different place from where I thought. I know we were both blown out of the hole by the RPG, because I went over the precipice. But Axe was a few hundred yards even farther away. No one quite knows how he got there.

Axe still had three magazines left for his pistol when the grenade hit us. But when they found him, he was on the last one. And that could mean only one thing: Axe must have fought on, recovering consciousness after the blast and going for those bastards again, firing maybe thirty more rounds at them; must have driven them mad. I guess that's why, when he inevitably succumbed to his most shocking injuries, they had accorded him that barbaric tribal finale.

I used to think Audie Murphy was the ultimate American warrior. I'm not so sure about that. Not now. Not anymore. And it upsets me more than I can say, thinking what they did, in the end, to Mikey and Axe. It upsets Morgan so bad, no one can even mention Axe's name without him having to leave the room. I guess you had to know him to understand that. There were not many like Matthew Axelson.

Well, by the time they brought Axe down, I was gone. They flew me out on the night of July 8, in a big military Boeing, the

C-141, on a long journey to Germany. Jeff Delapenta accompanied me, never left my side once. And there I checked in to the regional medical center at the U.S. Air Force base at Landstuhl, up near the western border with France, about fifty-five miles southwest of Frankfurt.

I was there for about nine days, recovering and receiving treatment for my wounds and therapy for the healing bones in my back, shoulder, and wrist. But that Pepsi bottle bug wouldn't budge from my stomach. It showed major resistance for long months and made it hard to regain my lost weight.

But I came through it and finally left Germany for the four-thousand-mile ride back to the U.S.A. This time Lieutenant Clint Burk, my swim buddy in BUD/S, accompanied me, along with Dr. Dickens. Clint and I have been closest friends forever, and the journey passed pretty quickly. We traveled in a C-17 cargo plane, upstairs in first class...well, nearly. But in seats. It was great. And we touched down nine hours later in Maryland. Then the navy hitched a ride for us in a Gulfstream private jet owned by a senator.

And I guess I arrived back in some style to San Antonio Airport, Texas, which stands almost two hundred miles west of Houston, right along Route 10 and over the Colorado River. Back home I guess there had been some talk that I might be taken on to San Diego, but apparently Morgan just said, "You can forget all about that. He's coming home, and we're going to get him."

They saddled up the family Suburban, Morgan and my kid brother, Scottie, plus the SEALs Lieutenant JJ, and JT. And they set off across the Lone Star State to collect the brother they had been told by the media was dead. I couldn't believe it when I saw them all waiting there when my private jet landed.

There were a few tears from all of us. Just tears of happiness, I guess, because they had all lived with the darkest of threats, that we would not see one another ever again. I have to say the thought had also crossed my mind a few times as well.

But mostly I remember the laughter. "Jesus, you look awful," said Morgan. "Mom'll have a nervous breakdown when she sees you." It reminded me of what I'd said to Axe when he'd been fatally wounded on the mountain—"Hey, man, you're all fucked up."

It's just the way we talk to each other. Remember, Morgan was a SEAL, and his words, even to his twin brother, were tempered with humor, like all of our words among ourselves. One day it could be Morgan trapped on the mountain and me waiting for him, beside myself with worry and fear for his life. I recall he did tell me he loved me, though, and so did Scottie. And that meant a lot to me.

In the absence of Commander Pero, Scottie rustled up a bag-ful of cheeseburgers for the five-hour journey home, and we guf-fawed our way across Texas; me making light of my ordeal, telling 'em it wasn't much really, none of them believing me. I guess it's impossible to look as bad as I did when it wasn't much really.

But we had some fun, and in the end, I told them a few of the bits that were on the serious side of horrendous. Morgan wept like a child when I told him about Axe. We all went pretty quiet while that was happening, because there were no words which could comfort him, nothing that could ever be said to ease his sadness. In my view, nothing ever will. Same with me and Mikey.

Eventually we ran into our little corner of East Texas. Every-one pulled together as we drove down that wide, red dirt road to the ranch, the home I thought I might never see again. Those big oaks still towered over the place, and Dad's dogs came running out to meet us, barking like hell, with Emma unusually out in the lead, wagging her tail, as if she knew something the others didn't.

Mom predictably broke down at the sight of me, because I was still more than thirty pounds lighter than when she last saw me. And I guess I still looked pretty ill. I never told her about the goddamned typhoid-laden Pepsi bottle. A ton of people were there, from all around the neighborhood, to greet me.

I didn't know at the time that these people had formed the bedrock of the five-day prayer vigil that had taken place on the property while I was missing. A vigil to which no one had been invited, and no one knew if anyone else would be there; a vigil born of pure friendship and concern, which started with such melancholy prophesies of doom and tenuous hopes, but ended on the sunlit uplands of answered prayers. I could scarcely believe it when I heard what had happened.

And yet, standing right before me, was the cast-iron evidence of the love those Texans must have had for me and for what I had tried to do on behalf of my country. It came in the form of a brand-new stone house standing across a new paved courtyard, maybe twenty feet from the main house. It was two floors high, with a wide, timbered upper deck around the bedrooms, which abutted a tall, stone-walled shower, custom-made for me. Inside, the house was perfectly decorated, carpeted, and furnished, with a big plasma television.

"How the hell did that get here?" I asked Mom. And what she then told me blew me away. It started with a visit, after the vigil had ended, from a marvelous Texan landowner called Scott Whitehead. He was just one of so many who came to see my parents and express his delight that I had been found. He'd never, by the way, met any of the family before.

And before he went, he explained he had a close friend who owned a construction company in Houston and wondered if there was anything Marcus might like when he came home.

Mom explained how I had always wanted a little space of my own where I could...well...chill, as the late Shane Patton would undoubtedly have expressed it. And perhaps a small extension off my lower-floor bedroom might be really nice. She was thinking rock-bottom price, and maybe she and Dad could manage that.

Next thing that happened, she said, two of the biggest trucks she'd ever seen came rolling into the drive, accompanied by a crane and a mechanical digger, a couple of architects, site engineers, and God knows what else. Then, Mom says, a team of around thirty guys, working twenty-four hours a day in shifts over three days, built me a house!

Scott Whitehead just said he was proud to have done a small favor for a very great Texan (Christ! He meant me, I think). And he still calls Mom every day, just to check we're all okay.

Anyway, Morgan and I moved in, freeing up space for the stream of SEALs who still kept coming to see us. And I stayed home with the family, resting for two weeks, during which time Mom fought a fierce running battle with the Pepsi bottle bug, trying to get some weight on me.

Scott Whitehead's boys had thought of everything. They even had the house phone wired up in my new residence, and the first call I received was a real surprise. I picked it up and a voice said, "Marcus, this is George Bush. I was forty-one."

Jesus! This was the forty-first president of the United States. I knew that real quick. President Bush lives in Houston.

"Yessir," I replied. "I very definitely know exactly who you are."

"Well, I just called you to tell you how proud we all are of you. And my son's real proud, and he wants you to know the United States of America is real proud of you, your gallantry, and your courage under fire."

Hell, you could tell he was a military man, right off. I knew about his record, torpedo bomber pilot in the Pacific, World War II, shot down by the Japanese, Distinguished Flying Cross. The man who appointed General Colin Powell as Chairman of the Joint Chiefs. Victor of the Gulf War.

Are you kidding! "I'm George, forty-one, calling you to let you know how proud we are of you!" That really broke me up. He told me if I needed anything, no matter what, "be sure to call me." Then he gave me his phone number. How about that? Me, Marcus? I mean, Jesus, he didn't have to do that. Are Texans the greatest people in the world or what? Maybe you don't think so, but I bet you see my point.

I was thrilled President Bush had called. And I thanked him sincerely. I just told him at the end, "Anything shakes loose, sir, I'll be sure to call. Yessir."

By mid-August, still being in the U.S. Navy, I had to go back to Hawaii (SDV Team 1). During my two weeks there I had a visit from the chief of Naval Operations, Admiral Mike Mullin, direct from the Pentagon.

He asked me to come over to the commanding officer's office and promoted me right there on the spot, made me a Petty Officer First Class, no bullshit.

He's the head of the U.S. Navy. And that was the greatest honor I had ever received. It was a moment I will never forget, just standing there in the presence of Admiral Mullin. He told me he was very proud of me. And it doesn't get a whole lot bigger than that. I nearly cracked up.

Perhaps civilians might not appreciate why an honor like that means all the world to all of us; that sacred recognition that you have served your country well, that you have done your duty and somehow managed to live up to the highest possible expectations.

Even though it may seem like a strange ritual in a foreign tribe, kinda like *lokhay*, probably, I hope y'all get my drift.

Anyway, he asked me if there was anything he could do for me and I told him there was just one thing. I had with me the Texas patch I'd worn on my chest throughout my service in Afghanistan, fighting the Taliban and al Qaeda. This is the patch that bears the Lone Star. It was burned from the blast of that last RPG, and it was still blood-spattered, though I'd tried to get it cleaned. But I'd wrapped it in plastic, and you could see the Star of Texas clearly. And I asked Admiral Mullin if he could give it to the president of the United States.

He replied that he most certainly would and that he believed that President George W. Bush would be honored to have it.

"Would you like to send a brief letter to the president to accompany the battle patch?" Admiral Mullin asked me.

But I told him no. "I'd be grateful if you'd just give it to him, sir. President Bush is a Texan. He'll understand."

I had another request to make as well, but I restricted that to my immediate superiors. I wanted to go back to Bahrain and rejoin my guys from SDV Team 1 and ultimately bring them home at the conclusion of their tour of duty.

"I deployed with them, and I want to come back with them," I said, and my very good friend Mario, the officer in charge of Alfa Platoon, considered this to be appropriate. And on September 12, 2005, I flew back to the Middle East, coming in to land at the U.S. air base on Muharraq Island, same place I'd left with

Mikey, Axe, Shane, James, and Dan Healy, bound for Afghanistan, five months ago. I was the only one left.

They drove me out over the causeway, back to the American base up in the northeast corner of the country on the western outskirts of the capital city of Manama. We drove through the downtown area, through the places where people made it so plain they hated us, and this time I admit there was an edge of wariness in my soul. I knew now, firsthand, what jihadist hatred was.

I was reunited with my guys, and I stayed in Bahrain until late October. Then we all returned to Hawaii, while I prepared for another arduous journey, the one I had promised myself, promised my departed brothers in my prayers, and promised the families, whenever I could. I intended to see all the relatives and to explain what exemplary conduct all of their sons, husbands, and brothers had displayed on the front line of the battle against world terror.

I suppose, in a sense, I was filling in a part of me, which had missed seeing the outpouring of grief as, one by one, my teammates returned from Afghanistan. I had missed the funerals, which mostly took place before I returned. And the memorial services immaculately conducted by the navy for my fallen comrades.

For instance, the funeral of Lieutenant Mikey Murphy on Long Island, New York, was enormous. They closed down entire roads, busy roads. There were banners hanging across the highway on the Long Island Expressway in memory of a Navy SEAL who had paid the ultimate price in our assault on the warriors of al Qaeda.

There were police escorts for the cortege as thousands of ordinary people turned out to pay their last respects to a local son who had given everything for his country. And they did not even know a quarter of what he had given. Neither did anyone else. Except for me.

I was shown a picture of the service at the cemetery graveside. It was held in a slashing downpour of rain, everyone soaked, with the stone-faced Navy SEALs standing there in dress uniform, solemn, unflinching in the rainstorm, as they lowered Mikey into the endless silence of the grave.

Every one of the bodies was flown home accompanied by a SEAL escort who wore full uniform and stood guard over each coffin, which was draped in the Stars and Stripes. As I mentioned, even in death, we never leave anyone behind.

They closed Los Angeles International Airport for the arrival of James Suh's plane. There were no arrivals and no takeoffs permitted while the aircraft was making its approach and landing. Nothing, until the escort had brought out the coffin and placed it in the hearse.

The State of Colorado damn near closed down for the arrival of the body of Danny Dietz, because the story of his heroism on the mountain had somehow been leaked to the press. But like the good citizens of Long Island, the people of Colorado never knew even a quarter of what that mighty warrior had done in the face of the enemy, on behalf of our nation.

They actually did close down the entire city of Chico, in northern California, when Axe came home. It's a small town, situated around seventy-five miles north of Sacramento, with its own municipal airport. The escort was met by an honor guard which carried out the coffin in front of a huge crowd, and the funeral a day later stopped the entire place in its tracks, so serious were the traffic jams.

It was all just people trying to pay their last respects. The same everywhere. And I am left feeling that no matter how much the drip-drip-drip of hostility toward us is perpetuated by the liberal press, the American people simply do not believe it. They are rightly proud of the armed forces of the United States of America. They innately understand what we do. And no amount of poison about our alleged brutality, disregard of the Geneva Convention, and abuse of the human rights of terrorists is going to change what most people think.

I doubt any editor of any media outfit would get a reception like the SEALs earned, even though these combat troops had achieved their highest moments in the enforced privacy of the Hindu Kush. Perhaps the media offered the American public a poisoned chalice and then chugged it back themselves.

Some members of the media might think they can brainwash the public any time they like, but I know they can't. Not here. Not in the United States of America.

Certainly on our long journey to visit the relatives, we were met only with warmth, friendship, and gratitude as representatives of the U.S. Navy. I think our presence in those scattered homes all over the country demonstrated once and for all that the memories of those beloved men will be forever treasured, not only by the families, but by the navy they served. Because the U.S. Navy cares enormously about these matters. Believe me, they really care.

The moment I suggested to my superiors that the remaining members of Alfa Platoon should make the journey, the navy offered their support and immediately agreed we should all go and that they would pay every last dollar the trip might cost.

We arrived back in San Diego and hired three SUVs. Then we drove up to Las Vegas to meet the family of my assistant Shane Patton, who died in the helicopter crash on the mountain. We arrived on Veterans Day. They made us guests of honor at the graveside for the memorial service. It was very upsetting for me.

Shane's dad had been a SEAL, and he understood how well I knew his son. I did the best I could.

Then we flew to New York to see Mikey's mother and fiancée, and after that I went to Washington, D.C., to see the parents of Lieutenant Commander Eric Kristensen, our acting commanding officer, the veteran SEAL commanding officer who dropped everything that afternoon and rushed out to the helicopter, piling in with the guys, slamming a magazine into his rifle, and telling them Mikey needed every gun he could get. I think it was Eric to whom Mikey spoke when he made that last fateful phone call.

I told Admiral Kristensen, his father, that Eric would always be a hero to me, as he was to all of those who died with him on the mountain. Our CO was buried at the U.S. Naval Academy in Annapolis.

We went to Arlington National Cemetery afterward to visit the graves of Lieutenant Mike McGreevy Jr. and Petty Officer First Class Jeff Lucas, of Corbett, Oregon. They both died in the helicopter and were laid to rest shoulder to shoulder in Arlington, as they had died in the Hindu Kush.

Next we flew back across the country to visit the huge family of Petty Officer James Suh. Everyone came to the cemetery to say a prayer for one of the most popular guys in the platoon.

Chief Dan Healy is buried in the military cemetery at Point Loma, San Diego, not far from Coronado. We all made the journey to northern California to see his family. Then we drove to Chico, and I told Axe's wife, Cindy, how hard he had fought, what a hero he was, and how his final words to me were "tell Cindy I love her."

Danny Dietz was from Colorado, and that's where he was buried. But his family lived in Virginia near the base at Virginia

Beach. I went to see his very beautiful, dark-haired wife, Patsy, and tried the best I could to explain what a critical role he had played in our team and how, in the end, he went down fighting as bravely as any man who ever served in the U.S. Armed Forces.

But grief like Patsy suffered is very hard to assuage. I know she felt her loss had smashed her life irrevocably, though she would try to put it together. But she sat with Danny's two big dogs, and before I went, she said simply, "I just know there will never be another man like Danny."

No argument from me about that.

As the year drew to an end, my injuries improved but remained, and I was posted back to Coronado. I detached from SDVT 1 and joined SEAL Team 5, where I was appointed leading petty officer (LPO) to Alfa Platoon. Like all SEAL platoons, it has a near-clockwork engine. The officer is responsible, the chief is in charge, the LPO runs it. They even gave me a desk, and the commanding officer, Commander Rico Lenway, instantly became like a father to me, as did Master Chief Pete Naschek, a super guy and veteran of damn near everywhere.

But it was a very reflective time for me, returning to Coronado, where I had not lived since BUD/S seven years ago. I walked back down to the beach where I'd first learned the realities of life as a Navy SEAL and what was expected and what I must tolerate; the cold, the freezing cold and the pain; the ability to obey an order instantly, without question, without rancor, the bedrocks of our discipline.

Right here I'd run, jumped, heaved, pushed 'em out, swum, floundered, and strived to within an inch of my life. I'd somehow kept going while others fell by the wayside. A million hopes and dreams had been smashed right here on this tide-washed sand. But not mine, and I had a funny feeling that for me this beach would forever be haunted by the ghost of the young, struggling Marcus Luttrell, laboring to keep up.

I walked back to my first barracks and nearly jumped out of my boots when that howling decom plant screamed into action. And I went and stood by the grinder, where the SEAL commanders had finally offered me warm wishes after presenting me with my Trident. Where I had first shaken the hand of Admiral Joe Maguire.

I looked at the silent bell outside the BUD/S office and at the place where the dropouts leave their helmets. Soon there would be more helmets, when the new BUD/S class began. Last time I was here I'd been in dress uniform, along with a group of immaculately turned-out new SEALs, many of whom I had subsequently served with.

And it occurred to me that any one of them, on any given day, would have done all the same things I had done in my last combat mission in the Hindu Kush. I wasn't any different. I was just, I hoped, the same Texas country boy who'd come through the greatest training system on earth, with the greatest bunch of guys anyone could ever meet. The SEALs, the warriors, the front line of United States military muscle. I still get a lump in my throat when I think of who we all are.

I remember my back ached a bit as I stood there on the grinder, lost in my own thoughts, and my wrist, as ever, hurt, pending another operation. And I suppose I knew deep down I would never be quite the same physically, never as combat-hard as I once was, because I cannot manage the running and climbing. Still, I never was Olympic standard!

But I did live my dream, and then some, and I guess I'll be asked many times whether it had all been worth it in the end. And my answer will always be the same one I gave so often on my first day.

"Affirmative, sir." Because I came through it, and I have my memories, and I wouldn't have traded any of it, not for the whole world. I'm a United States Navy SEAL.

Epilogue: Lone Star

On September 13, 2005, Danny Dietz and Matthew Axelson were awarded the highest honor which either the United States Navy or the Marine Corps can bestow on anyone—the Navy Cross for combat heroism. I was summoned to the White House to receive mine on July 18 the following year.

I was accompanied by my brothers, Morgan and Scottie, my mom and dad, and my close friend Abbie. SEAL Team 5's Commander Lenway and Master Chief Pete Naschek were also there, with Lieutenant Drexler, Admiral Maguire's aide.

Attired in full dress blues, my new Purple Heart pinned on my chest, close to my Trident, I walked into the Oval Office. The president of the United States, George W. Bush, stood up to greet me.

"It's an honor to meet you, sir," I said.

And the president gave me that little smile of his, which I took to mean, We're both Texans, right? And he said, a little bit knowingly, "It's my pleasure to meet you, son."

He looked at the cast on my left wrist, and I told him, "I'm just trying to get back into the fight, sir."

I shook his hand, and he had a powerful handshake. And he looked me right in the eye with a hard, steady gaze. Last time anyone looked at me like that was Ben Sharmak in Afghanistan. But that was born of hatred. This was a look between comrades.

Our handshake was prolonged and, for me, profound. This was my commander in chief, and right now I had his total attention, as I would have every time he spoke to me. President Bush does that naturally, speaking as if there is no one else in the room for him. This was one powerful man.

I remember I wanted to tell him how all my buddies love him, believe in him, and that we're out there ready to bust our asses for him anytime he needs us. But he knows that. He's our guy. Even Shane in his leopard-skin coat recognized our C in C as "a real dude."

President Bush seemed to know what I was thinking. And he slapped me on the shoulder and said, "Thank you, Marcus. I'm proud of you, son."

I have no words to describe what that meant to me, how much it all mattered. I came to attention, and Lieutenant Drexler read out my citation. And the president once more came toward me. In his hand he carried the fabled Navy Cross, with its dark blue ribbon that's slashed down the center by a white stripe, signifying selflessness.

The cross itself features a navy ship surrounded by a wreath. The president pinned it directly below my Trident. And he said again, "Marcus, I'm very proud of you. And I really like the SEALs."

Again I thanked him. And then he saw me glance at his desk, and on it was the battle patch I'd asked Admiral Mullin to present to him. The president grinned and said, "Remember this?"

"Yessir." Did I ever remember it. I'd hidden that baby in my Afghan trousers, just to make sure those Taliban bastards didn't get it. And now here it was again, right on the desk of the president of the United States, the Lone Star of Texas, battle worn but still there.

We talked privately for a few minutes, and it was clear to me, President Bush knew all about the firefight on Murphy's Ridge. And indeed how I had managed to get out of there.

At the end of our chat, I reached over and picked up the patch, just for old times' sake. And the president suddenly said, in that rich Texan accent, "Now you put that down, boy! That doesn't belong to you anymore."

We both laughed, and he told me my former battle patch was going to his future museum. As I left the Oval Office he told me, "Anything you need, Marcus. That's *anything*. You call me right here, on that phone, understand?"

"Yessir." And it still felt to me like two Texans meeting for the first time. One of 'em kinda paternal, understanding. The other absolutely awestruck in the presence of a very great United States president, and my commander in chief.

Afterword

by Patrick Robinson

In the fall of 2006, Marcus Luttrell was redeployed with SEAL Team 5 in Iraq. At 0900 on Friday, October 6, thirty-six of them took off in a military Boeing C-17 from North Air Station, Coronado, bound for Ar Ramadi, the U.S. base which lies sixty miles west of Baghdad—a notorious trouble spot, of course. That's why the SEALs were going.

The fact that the navy had deployed their wounded, decorated hero of the Afghan mountains was a considerable surprise to many people, most of whom thought he would leave SPEC-WARCOM for the less dangerous life of a civilian. Because even after more than a year, his back was still painful, his battered wrist was less than perfect, and he still suffered from that confounded Afghan stomach bug he had contracted from the Pepsi bottle.

But the deployment of Marcus Luttrell was a personal matter. He alone called the shots, not the navy. His contract with the SEALs still had many months to run, and there was no way he was going to quit. I think we mentioned, there ain't no quit in him. Marcus wanted to stay, to fulfill his new obligations as leading petty officer (Alfa Platoon), a position which carries heavy responsibilities.

To me, he said, "I don't want my guys to go without me. Because if anything happened to them and I wasn't there, I guess I would not forgive myself."

And so Marcus Luttrell went back to war. The C-17 was packed with all the worldly goods of SEAL Team 5, from machine guns to hand grenades. On board the flight was Petty Officer Morgan Luttrell (Bravo Platoon), a new posting not absolutely guaranteed to delight their mother.

Marcus had a new patch on his chest, identical to the one on the president's desk in the Oval Office. "That's who I'm fighting for, boy," he told me. "My country, and the Lone Star State."

The last words to me from this consummate Navy SEAL were "I'm outta here with my guys for a few months. God help the enemy, and God bless Texas."

Acknowledgments

Many thanks to my coauthor, Patrick Robinson, whose admiration and respect for the SEALs is reflected in so many of his novels. He understood I had made a solemn, private vow to the guys that I would somehow get out and relate the story of their gallantry and unending courage. Patrick made this possible, beyond my hopes. I could not possibly have done it without him.

I also owe thanks to the senior commanders of SPECWARCOM, who granted me permission to tell my story: in particular to Admiral Joe Maguire; to our judge advocate general, Captain Jo King; and to Captain Barbara Ford, who helped me through the network of naval administration prior to publication.

My skipper in SEAL Team 5, Commander Rico Lenway, and Master Chief Pete Naschek unfailingly understood my requests for latitude during the long process of writing the book. As their leading petty officer (Alfa Platoon) I owe them my thanks, not only for their cooperation but also for their certainty that the story of the guys on the mountain should be made public.

I would also like to express my appreciation to ex–Navy SEAL Dick Couch, author of the excellent book *The Warrior Elite*, the story of the training of BUD/S Class 228. I, of course, was there and appear in his book from time to time, but I referred to Captain Couch's well-kept log of events for accurate times, dates, sequences, and rate of dropouts. I had notes, but not as good as his, and I'm grateful.

Thanks are also due to my mom and dad, David and Holly Luttrell, for so many things, but especially, in this context, for sitting down and relating, chapter and verse, the extraordinary events that took place back at the ranch in the early summer of 2005 while I was missing in action.

Finally, my fellow SEAL and twin brother, Morgan, who came storming into the ranch within hours of the Battle for Murphy's Ridge, swore to God I was alive, and never stopped encouraging everyone. Devastated by the death of his great friend Matthew Axelson, still too upset to talk about it, he was nonetheless there for me, helping to correct and improve the manuscript...still with me, as he's always been and I hope always will be.

Just like we say, bro, *From the womb to the tomb!* And no one's ever going to change that.

—Marcus Luttrell

About the Authors

Petty Officer Marcus Luttrell was raised on his parents' horse ranch in Texas. He joined the United States Navy in March 1999, was awarded his Trident as a combat-trained Navy SEAL in January 2002, and joined SEAL Team 5 in Baghdad in April 2003. In the spring of 2005 he was deployed to Afghanistan. He was awarded the Navy Cross for combat heroism in 2003 by President Bush.

Patrick Robinson is known for his bestselling U.S. Navy–based novels, most notably, *Nimitz Class, Kilo-Class,* and *Seawolf.* His autobiography of Admiral Sir Sandy Woodward, *One Hundred Days,* was an international bestseller. He lives in England but spends his summers on Cape Cod, Massachusetts, where he and Marcus Luttrell wrote *Lone Survivor.*